WORKBOOK FOR ANALYZING RHETORIC

A Handbook for the
Informed Citizen in
A New Millennium

Fifth Edition

Robert C. Rowland
The University of Kansas

Kendall Hunt
publishing company

Copyright © 1999, 2002, 2008, 2012, 2019 by Robert C. Rowland

ISBN 978-1-5249-9402-0

Kendall Hunt Publishing Company has the exclusive rights to reproduce this work,
to prepare derivative works from this work, to publicly distribute this work,
to publicly perform this work and to publicly display this work.

Published in the United States of America
10 9 8 7 6 5 4 3 2 1

CONTENTS

CHAPTER 8
Generic Rhetoric

CHAPTER 9
The Informed Citizen

RHETORICAL STRATEGIES

INTRODUCTION

This workbook is the companion volume to *Analyzing Rhetoric: A Handbook for the Informed Citizen in a New Millennium.* It is organized in sections that match the system of rhetorical analysis and evaluation developed in that book. The primary purposes of this volume are to provide samples of rhetoric to illustrate each of the main categories of rhetoric and to include analysis and evaluation forms that will assist the student in critiquing the material. To fulfill these purposes, each chapter introduces a number of works of rhetoric that illustrate the principles developed in *Analyzing Rhetoric: A Handbook for the Informed Citizen in a New Millennium.* At the end of the volume, I include rhetorical analysis forms for describing, analyzing, and evaluating any work of rhetoric.

CHAPTER 1
Analysis, Historical Context, and Rhetorical Effectiveness

The works contained in this chapter provide examples to illustrate the analysis process, the importance of considering historical context in understanding any work of rhetoric, and the method of internal evaluation of effectiveness, in which the critic considers whether the rhetor did an effective job of overcoming rhetorical barriers in order to achieve his/her purpose.

In considering each of these works, the critic first should apply the analysis system and then identify the rhetorical barriers (and advantages) faced by each rhetor. Finally, the critic should apply the system for internal evaluation of effectiveness in order to judge the success or failure of the rhetoric.

AMERICA'S BEST DAYS ARE YET TO COME

In his final major speech, "America's Best Days Are Yet to Come," Ronald Reagan presented his vision of America to the 1992 Republican party convention. In speaking to his party's national convention, Reagan had immense rhetorical advantages. He was a beloved figure among Republicans, the man credited with revitalizing the party. But in this address, Reagan did more than act as a cheerleader for his party. He also included warnings about the direction the party was moving. And, despite his immense popularity with Republicans, he also faced rhetorical barriers. It is possible, for instance, that many Republicans were not there to listen to Reagan's content, but simply to applaud for the old days. And despite his popularity, his day was past. Finally, while Reagan was speaking primarily to Republicans, his nationally televised address also was aimed at moderates and even some conservative Democrats (the so-called "Reagan Democrats") who had been so instrumental in his own political success.

America's Best Days Are Yet to Come

We Must Be Equal in the Eyes of Each Other

Ronald Reagan

Delivered at the Republican National Convention, Houston, Texas, August 17, 1992

Thank you. Thank you very much. Thank you, Paul for that kind introduction. And Mr. Chairman, delegates, friends, fellow Americans, thank you so very much for that welcome.

You've given Nancy and me so many wonderful memories, so much of your warmth and affection, we cannot thank you enough for the honor of your friendship.

Over the years, I've addressed this convention as a private citizen, as a governor, as a presidential candidate, as a president. And now, once again tonight, as private citizen Ronald Reagan.

Tonight is a very special night for me. Of course, at my age, every night's a special night. After all—after all, I was born in 1911. Indeed, according to the experts, I have exceeded my life expectancy by quite a few years. Now, this is a source of great annoyance to some, especially those in the Democratic party.

But, here's the remarkable thing about being born in 1911. In my life's journey over these past eight decades, I have seen the human race through a period of unparalleled tumult and triumph. I have seen the birth of communism and the death of communism. I have witnessed the bloody futility of two World Wars, and Korea, Vietnam and the Persian Gulf. I have seen Germany united, divided and united again. I have seen television grow from a parlor novelty to become the most powerful vehicle of communication in history. As a boy, I saw streets filled with model-T's. As a man, I have met men who walked on the moon.

I have not only seen, but lived the marvels of what historians have called the "American Century." Yet, tonight is not a time to look backward. For while I take inspiration from the past, like most Americans, I live for the future.

So this evening, for just a few minutes, I hope you will let me talk about a country that is forever young.

There was a time when empires were defined by land mass, subjugated peoples, and military might. But the United States is unique because we are an empire of ideals. For two hundred years we have been set apart by our faith in the ideals of democracy, of free men and free markets, and of the extraordinary possibilities that lie within seemingly ordinary men and women. We believe that no power of government is as formidable a force for good as the creativity and entrepreneurial drive of the American people.

Those are the ideals that invented revolutionary technologies and a culture envied by people everywhere. This powerful sense of energy has made American synonymous for opportunity the world over. And after generations of struggle, America is the moral force that defeated communism—and all those who would put the human soul itself into bondage.

But in a few short years, we Americans have experienced the most sweeping changes of this century—the fall of the Soviet Union and the rise of the global economy. No transition is without its problems, but as uncomfortable as it may feel at the moment, the changes of the 1990s will leave America more dynamic and less in danger than at any time in my life.

A fellow named James Allen once wrote in his diary, "many thinking people believe America has seen its best days." He wrote that July 26, 1775. There are still those who believe America is weakening, that our glory was the brief flash of time called the 20th Century, that ours was a burst of greatness too bright and brilliant to sustain, that America's purpose is past. My friends, I utterly reject those views. That's not the America we know.

We were meant to be masters of destiny, not victims of fate. Who among us would trade America's future for that of any other country in the world? And who could possibly have so little faith in our American people that they would trade our tomorrow for our yesterday? I'll give you a hint. They put on quite a production in New York a few weeks ago.

You might even call it "slick."

A stone's throw from Broadway, it was. And how appropriate. Over and over they told us they were not the party they were. They kept telling us with straight face that they're for family values, they're for a strong America, they're for less intrusive government. And they call me an actor!

To hear them—to hear them talk, you'd never know that the nightmare of nuclear annihilation has been lifted from our sleep. You'd never know that our standard of living remains the highest in the world. You'd never know that our air is cleaner than it was 20 years ago. You'd never know that we remain the one nation the rest of the world looks to for leadership.

All right. All right, thank you.

It always—or wasn't always this way. We mustn't forget, even if they would like to, the very different America that existed just twelve years ago—an America with 21 percent interest rates and back-to-back years of double-digit inflation; an America where mortgage payments doubled, paychecks plunged, and motorists sat in gas lines; an America whose leaders told us it was our own fault, that ours was a future of scarcity and sacrifice, and that what we really needed was another good dose of government control and higher taxes.

It wasn't so long ago that the world was a far more dangerous place as well. It was a world where aggressive Soviet communism was on the rise and America's strength was in decline. It was a world where our children came of age under the threat of nuclear holocaust. It was a world where our leaders told us that standing up to aggressors was dangerous, that America might and determination were somehow obstacles to peace.

But we stood tall and proclaimed that communism was destined for the ash-heap of history. We never heard so much ridicule from our liberal friends. The only thing that got them more upset was two simple words: "Evil Empire."

But we knew then what the liberal Democrat leaders just couldn't figure out—the sky would not fall if America restored her strength and resolve, the sky would not fall if an American president spoke the truth. The only thing that would fall was the Berlin Wall.

I heard those speakers at that other convention saying "we won the Cold War." And I couldn't help wondering, just who exactly do they mean by "we?" All right. And to top it off—to top it off, they even tried to portray themselves as sharing the same fundamental values of our party. But, they truly don't understand the principle so eloquently stated by Abraham Lincoln:

> You cannot strengthen the weak by weakening the strong. You cannot help the wage-earner by pulling down the wage-payer. You cannot help the poor by destroying the rich. You cannot help men permanently by doing for them what they could and should do for themselves.

If we ever hear the Democrats quoting that passage by Lincoln and acting like they mean it, then my friends, we will know that the opposition has really changed. Until then, when we see all that rhetorical smoke blowing out from the Democrats, well Ladies and Gentlemen, I'd follow the example of their nominee—don't inhale.

All right. But listen to me. This fellow they've nominated claims he's the new Thomas Jefferson. Well, let me tell you something—I knew Thomas Jefferson. He was a friend of mine. And, governor, you're no Thomas Jefferson.

But now, let's not dismiss our current troubles. But where they see only problems, I see possibilities as vast and diverse as the American family itself. Even as we meet, the rest of the world is astounded by the pundits and fingerpointers who are so down on us as a nation.

Well I've said it before and I'll say it again: America's best days are yet to come.

Our proudest moments are yet to be. Our most glorious achievements are just ahead. America remains what Emerson called her 150 years ago, "the country of tomorrow." What a wonderful description and how true. And yet tomorrow might never have happened had we lacked the courage in the 1980s to chart a course of strength and honor.

All the more reason—all the more reason no one should underestimate the importance of this campaign and what the outcome will mean. The stakes are high. The presidency is serious business. We cannot afford to take a chance. We need a man of serious purpose, unmatched experience, knowledge and ability—a man who understands government, who understands our country and who understands the world—a man who has been at the table with Gorbachev and Yeltsin—a man whose performance as commander-in-chief of the bravest and most effective fighting force in history left the world in awe and the people of Kuwait free of foreign tyranny—yes, yes, yes, four more years, a man who has devoted more than half of his life to serving his country—a man of decency, integrity and honor.

And tonight I come to tell you that I warmly, genuinely, wholeheartedly support the reelection of George Bush as President of the United States.

All right. Okay. All right.

We know President Bush. By his own admission, he is a quiet man, not a showman. He is a trustworthy and level-headed leader who is respected around the world. His is a steady hand on the tiller through the choppy waters of the '90s, which is exactly what we need. We need George Bush!

Yes—yes—yes—we need Bush. We also need another real fighter, a man who happens to be with us this evening, someone—someone who has repeatedly stood up for his deepest convictions. We need our vice president, Dan Quayle.

Now—now—now, it's true. A lot of liberal Democrats are saying it's time for a change. And they're right. The only trouble is they're pointing to the wrong end of Pennsylvania Avenue.

What we should change is a Democratic Congress that wastes precious time on partisan matters of absolutely no relevance to the needs of the average American. So to all the entrenched interests along the Potomac—the gavel-wielding chairmen, the bloated staffs, the taxers and takers and congressional rulemakers—we have a simple slogan for November 1992: Clean House!

Yes, yes—

For you see, my fellow Republicans, we are the change! For 50 of the last 60 years, the Democrats have controlled the Senate. And they've had the House of Representatives for 56 of the last 60 years. It is time to clean house, to clean out the privileges and perks, clean out the arrogance and the big egos, clean out the scandals, the corner-cutting and the foot-dragging. What kind of job do you think they've done during all those years they've been running the Congress?

You're absolutely right.

You know, I used to say to some of those Democrats who chair every committee in the House:

"You need to balance the Government's checkbook the same way you balance your own."

Then I learned how they ran the House bank—and I realized that was exactly what they had been doing!

Now just imagine what they would do if they controlled the Executive Branch, too!

This is the 21st presidential election in my lifetime, the 16th in which I will cast a ballot. Each of those elections had its shifting moods of the moment, its headlines of one day that were forgotten the next.

There have been a few more twists and turns this year than in others, a little more shouting about who was up or down, in or out, as we went about selecting our candidates. But now we have arrived, as we always do, at the moment of truth—the serious business of selecting a president.

Now is the time for choosing.

As it did twelve years ago, and as we have seen many times in history, our country stands at a crossroads. There is widespread doubt about our public institutions and profound concern, not merely about the economy but about the overall direction of this great country. And as they did then, the American people are clamoring for change and sweeping reform. The kind of question we had to ask twelve years ago is the question we ask today, what kind of change can we Republicans offer the American people?

Some might believe that the things we've talked about tonight are irrelevant to the choice. These new isolationists claim that the American people don't care about how or why we prevailed in the great defining struggle of our age, the victory of liberty over our adversaries. They insist that our triumph is yesterday's news, part of a past that holds no lessons for the future.

Well nothing could be more tragic, after having come all this way on the journey of renewal we began 12 years ago, than if America herself forgot the lessons of individual liberty that she has taught to a grateful world.

Emerson was right. We are the country of tomorrow. Our revolution did not end at Yorktown. More than two centuries later, America remains on a voyage of discovery, a land that has never become, but is always in the act of becoming.

But just as we have led the crusade for democracy beyond our shores, we have a great task to do together in our own home. Now, I would appeal to you to invigorate democracy in your own neighborhoods.

Whether we come from poverty or wealth; whether we are Afro-American or Irish-American; Christian or Jewish, from the big cities or small towns, we are all equal in the eyes of God. But as Americans, that is not enough. We must be equal in the eyes of each other. We can no longer judge each other on the basis of what we are, but must, instead, start finding out who we are. In America, our origins matter less than our destinations and that is what democracy is all about.

A decade after we summoned America to a new beginning, we are beginning still. Every day brings fresh challenges and opportunities to match. With each sunrise we are reminded that millions of our citizens have yet to share in the abundance of American prosperity. Many languish in neighborhoods riddled with drugs and bereft of hope. Still others hesitate to venture out on the streets for fear of criminal violence. Let us pledge ourselves to a new beginning for them.

Let us apply our ingenuity and remarkable spirit to revolutionize education in America so that everyone among us will have the mental tools to build a better life. And while we do so, let's remember that the most profound education begins in the home.

And let us harness the competitive energy that built America into rebuilding our inner cities so that real jobs can be created for those who live there and real hope can rise out of despair.

Let us strengthen our health care system so that Americans of all ages can be secure in their futures without the fear of financial ruin.

And my friends, once and for all, let us get control of the federal deficit through a Balanced Budget Amendment—yes—yes—yes—, a budget amendment and a line item veto for the president.

And let us all renew our commitment. Renew our pledge to day by day, person by person, make our country and the world a better place to live. Then when the nations of the world turn to us and say, "America, you are the model of freedom and prosperity," we can turn to them and say, "you ain't seen nothing, yet."

For me, tonight is the latest chapter in a story that began a quarter of a century ago, when the people of California entrusted me with the stewardship of their dreams.

My fellow citizens—those of you here in this hall and those of you at home—I want you to know that I have always had the highest respect for you, for your common sense and intelligence and for your decency. I have always believed in you and in what you could accomplish for yourselves and for others.

And whatever else history may say about me when I'm gone, I hope it will record that I appealed to your best hopes, not your worst fears, to your confidence rather than your doubts. My dream is that you will travel the road ahead with liberty's lamp guiding your steps and opportunity's arm steadying your way.

My fondest hope for each one of you, and especially for the young people here—Friends, what this is, is my hope that you will love your country, not for her power or wealth, but for her selflessness and her idealism. May each of you have the heart to conceive, the understanding to direct, and the hand to execute works that will make the world a little better for your having been here.

May all of you as Americans never forget your heroic origins, never fail to seek divine guidance, and never lose your natural, God-given optimism.

And finally, my fellow Americans, may every dawn be a great new beginning for America and every evening bring us closer to that shining city upon a hill.

Before I go, I would like to ask the person who has made my life's journey so meaningful, someone I have been so very proud of over the years, to join me. Nancy—

My fellow Americans—my fellow Americans, on behalf of both of us, goodbye and God bless each and every one of you. And God bless this country we love.

"THE NEW SOUTH ADDRESS"

Henry Grady, the editor of the *Atlanta Constitution*, was the first Southerner to give a major speech in the North following the Civil War. He spoke in New York City to the New England Society in 1886.[1] Although twenty years had passed since the end of the war, there were still strong feelings in the North, both about slavery and the war itself. To make matters more difficult for Grady, previous speakers had praised the Union army for its conduct of the war and even sung "Marching Through Georgia," a song referring to General William Tecumseh Sherman's campaign in Georgia, which resulted in the burning of Atlanta. And Sherman himself was there and spoke prior to Grady. This speech is considered because Grady faced extremely daunting rhetorical barriers and by all historical accounts overcame them, producing a very strong audience reaction.

The New South
Henry Grady

"There was a South of slavery and secession—that South is dead. There is a South of union and freedom—that South, thank God, is living, breathing, growing every hour." These words, delivered from the immortal lips of Benjamin H. Hill, at Tammany Hall in 1866, true then, and truer now, I shall make my text to-night.

Mr. President and Gentlemen: Let me express to you my appreciation of the kindness by which I am permitted to address you. I make this abrupt acknowledgment advisedly, for I feel that if, when I raise my provincial voice in this ancient and august presence, I could find courage for no more than the opening sentence, it would be well if, in that sentence, I had met in a rough sense my obligation as a guest, and had perished, so to speak, with courtesy on my lips and grace in my heart. *[Laughter.]* Permitted through your kindness to catch my second wind, let me say that I appreciate the significance of being the first Southerner to speak at this board, which bears the substance, if it surpasses the semblance, of original New England hospitality *[Applause],* and honors a sentiment that in turn honors you, but in which my personality is lost, and the compliment to my people made plain. *[Laughter.]*

I bespeak the utmost stretch of your courtesy to-night. I am not troubled about those from whom I come. You remember the man whose wife sent him to a neighbor with a pitcher of milk, and who, tripping on the top step, fell, with such casual interruptions as the landing afforded, into the basement; and while picking himself up had the pleasure of hearing his wife call out: "John, did you break the pitcher?"

"No, I didn't," said John, "but I be dinged if I don't!" *[Laughter.]*

So, while those who call to me from behind may inspire me with energy if not with courage, I ask an indulgent hearing from you. I beg that you will bring your full faith in American fairness and frankness to judgment upon what I shall say. There was an old preacher once who told some boys of the Bible lessons he was going to read in the morning. The boys finding the place, glued together the connecting pages. *[Laughter.]* The next morning he read on the bottom of one page: "When Noah was one hundred and twenty years old he took unto himself a wife, who was"—then turning the page—"one hundred and forty cubits long *[Laughter]*, forty cubits wide, built of gopher-wood *[Laughter]*, and covered with pitch inside and out." *[Loud and continued laughter.]* He was naturally puzzled at this. He read it again, verified it, and then said: "My friends, this is the first time I ever met this in the Bible, but I accept it as an evidence of the assertion that we are fearfully and

Delivered in New York City on December 31, 1886.

wonderfully made." *[Immense laughter.]* If I could get you to hold such faith to-night I could proceed cheerfully to the task I otherwise approach with a sense of consecration.

Pardon me one word, Mr. President, spoken for the sole purpose of getting into the volumes that go out annually freighted with the right eloquence of your speakers—the fact that the Cavalier as well as the Puritan was on the continent in its early days, and that he was "up and able to be about." *[Laughter.]* I have read your books carefully and I find no mention of that fact, which seems to me an important one for preserving a sort of historical equilibrium if for nothing else.

Let me remind you that the Virginia Cavalier first challenged France on this continent—that Cavalier John Smith gave New England its very name, and was so pleased with the job that he has been handing his own name around ever since—and that while Miles Standish was cutting off men's ears for courting a girl without her parents' consent, and forbade men to kiss their wives on Sunday, the Cavalier was courting everything in sight, and that the Almighty had vouchsafed great increase to the Cavalier colonies, the huts in the wilderness being full as the nests in the woods.

But having incorporated the Cavalier as a fact in your charming little books I shall let him work out his own salvation, as he has always done with engaging gallantry, and we will hold no controversy as to his merits. Why should we? Neither Puritan nor Cavalier long survived as such. The virtues and traditions of both happily still live for the inspiration of their sons and the saving of the old fashion. *[Applause.]* But both Puritan and Cavalier were lost in the storm of the first Revolution; and the American citizen, supplanting both and stronger than either, took possession of the Republic bought by their common blood and fashioned to wisdom, and charged himself with teaching men government and establishing the voice of the people as the voice of God. *[Applause.]*

My friend Dr. Talmadge has told you that the typical American has yet to come. Let me tell you that he has already come. *[Applause.]* Great types like valuable plants are slow to flower and fruit. But from the union of these colonist Puritans and Cavaliers, from the straightening of their purposes and the crossing of their blood, slow perfecting through a century, came he who stands as the first typical American, the first who comprehended within himself all the strength and gentleness, all the majesty and grace of this Republic—Abraham Lincoln. *[Loud and continued applause.]* He was the sum of Puritan and Cavalier, for in his ardent nature were fused the virtues of both, and in the depths of his great soul the faults of both were lost. *[Renewed applause.]* He was greater than Puritan, greater than Cavalier, in that he was American *[Renewed applause.]* and that in his homely form were first gathered the vast and thrilling forces of his ideal government—charging it with such tremendous meaning and so elevating it above human suffering that martyrdom, though infamously aimed, came as a fitting crown to a life consecrated from the cradle to human liberty. *[Loud and prolonged cheering.]* Let us, each cherishing the traditions and honoring his fathers, build with reverent hands to the type of this simple but sublime life, in which all types are honored; and in our common glory as Americans there will be plenty and to spare for your forefathers and for mine. *[Renewed cheering.]*

In speaking to the toast with which you have honored me, I accept the term, "The New South," as in no sense disparaging to the Old. Dear to me, sir, is the home of my childhood and the traditions of my people. I would not, if I could, dim the glory they won in peace and war, or by word or deed take aught from the splendor and grace of their civilization—never equaled and, perhaps never to be equaled in its chivalric strength and grace. There is a New South, not through protest against the Old, but because of new conditions, new adjustments and, if you please, new ideas and aspirations. It is to this that I address myself, and to the consideration of which I hasten lest it become the Old South before I get to it. Age does not endow all things with strength and virtue, nor are all new things to be despised. The shoemaker who put over his door "John Smith's shop. Founded in 1760," was more than matched by his young rival across the street who hung out this sign: "Bill Jones. Established 1886. No old stock kept in this shop."

Dr. Talmadge has drawn for you, with a master's hand, the picture of your returning armies. He has told you how, in the pomp and circumstance of war, they came back to you, marching with proud and victorious tread, reading their glory in a nation's eyes! Will you bear with me while I tell you of another army that sought its home at the close of the late war—an army that marched home in defeat and not in victory—in pathos and not in splendor, but in glory that equaled yours, and to hearts as loving as ever welcomed heroes home. Let me picture to you the footsore Confederate soldier, as, buttoning up in his faded gray jacket the parole which was to bear testimony to his children of his fidelity and faith, he turned his face southward from Appomattox in April, 1865. Think of him as ragged, half-starved, heavy-hearted, enfeebled by want and wounds;

having fought to exhaustion, he surrenders his gun, wrings the hands of his comrades in silence, and lifting his tear-stained and pallid face for the last time to the graves that dot the old Virginia hills, pulls his gray cap over his brow and begins the slow and painful journey. What does he find—let me ask you, who went to your homes eager to find in the welcome you had justly earned, full payment for four years' sacrifice—what does he find when, having followed the battle-stained cross against overwhelming odds, dreading death not half so much as surrender, he reaches the home he left so prosperous and beautiful? He finds his house in ruins, his farm devastated, his slaves free, his stock killed, his barns empty, his trade destroyed, his money worthless; his social system, feudal in its magnificence, swept away; his people without law or legal status, his comrades slain, and the burdens of others heavy on his shoulders. Crushed by defeat, his very traditions are gone; without money, credit, employment, material or training; and, besides all this, confronted with the gravest problem that ever met human intelligence—the establishing of a status for the vast body of his liberated slaves.

What does he do—this hero in gray with a heart of gold? Does he sit down in sullenness and despair? Not for a day. Surely God, who had stripped him of his prosperity, inspired him in his adversity. As ruin was never before so overwhelming, never was restoration swifter. The soldier stepped from the trenches into the furrow; horses that had charged Federal guns march before the plow, and fields that ran red with human blood in April were green with the harvest in June; women reared in luxury cut up their dresses and made breeches for their husbands, and, with a patience and heroism that fit women always as a garment, gave their hands to work. There was little bitterness in all this. Cheerfulness and frankness prevailed. "Bill Arp" struck the keynote when he said: "Well, I killed as many of them as they did of me, and now I am going to work." *[Laughter and applause.]* Or the soldier returning home after defeat and roasting some corn on the roadside, who made the remark to his comrades: "You may leave the South if you want to, but I am going to Sandersville, kiss my wife and raise a crop, and if the Yankees fool with me anymore I will whip 'em again." *[Renewed applause.]* I want to say to General Sherman—who is considered an able man in our hearts, though some people think he is a kind of careless man about fire—that from the ashes he left us in 1864 we have raised a brave and beautiful city; that somehow or other we have caught the sunshine in the bricks and mortar of our homes, and have builded therein not one ignoble prejudice or memory. *[Applause.]*

But in all this what have we accomplished? What is the sum of our work? We have found out that in the general summary the free negro counts more than he did as a slave. We have planted the schoolhouse on the hilltop and made it free to white and black. We have sowed towns and cities in the place of theories and put business above politics. *[Applause.]* We have challenged your spinners in Massachusetts and your iron-makers in Pennsylvania. We have learned that the $400,000,000 annually received from our cotton crop will make us rich, when the supplies that make it are home-raised. We have reduced the commercial rate of interest from twenty-four to six percent, and are floating four percent bonds. We have learned that one Northern immigrant is worth fifty foreigners, and have smoothed the path to southward, wiped out the place where Mason and Dixon's line used to be, and hung our latch-string out to you and yours. *[Prolonged cheers.]* We have reached the point that marks perfect harmony in every household, when the husband confesses that the pies which his wife cooks are as good as those his mother used to bake; and we admit that the sun shines as brightly and the moon as softly as it did "before the war." *[Laughter.]* We have established thrift in city and country. We have fallen in love with work. We have restored comfort to homes from which culture and elegance never departed. We have let economy take root and spread among us as rank as the crabgrass which sprang from Sherman's cavalry camps, until we are ready to lay odds on the Georgia Yankee, as he manufactures relics of the battlefield in a one-story shanty and squeezes pure olive oil out of his cottonseed, against any down-easter that ever swapped wooden nutmegs for flannel sausages in the valleys of Vermont. *[Loud and continuous laughter.]* Above all, we know that we have achieved in these "piping times of peace" a fuller independence for the South than that which our fathers sought to win in the forum by their eloquence or compel on the field by their swords. *[Loud applause.]*

It is a rare privilege, sir, to have had part, however humble, in this work. Never was nobler duty confided to human hands than the uplifting and upbuilding of the prostrate and bleeding South, misguided perhaps, but beautiful in her suffering, and honest, brave and generous always. *[Applause.]* In the record of her social, industrial, and political illustrations we await with confidence the verdict of the world.

But what of the negro? Have we solved the problem he presents or progressed in honor and equity towards the solution? Let the record speak to the point. No section shows a more prosperous laboring population than the negroes of the South; none in fuller sympathy with the employing and land-owning class. He shares our school fund, has the fullest protection of our laws and the friendship of our people. Self-interest, as well as honor, demand that he should have this. Our future, our very existence depend upon our working out this problem in full and exact justice. We understand that when Lincoln signed the Emancipation Proclamation, your victory was assured; for he then committed you to the cause of human liberty, against which the arms of man cannot prevail [Applause]; while those of our statesmen who trusted to make slavery the cornerstone of the Confederacy doomed us to defeat as far as they could, committing us to a cause that reason could not defend or the sword maintain in the sight of advancing civilization. [Renewed applause.] Had Mr. Toombs said, which he did not say, that he would call the roll of his slaves at the foot of Bunker Hill, he would have been foolish, for he might have known that whenever slavery became entangled in war it must perish, and that the chattel in human flesh ended forever in New England when your fathers—not to be blamed for parting with what didn't pay—sold their slaves to our fathers—not to be praised for knowing a paying thing when they saw it. [Laughter.] The relations of the Southern people with the negro are close and cordial. We remember with what fidelity for four years he guarded our defenseless women and children, whose husbands and fathers were fighting against his freedom. To his eternal credit be it said that whenever he struck a blow for his own liberty he fought in open battle, and when at last he raised his black and humble hands that the shackles might be struck off, those hands were innocent of wrong against his helpless charges, and worthy to be taken in loving grasp by every man who honors loyalty and devotion. [Applause.] Ruffians have maltreated him, rascals have misled him, philanthropists established a bank for him, but the South, with the North, protects against injustice to this simple and sincere people. To liberty and enfranchisement is as far as law can carry the negro. The rest must be left to conscience and common sense. It should be left to those among whom his lot is cast, with whom he is indissolubly connected and whose prosperity depends upon their possessing his intelligent sympathy and confidence. Faith has been kept with him in spite of calumnious assertions to the contrary by those who assume to speak for us or by frank opponents. Faith will be kept with him in the future, if the South holds her reason and integrity. [Applause.]

But have we kept faith with you? In the fullest sense, yes. When Lee surrendered—I don't say when Johnston surrendered, because I understand he still alludes to the time when he met General Sherman last as the time when he "determined to abandon any further prosecution of the struggle"—when Lee surrendered, I say, and Johnston quit, the South became and has since been, loyal to this Union. We fought hard enough to know that we were whipped, and in perfect frankness accepted as final the arbitrament of the sword to which we had appealed. The South found her jewel in the toad's head of defeat. The shackles that had held her in narrow limitations fell forever when the shackles of the negro slave were broken. [Applause.] Under the old regime the negroes were slaves to the South, the South was slave to the system. The old plantation, with its simple police regulation and its feudal habit, was the only type possible under slavery. Thus we gathered in the hands of a splendid and chivalric oligarchy the substance that should have been diffused among the people, as the rich blood, under certain artificial conditions, is gathered at the heart, filling that with affluent rapture, but leaving the body chill and colorless. [Applause.]

The Old South rested everything on slavery and agriculture, unconscious that these could neither give nor maintain healthy growth. The New South presents a perfect democracy, the oligarchs leading in the popular movement—a social system compact and closely knitted, less splendid on the surface but stronger at the core—a hundred farms for every plantation, fifty homes for every palace, and a diversified industry that meets the complex needs of this complex age.

The New South is enamored of her new work. Her soul is stirred with the breath of a new life. The light of a grander day is falling fair on her face. She is thrilling with the consciousness of growing power and prosperity. As she stands upright, full-statured and equal among the people of the earth, breathing the keen air and looking out upon the expanding horizon, she understands that her emancipation came because in the inscrutable wisdom of God her honest purpose was crossed and her brave armies were beaten. [Applause.]

This is said in no spirit of time-serving or apology. The South has nothing for which to apologize. She believes that the late struggle between the States was war and not rebellion, revolution and not conspiracy, and that her convictions were as honest as yours. I should be unjust to the dauntless spirit of the South and to my own convictions if I did not make this plain in this presence. The South has nothing to take back. In my native town of Athens it is a monument that crowns its central hills—a plain, white shaft. Deep cut into its shining side is a name dear to me above the names of men, that of a brave and simple man who died in brave and simple faith. Not for all the glories of New England—from Plymouth Rock all the way—would I exchange the heritage he left me in his soldier's death. To the foot of that shaft I shall send my children's children to reverence him who ennobled their name with his heroic blood. But, sir, speaking from the shadow of that memory, which I honor as I do nothing else on earth, I say that the cause in which he suffered and for which he gave his life was adjudged by higher and fuller wisdom than his or mine, and I am glad that the omniscient God held the balance of battle in His Almighty hand, and that human slavery was swept forever from American soil—the American Union saved from the wreck of war. *[Loud applause.]*

This message, Mr. President, comes to you from consecrated ground. Every foot of the soil about the city in which I live is sacred as a battleground of the Republic. Every hill that invests it is hallowed to you by the blood of your brothers, who died for your victory, and doubly hallowed to us by the blood of those who died hopeless, but undaunted, in defeat—sacred soil to all of us, rich with memories that make us purer and stronger and better, silent but stanch witnesses in its red desolation of the matchless valor of American hearts and the deathless glory of American arms—speaking an eloquent witness in its white peace and prosperity to the indissoluble union of American States and the imperishable brotherhood of the American people. *[Immense cheering.]*

Now, what answer has New England to this message? Will she permit the prejudices of war to remain in the hearts of the conquerors, when it has died in the hearts of the conquered? *[Cries of "No! No!"]* Will she transmit this prejudice to the next generation, that in their hearts, which never felt the generous ardor of conflict, it may perpetuate itself? *["No! No!"]* Will she withhold, save in strained courtesy, the hand which straight from his soldier's heart Grant offered to Lee at Appomattox? Will she make the vision of a restored and happy people, which gathered above the couch of your dying captain, filling his heart with grace, touching his lips with praise and glorifying his path to the grave; will she make this vision on which the last sight of his expiring soul breathed a benediction, a cheat and a delusion? *[Tumultous cheering and shouts of "No! No!"]* If she does, the South will never abject in asking for comradeship, must accept with dignity its refusal; but if she does not; if she accepts frankness and sincerity this message of goodwill and friendship, then will the prophecy of Webster, delivered in this very Society forty years ago amid tremendous applause, be verified in its fullest and final sense, when he said: "Standing hand to hand and clasping hands, we should remain united as we have been for sixty years, citizens of the same country, members of the same government, united, all united now and united forever. There have been difficulties, contentions, and controversies, but I tell you that in my judgment

Those opposed eyes,
Which like the meteors of a troubled heaven,
All of one nature, of one substance bred,
Did lately meet in th' intestine shock,
Shall now, in mutual well-beseeming ranks,
March all one way.

[Prolonged applause.]

SENATOR BERNIE SANDERS ON THE TRUMP TAX BILL AND ADDRESSING THE NEEDS OF THE MIDDLE CLASS

Senator Bernie Sanders of Vermont made an unexpectedly strong run at winning the Democratic nomination for president in 2016. Although he ultimately lost the nomination battle to former Senator and Secretary of State Hillary Clinton, Sanders, a self-proclaimed democratic socialist, received quite strong support. The most important issue that Senator Sanders focused upon was income inequality. In a speech in the Senate shortly after the Trump administration passed a tax bill, Sanders critiqued the bill and other administration policies as designed to help the rich. It is important to consider how Sanders has been able to build strong support despite the nation's history of rejecting socialism.

Trump Tax Bill and Addressing the Needs of the Middle Class

Bernie Sanders

I understand that my Republican colleagues and President Trump are busy celebrating the passage of the tax bill that was voted on at 1:30 in the morning. They are very excited, and they are very happy about it. I understand that. I guess, if one is a billionaire like President Trump or is a wealthy campaign contributor, you do have a whole lot to celebrate. Maybe, if you are one of the 6,000 lobbyists here in Washington, DC, who helped to write the bill, you are celebrating a lot today. Yet, if you are one of the vast majority of the American people who is in the middle class, you should not be celebrating today. In fact, you should be pretty nervous.

The passage of this legislation marks a great victory for the Koch brothers and other wealthy campaign contributors who will see, at a time of massive income and wealth inequality, huge tax breaks for themselves. In other words, the wealthiest people will become much wealthier. Meanwhile, the deficit—what is owed by our kids and our grandchildren—will increase by $1.5 trillion as a result of this bill. The largest and most profitable corporations—companies like Apple, Microsoft, Pfizer, and General Electric—despite record breaking profits, are going to see very, very large tax breaks to the tune of many billions of dollars.

Now, at a time when the very wealthy are becoming much richer, tens of millions of American families are struggling to keep their heads above water economically. There are 40 million Americans who are living in poverty. The nonpartisan Tax Policy Center tells us that in terms of this legislation, 83 percent of the tax benefits will go to the top one percent by the end of the decade, who are already doing phenomenally well, and that 60 percent of the benefits will go to the top one-tenth of one percent. Meanwhile, at the end of 10 years, some 92 million middle-class households will be paying more in taxes.

On top of all of that, as the only nation—major country—on Earth not to guarantee healthcare to all people, this bill will result in 13 million Americans losing their health insurance. I understand the President was really excited about this. Hey, what a great day. There are 13 million more Americans who are losing their health insurance when we are the only major country on Earth not to guarantee healthcare to all people.

In the ending of the individual mandate, what all of the experts tell us is that our healthcare premiums will go up. If you are an average person out there, your healthcare premiums will very likely go up as a result of this legislation. Meanwhile, starting next year—I am not talking about 10 years from now—some eight million middle-class families will pay more in taxes.

Doesn't it say a lot about Republican priorities when they make permanent the tax breaks for corporations; yet they make temporary the tax breaks for working families, which will expire in eight years?

Furthermore, I would hope that every American is listening closely to what Speaker of the House Paul Ryan is talking about. I have to give Ryan credit for being pretty honest about the intentions of the Republican Party. Just this morning, he was on ABC, saying what he has said for quite a while, and that is that the Republican plan is a two-step approach. Step No. 1 is passing the legislation that passed last night here and today in the House. Step No. 2 is, having run up a deficit of $1.5 trillion, they are now going to come back and offset that deficit by making massive cuts to Social Security, Medicare, and Medicaid.

According to Ryan, they have a two- step program. Step No. 1 is to give massive tax breaks to the rich and large corporations and to run up the deficit by $1.5 trillion. Step No. 2 is to offset that deficit by cutting Social Security, Medicare, and Medicaid. How unspeakable and outrageous is this plan? How much does it go against what the American people want? This gives huge tax breaks to billionaires— to the Trump family, to the Koch brothers—and then pays for those tax breaks by cutting Social Security, Medicare, and Medicaid.

There are millions of senior citizens and people with disabilities in Vermont and all across this country who, today, are struggling to buy food, to heat their homes, and to buy the prescription drugs that they need because they are trying to survive on $12,000, $13,000, $14,000 a year in Social Security. There are people who have worked their entire lives and have exhausted themselves as they approach retirement. Do not tell those people who live on $12,000, $13,000 a year in Social Security that you are going to cut their benefits through a Chained CPI or by some other mechanism in order to give tax breaks to billionaires. How outrageous that would be.

Senator Bernie Sanders on the Trump Tax Bill and Addressing the Needs of the Middle Class, December 20, 2017

Don't tell older workers—many of them with health problems after their having worked 20, 30, 40 years—that you are going to give billions of dollars in tax breaks to Microsoft, Pfizer, or General Electric, but then you are going to ask them to work more years in order to be eligible for Medicare.

I understand that every Member of the Congress would like to go home for the holiday season, and so would I. This is the time of year during which Vermont is very, very beautiful. The truth is that it would really be unconscionable for us to leave Washington after giving tax breaks to billionaires and large corporations while we ignore the enormous problems that are facing the middle class and working families of our country.

When Donald Trump ended the Deferred Action for Childhood Arrivals Program, the DACA Program, nearly 800,000 lives were thrown into chaos and uncertainty. Without the legal protections afforded by the DACA Program, hundreds of thousands of young people today are living in terrible fear and anxiety about losing the legal status they currently have in the only country they have ever known. These are young people who grew up in the United States, went to school in the United States, are working in the United States, and are in our military. This is their home. It would be unspeakable to take away their legal status and subject them to deportation.

Since the President's announcement in September, more than 11,000 people have already lost their protections under DACA, with approximately 22,000 set to lose their legal protections by the March 5, 2018, deadline. These are hundreds of thousands of wonderful young people. We cannot turn our backs on them. We must deal with DACA before we leave for the holiday break. Any end-of-the-year spending agreement must address the fear and uncertainty caused by the administration's reckless actions, and a clean Dream Act must be signed into law.

This is not just what Bernie Sanders wants; this is what the American people in overwhelming numbers want. A Quinnipiac poll came out just the other day in which 77 percent of the American people supported maintaining legal status for these young people and allowing them to move forward toward citizenship—77 percent—and that is consistent with other polls that have been taken. A vast majority of Democrats, Republicans, and Independents understand that it would be incredibly cruel and harmful to our country in so many ways to deny legal status to the Dreamers. We cannot turn our backs on the Dreamers. We must address their crisis right now.

It has been almost three months since funding for community health centers has lapsed. Our nation's 1,400 community health centers serve more than 27 million people in roughly 10,000 communities throughout the country. In my home State of Vermont, one out of four Vermonters gets their primary healthcare, dental care, low-cost prescription drugs, and mental health counseling at a community health center.

How does it happen that the Republican leadership can spend months on a bill to give tax breaks to billionaires but not address the lack of funding, the reauthorization of the Community Health Centers Program or the Children's Health Insurance Program, which provides healthcare to nine million children?

In this country, there are 1.5 million workers and retirees in multi-employer pension plans who could see the pensions that they worked for over their entire lives cut by up to 60 percent. People were promised these pensions a few years ago, and in a disastrous act, Congress took away that promise, and working people could lose the pensions they were promised by up to 60 percent cuts in those pensions. Congress needs to act before the end of the year to make sure that no one in America in a multi-employer pension plan will see their pension cut.

Those are real issues impacting real people, but there are more. There was an article recently in the Washington Post, and it said that because of major cuts to the Social Security Administration, people with disabilities are not getting their claims processed in a timely manner. The result was that in one year, if you can believe it, 10,000 people with disabilities died before they got their claims processed.

What the Republicans have been very active on is making sure that the Social Security Administration does not get the funding it needs, which means that it is harder for people who have retired and people who have disabilities to get the information they need or the claims that they have processed in a timely manner. We must make sure that every senior and person with a disability gets treated with dignity. We have to restore adequate funding to the Social Security Administration.

One of the great outrages that currently is taking place in this country and really is quite beyond belief is that at a time when we live in a competitive global economy and when we need the best educated workforce in the world to be able to do the new jobs that are being created, which require more education, we have over 40 million people in our country who have left college or graduate school in debt and sometimes deeply in debt. I am talking about people

I have met who have gone to medical school or dental school and are $300,000 or $400,000 in debt. People graduate college $100,000 or $150,000 in debt. This is a crisis that is impacting millions of people. It is impacting our entire economy. It is an issue that must be addressed. Maybe, just maybe, before we give tax breaks to billionaires, we might want to significantly lower the debt burden so many people in this country have in their student debt.

This is the year 2017, soon to be 2018. This is the wealthiest country in the history of the world. Yet there are communities in Vermont, Utah, and communities all over this country that do not have adequate broadband service. How does a business start up in a community if that community does not have rapid broadband or good cell phone service? The answer is, it doesn't. It can't. That is one of the reasons why rural America is hurting so badly. We must invest in rural infrastructure to make sure every community in this country has quality, affordable broadband.

There is an opioid epidemic sweeping this country, impacting Vermont, my neighboring State of New Hampshire, West Virginia, Kentucky, and all parts of this country are seeing people dying from overdoses from opioids and heroin. This is an epidemic that must be addressed. We can't simply walk out of here and leave people all across the country without the resources they need to treat people who are addicted and to prevent our young people from becoming addicts. We need to invest in treatment and prevention for the opioid epidemic.

As we speak, there are over 30,000 vacancies in the Veterans' Administration. That means that we have to make sure every veteran in this country who goes to the VA gets the quality and timely healthcare he or she needs. We can't turn our backs on the veterans. We have to invest in the VA.

The bottom line is that, as much as all of us would like to get out of Washington and go home, we simply cannot turn our backs on tens of millions of working people and people in the middle class. It is not good enough to pass tax breaks for billionaires and then leave town. So I hope the Republican leadership will immediately bring to this floor the legislation that we need to address the many crises facing the middle class of this country.

JIMMY SWAGGART'S SPEECH

Television evangelist Jimmy Swaggart's address was delivered on 21 February 1988. His speech is what is known as an apologia or a speech of self-defense. It was presented by Swaggart after he was accused of sexual misconduct. Because of the very conservative moral values of his congregation and television ministry, and also because of his own statements about the immorality of extramarital sex, Swaggart faced very difficult rhetorical barriers.

Jimmy Swaggart's Speech

Everything I will attempt to say to you this morning will be from my heart. I will not speak from a prepared script. Knowing the consequences of what I will say, that much of it will be taken around the world as it should be, I am positive that all I want to say I will not be able to articulate as I would desire. What I pray is that you will somehow feel the anguish, the pain, and the love in my heart.

I've always, every single time I have stood before a congregation and the television cameras, I have met and faced the issues head on. I have never sidestepped or skirted unpleasantries. I have tried to be like a man and preach this Gospel exactly as I have seen it without fear or reservation.

I can do no less this morning. I do not plan in any way to whitewash my sin. I do not call it a mistake, a mendacity. I call it sin. I would much rather if possible—and in my estimation it would not be possible—to make it worse or less than it actually is. I have no one but myself to blame, I do not lay the fault or the blame or the charge at anyone else but me. For no one is to blame but Jimmy Swaggart. I take the responsibility. I take the blame. I take the fault.

Many times I have addressed the media in a very stern manner and I have chastised them for what I thought and believed was error in their reporting or investigation. This time I do not. I commend them. I feel that the media, both by print and by television, radio, have been fair and objective and even compassionate.

Ted Koppel of (ABC News') Nightline, I feel did everything within his power, going the second, third, fourth, fifth, and tenth mile to make doubly certain to make sure that what he reported was as at least as fair and as honest as he, the spokesman for this world-famed news program, could make it. And I thank him for his objectivity, his kindness and his fairness. And I also want to express appreciation to the entire media everywhere, but especially

Reprinted by permission of the Baton Rouge Morning Advocate. Delivered February 21, 1988.

here in Baton Rouge—Channels 9, 2, and 33, the newspapers and the radio stations. They've been hard but they have been fair. They have been objective and at times, I believe, they have even been compassionate.

Even my old nemesis, (WBRZ reporter) John Camp, that we have disagreed with very strongly, and I love you, John, in spite of our differences. I think he's one of the finest investigative reporters in the world, and I mean that.

I want to address myself as best as I know how to those that I have sinned against. First of all, my wife Frances. God never gave a man a better helpmate and companion to stand beside him and as far as this Gospel has been taken through the ether waves to the great cities of the world and covered this globe. It would never have been done were it not for her strength, her courage, her consecration to her Redeemer, the Lord Jesus Christ. I have sinned against you and I beg your forgiveness.

God said to David 3,000 years ago, you have done this thing in secret but I will do what I do openly before all Israel. My sin was done in secret and God has said to me, "I will do what I do before the whole world." Blessed be the name of the Lord.

God could not give a man, a father, a minister of the Gospel a finer son than he has given me and his mother. Donnie and my beautiful and lovely daughter-in-law Debbie. Donnie has stood with me and I have relied upon him these trying days, he and his mother and myself. We do not know what we would have done without his strength, his courage and his utter devotion to the Lord Jesus Christ. Donnie and Debbie, I have sinned against you. And I beg you to forgive me.

To the Assemblies of God, which helped bring the Gospel to my little beleaguered town where my family was lost without Jesus, this movement and fellowship that girdles the globe, that has been more instrumental in taking this Gospel through the stringent night of darkness to the far-flung hundreds of millions, that may beat any effort in the annals of human history; its leadership has been compassionate, kind and considerate and long suffering toward me without exception, but never for one moment condoning sin both on the national level and this esteemed district level; to it thousands and thousands of pastors that are Godly, that uphold the standard of righteousness; its evangelists through that are heralds and criers of redemption; its missionaries, on the front lines of darkness holding back the tides of Hell; I have sinned against you and I have brought disgrace and humiliation and embarrassment upon you. I beg your forgiveness.

This church, this ministry, this Bible college, these professors, this choir, these musicians, these singers that have stood with me on a thousand crusades platforms around the world, that have labored . . . tirelessly to lift the great name of Jesus Christ and to tell the weary that He is rest and the same Christ, the He, Jesus, is victory.

To my associates—and no evangelist ever had a greater group of men and women—given by the hand of God who worked with me . . . unflaggingly, I have sinned against you. I have brought shame and embarrassment to you. And I beg you your forgiveness.

To my fellow television ministers and evangelists, you that are already bearing an almost unbearable load, to continue to save and tell the great story of Jesus' love, I have made your load heavier and I have hurt you. Please forgive me for sinning against you.

And to the hundreds of millions that I have stood before in over 100 countries of the world, I've looked into the cameras and so many of you with a heart of loneliness that needed help reached out to the minister of the Gospel, the beacon of light, you that are nameless—most I will never be able to see you except in faith—I sinned against you. I beg you forgive me.

And most of all to my Almighty and My Savior, My Redeemer, the one who I serve and I love and I worship . . . who had saved me and washed me and cleansed me. I have sinned against you my lord and I would ask that your precious blood would wash and cleanse every stain until it is in the seas of God's forgetfulness, never to be remembered against me anymore.

I say unto you that watch me today, through his mercy and his grace and his love the sin of which I speak is not a present sin, it is a past sin.

I know that so many would ask, 'Why, why?' I have asked myself that 10,000 times through 10,000 tears. Maybe Jimmy Swaggart has tried to live his entire life as though he were not human. And I have thought that with the Lord—knowing his is omnipotent and omniscient—that there was nothing I could not do and I emphasize with his help and with his kindness. And I think this is the reason, in my limited knowledge, that I did not find the victory I sought because I did not seek the help of my brother and my sister in the Lord.

I have come to the realization this Gospel is flawless, even though it is ministered at times by flawed men. If I could have sought the help of those who loved me with the added strength, I look back now, and know victory could have been mine. They have given me strength along with the compassion of our

Savior in these last few days that I have needed for a long, long time.

Many ask as I close, this: 'Will the ministry continue?' Yes, the ministry will continue.

Under the guidance, leadership and direction as best as we know how and can, the Louisiana District of the Assemblies of God will continue to take this Gospel of Jesus Christ all over the World. I will step out of this pulpit for the moment, for an undetermined, indeterminate period of time and we will leave that in the hands of the Lord.

BARACK OBAMA, KEYNOTE ADDRESS AT THE 2004 DEMOCRATIC NATIONAL CONVENTION

Barack Obama, then an almost unknown state senator from Illinois running for the United States Senate, presented an address at the 2004 Democratic National Convention that electrified the audience in the hall and the nation as a whole. Obama went on to win his senate race by a wide margin and quickly became a leading figure in the Democratic party and possible presidential candidate. The address is important for many reasons, including the way that it illustrates the power of well-designed audience adaptation strategies.

Keynote Address at the 2004 Democratic National Convention

Barack Obama

On behalf of the great state of Illinois, crossroads of a nation, land of Lincoln, let me express my deep gratitude for the privilege of addressing this convention. Tonight is a particular honor for me because, let's face it, my presence on this stage is pretty unlikely. My father was a foreign student, born and raised in a small village in Kenya. He grew up herding goats, went to school in a tin-roof shack. His father, my grandfather, was a cook, a domestic servant.

But my grandfather had larger dreams for his son. Through hard work and perseverance my father got a scholarship to study in a magical place: America, which stood as a beacon of freedom and opportunity to so many who had come before. While studying here, my father met my mother. She was born in a town on the other side of the world, in Kansas. Her father worked on oil rigs and farms through most of the Depression. The day after Pearl Harbor he signed up for duty, joined Patton's army and marched across Europe. Back home, my grandmother raised their baby and went to work on a bomber assembly line. After the war, they studied on the GI Bill, bought a house through FHA, and moved west in search of opportunity.

And they, too, had big dreams for their daughter, a common dream, born of two continents. My parents shared not only an improbable love; they shared an abiding faith in the possibilities of this nation. They would give me an African name, Barack, or "blessed," believing that in a tolerant America your name is no barrier to success. They imagined me going to the best schools in the land, even though they weren't rich, because in a generous America you don't have to be rich to achieve your potential. They are both passed away now. Yet, I know that, on this night, they look down on me with pride.

I stand here today, grateful for the diversity of my heritage, aware that my parents' dreams live on in my precious daughters. I stand here knowing that my story is part of the larger American story, that I owe a debt to all of those who came before me, and that, in no other country on earth, is my story even possible. Tonight, we gather to affirm the greatness of our nation, not because of the height of our skyscrapers, or the power of our military, or the size of our economy. Our pride is based on a very simple premise, summed up in a declaration made over two hundred years ago, "We hold these truths to be self-evident, that all men are created equal. That they are endowed by their Creator with certain inalienable rights. That among these are life, liberty and the pursuit of happiness."

That is the true genius of America, a faith in the simple dreams of its people, the insistence on small miracles. That we can tuck in our children at night and know they are fed and clothed and safe from harm. That we can say what we think, write what we think, without hearing a sudden knock on the door. That we can have an idea and start our own business without paying a bribe or hiring somebody's son. That we can participate in the political process without fear of retribution, and that our votes will be counted—or at least, most of the time.

This year, in this election, we are called to reaffirm our values and commitments, to hold them against a hard reality and see how we are measuring up, to the legacy of our forbearers, and the promise of future generations. And fellow Americans—Democrats, Republicans, Independents—I say to you tonight: we have more work to do. More to do for the workers I met in Galesburg, Illinois, who are losing their union jobs at the Maytag plant that's moving to Mexico, and now are having to compete with their own children for jobs that pay seven bucks an hour. More to do for the father I met who was losing his job and choking back tears, wondering how he would pay $4,500 a month for the drugs his son needs without the health benefits he counted on. More to do for the young woman in East St. Louis, and thousands more like her, who has the grades, has the drive, has the will, but doesn't have the money to go to college.

Don't get me wrong. The people I meet in small towns and big cities, in diners and office parks, they don't expect government to solve all their problems. They know they have to work hard to get ahead and they want to. Go into the collar counties around Chicago, and people will tell you they don't want their tax money wasted by a welfare agency or the Pentagon. Go into any inner city neighborhood, and folks will tell you that government alone can't teach kids to learn. They know that parents have to parent, that children can't achieve unless we raise their expectations and turn off the television sets and eradicate the slander that says a black youth with a book is acting white. No, people don't expect government to solve all their problems. But they sense, deep in their bones, that with just a change in priorities, we can make sure that every child in America has a decent shot at life, and that the doors of opportunity remain open to all. They know we can do better. And they want that choice.

In this election, we offer that choice. Our party has chosen a man to lead us who embodies the best this country has to offer. That man is John Kerry. John Kerry understands the ideals of community, faith, and sacrifice, because they've defined his life. From his heroic service in Vietnam to his years as prosecutor and lieutenant governor, through two decades in the United States Senate, he has devoted himself to this country. Again and again, we've seen him make tough choices when easier ones were available. His values and his record affirm what is best in us.

John Kerry believes in an America where hard work is rewarded. So instead of offering tax breaks to companies shipping jobs overseas, he'll offer them to companies creating jobs here at home. John Kerry believes in an America where all Americans can afford the same health coverage our politicians in Washington have for themselves. John Kerry believes in energy independence, so we aren't held hostage to the profits of oil companies or the sabotage of foreign oil fields. John Kerry believes in the constitutional freedoms that have made our country the envy of the world, and he will never sacrifice our basic liberties nor use faith as a wedge to divide us. And John Kerry believes that in a dangerous world, war must be an option, but it should never be the first option.

A while back, I met a young man named Shamus at the VFW Hall in East Moline, Illinois. He was a good-looking kid, six-two or six-three, clear-eyed, with an easy smile. He told me he'd joined the Marines and was heading to Iraq the following week. As I listened to him explain why he'd enlisted, his absolute faith in our country and its leaders, his devotion to duty and service, I thought this young man was all any of us might hope for in a child. But then I asked myself: Are we serving Shamus as well as he was serving us? I thought of more than 900 service men and women, sons and daughters, husbands and wives, friends and neighbors, who will not be returning to their hometowns. I thought of families I had met who were struggling to get by without a loved one's full income, or whose loved ones had returned with a limb missing or with nerves shattered, but who still lacked long-term health benefits because they were reservists. When we send our young men and women into harm's way, we have a solemn obligation not to fudge the numbers or shade the truth about why they're going, to care for their families while they're gone, to tend to the soldiers upon their return, and to never ever go to war without enough troops to win the war, secure the peace, and earn the respect of the world.

Now let me be clear. We have real enemies in the world. These enemies must be found. They must be pursued and they must be defeated. John Kerry knows this. And just as Lieutenant Kerry did not hesitate to risk his life to protect the men who served with him in Vietnam, President Kerry will not hesitate one moment to use our military might to keep America safe and secure. John Kerry believes in America. And he knows it's not enough for just some of us to prosper. For alongside our famous individualism, there's another ingredient in the American saga.

A belief that we are connected as one people. If there's a child on the south side of Chicago who can't read, that matters to me, even if it's not my child. If there's a senior citizen somewhere who can't pay for her prescription and has to choose between medicine and the rent, that makes my life poorer, even if it's not my grandmother. If there's an

Arab American family being rounded up without benefit of an attorney or due process, that threatens my civil liberties. It's that fundamental belief—I am my brother's keeper, I am my sister's keeper—that makes this country work. It's what allows us to pursue our individual dreams, yet still come together as a single American family. "E pluribus unum." Out of many, one.

Yet even as we speak, there are those who are preparing to divide us, the spin masters and negative ad peddlers who embrace the politics of anything goes. Well, I say to them tonight, there's not a liberal America and a conservative America—there's the United States of America. There's not a black America and white America and Latino America and Asian America; there's the United States of America. The pundits like to slice-and-dice our country into Red States and Blue States; Red States for Republicans, Blue States for Democrats. But I've got news for them, too. We worship an awesome God in the Blue States, and we don't like federal agents poking around our libraries in the Red States. We coach Little League in the Blue States and have gay friends in the Red States. There are patriots who opposed the war in Iraq and patriots who supported it. We are one people, all of us pledging allegiance to the stars and stripes, all of us defending the United States of America.

In the end, that's what this election is about. Do we participate in a politics of cynicism or a politics of hope? John Kerry calls on us to hope. John Edwards calls on us to hope. I'm not talking about blind optimism here—the almost willful ignorance that thinks unemployment will go away if we just don't talk about it, or the health care crisis will solve itself if we just ignore it. No, I'm talking about something more substantial. It's the hope of slaves sitting around a fire singing freedom songs; the hope of immigrants setting out for distant shores; the hope of a young naval lieutenant bravely patrolling the Mekong Delta; the hope of a millworker's son who dares to defy the odds; the hope of a skinny kid with a funny name who believes that America has a place for him, too. The audacity of hope!

In the end, that is God's greatest gift to us, the bedrock of this nation; the belief in things not seen; the belief that there are better days ahead. I believe we can give our middle class relief and provide working families with a road to opportunity. I believe we can provide jobs to the jobless, homes to the homeless, and reclaim young people in cities across America from violence and despair. I believe that as we stand on the crossroads of history, we can make the right choices, and meet the challenges that face us. America!

Tonight, if you feel the same energy I do, the same urgency I do, the same passion I do, the same hopefulness I do—if we do what we must do, then I have no doubt that all across the country, from Florida to Oregon, from Washington to Maine, the people will rise up in November, and John Kerry will be sworn in as president, and John Edwards will be sworn in as vice president, and this country will reclaim its promise, and out of this long political darkness a brighter day will come. Thank you and God bless you.

BARACK OBAMA, REMARKS BY THE PRESIDENT ON THE ACCEPTANCE OF THE NOBEL PEACE PRIZE

President Barack Obama received the 2009 Nobel Peace Prize. The awarding of the prize to Obama was controversial due to his short time in office. In addition, the new president was a war president. He faced the problem of accepting a prize honoring his work for peace, while he was Commander-in-Chief of United States forces involved in combat in Iraq and Afghanistan and involved in covert activities around the world. In the address, President Obama attempted to overcome these problems and lay out a consistent foreign policy justification for both taking steps to achieve peace around the world and using military force to fight against threats to peace and freedom.

Remarks by the President at the Acceptance of the Nobel Peace Prize
Oslo, Norway

Your Majesties, Your Royal Highnesses, distinguished members of the Norwegian Nobel Committee, citizens of America, and citizens of the world:

I receive this honor with deep gratitude and great humility. It is an award that speaks to our highest aspirations—that for all the cruelty and hardship of our world, we are not mere prisoners of fate. Our actions matter, and can bend history in the direction of justice.

And yet I would be remiss if I did not acknowledge the considerable controversy that your generous decision has generated. *[Laughter]* In part, this is because I am at the beginning, and not the end, of my labors on the world stage. Compared to some of the giants of history who've received this prize—Schweitzer and King; Marshall and Mandela—my accomplishments are slight. And then there are the men and women around the world who have been jailed and beaten in the pursuit of justice; those who toil in humanitarian organizations to relieve suffering; the unrecognized millions whose quiet acts of courage and compassion inspire even the most hardened cynics. I cannot argue with those who find these men and women—some known, some obscure to all but those they help—to be far more deserving of this honor than I.

But perhaps the most profound issue surrounding my receipt of this prize is the fact that I am the Commander-in-Chief of the military of a nation in the midst of two wars. One of these wars is winding down. The other is a conflict that America did not seek; one in which we are joined by 42 other countries including Norway in an effort to defend ourselves and all nations from further attacks.

Still, we are at war, and I'm responsible for the deployment of thousands of young Americans to battle in a distant land. Some will kill, and some will be killed. And so I come here with an acute sense of the costs of armed conflict—filled with difficult questions about the relationship between war and peace, and our effort to replace one with the other.

Now these questions are not new. War, in one form or another, appeared with the first man. At the dawn of history, its morality was not questioned; it was simply a fact, like drought or disease—the manner in which tribes and then civilizations sought power and settled their differences.

And over time, as codes of law sought to control violence within groups, so did philosophers and clerics and statesmen seek to regulate the destructive power of war. The concept of a "just war" emerged, suggesting that war is justified only when certain conditions were met: if it is waged as a last resort or in self-defense; if the force used is proportional; and if, whenever possible, civilians are spared from violence.

Of course, we know that for most of history, this concept of "just war" was rarely observed. The capacity of human beings to think up new ways to kill one another proved inexhaustible, as did our capacity to exempt from mercy those who look different or pray to a different God. Wars between armies gave way to wars between nations—total wars in which the distinction between combatant and civilian became blurred. In the span of 30 years, such carnage would twice engulf this continent. And while it's hard to conceive of a cause more just than the defeat of the Third Reich and the Axis powers, World War II was a conflict in which the total number of civilians who died exceeded the number of soldiers who perished.

In the wake of such destruction, and with the advent of the nuclear age, it became clear to victor and vanquished alike that the world needed institutions to prevent another world war. And so, a quarter-century after the United States Senate rejected the League of Nations—an idea for which Woodrow Wilson received this prize—America led the world in constructing an architecture to keep the peace: a Marshall Plan and a United Nations, mechanisms to govern the waging of war, treaties to protect human rights, prevent genocide, restrict the most dangerous weapons.

In many ways, these efforts succeeded. Yes, terrible wars have been fought, and atrocities committed. But there has been no Third World War. The Cold War ended with jubilant crowds dismantling a wall. Commerce has stitched much of the world together. Billions have been lifted from poverty. The ideals of liberty and self-determination, equality and the rule of law have haltingly advanced. We are the heirs of the fortitude and foresight of generations past, and it is a legacy for which my own country is rightfully proud.

And yet, a decade into a new century, this old architecture is buckling under the weight of new threats. The world may no longer shudder at the prospect of war between two nuclear superpowers, but proliferation may increase the risk of catastrophe. Terrorism has long been a tactic, but modern technology allows a few small men with outsized rage to murder innocents on a horrific scale.

Moreover, wars between nations have increasingly given way to wars within nations. The resurgence of ethnic or sectarian conflicts; the growth of secessionist movements, insurgencies, and failed states—all these things have increasingly trapped civilians in unending chaos. In today's wars, many more civilians are killed than soldiers; the seeds of future conflict are sown, economies are wrecked, civil societies torn asunder, refugees amassed, children scarred.

I do not bring with me today a definitive solution to the problems of war. What I do know is that meeting these challenges will require the same vision, hard work, and persistence of those men and women who acted so boldly decades ago. And it will require us to think in new ways about the notions of just war and the imperatives of a just peace.

We must begin by acknowledging the hard truth: We will not eradicate violent conflict in our lifetimes. There will be times when nations—acting individually or in concert—will find the use of force not only necessary but morally justified.

I make this statement mindful of what Martin Luther King Jr. said in this same ceremony years ago: "Violence never brings permanent peace. It solves no social problem: It merely creates new and more complicated ones." As someone who stands here as a direct consequence of Dr. King's life work, I am living testimony to the moral force of nonviolence. I know there's nothing weak—nothing passive—nothing naïve—in the creed and lives of Gandhi and King.

But as a head of state sworn to protect and defend my nation, I cannot be guided by their examples alone. I face the world as it is, and cannot stand idle in the face of threats to the American people. For make no mistake: Evil does exist in the world. A nonviolent movement could not have halted Hitler's armies. Negotiations cannot convince al Qaeda's leaders to lay down their arms. To say that force may sometimes be necessary is not a call to cynicism—it is a recognition of history; the imperfections of man, and the limits of reason.

I raise this point, I begin with this point because in many countries there is a deep ambivalence about military action today, no matter what the cause. And at times, this is joined by a reflexive suspicion of America, the world's sole military superpower.

But the world must remember that it was not simply international institutions—not just treaties and declarations—that brought stability to a post World War II world. Whatever mistakes we have made, the plain fact is this: The United States of America has helped underwrite global security for more than six decades with the blood of our citizens and the strength of our arms. The service and sacrifice of our men and women in uniform has promoted peace and prosperity from Germany to Korea, and enabled democracy to take hold in places like the Balkans. We have borne this burden not because we seek to impose our will. We have done so out of enlightened self-interest—because we seek a better future for our children and grandchildren, and we believe that their lives will be better if others' children and grandchildren can live in freedom and prosperity.

So yes, the instruments of war do have a role to play in preserving the peace. And yet this truth must coexist with another—that no matter how justified, war promises human tragedy. The soldier's courage and sacrifice is full of glory, expressing devotion to country, to cause, to comrades in arms. But war itself is never glorious, and we must never trumpet it as such.

So part of our challenge is reconciling these two seemingly irreconcilable truths—that war is sometimes necessary, and war at some level is an expression of human folly. Concretely, we must direct our effort to the task that President Kennedy called for long ago. "Let us focus," he said, "on a more practical, more attainable peace, based not on a sudden revolution in human nature but on a gradual evolution in human institutions." A gradual evolution of human institutions.

What might this evolution look like? What might these practical steps be?

To begin with, I believe that all nations—strong and weak alike—must adhere to standards that govern the use of force. I—like any head of state—reserve the right to act unilaterally if necessary to defend my nation. Nevertheless, I am convinced that adhering to standards, international standards, strengthens those who do, and isolates and weakens those who don't.

The world rallied around America after the 9/11 attacks, and continues to support our efforts in Afghanistan, because of the horror of those senseless attacks and the recognized principle of self-defense. Likewise, the world recognized the need to confront Saddam Hussein when he invaded Kuwait—a consensus that sent a clear message to all about the cost of aggression.

Furthermore, America—in fact, no nation—can insist that others follow the rules of the road if we refuse to follow them ourselves. For when we don't, our actions appear arbitrary and undercut the legitimacy of future interventions, no matter how justified.

And this becomes particularly important when the purpose of military action extends beyond self-defense or the defense of one nation against an aggressor. More and more, we all confront difficult questions about how to prevent the slaughter of civilians by their own government, or to stop a civil war whose violence and suffering can engulf an entire region.

I believe that force can be justified on humanitarian grounds, as it was in the Balkans, or in other places that have been scarred by war. Inaction tears at our conscience and can lead to more costly intervention later. That's why all responsible nations must embrace the role that militaries with a clear mandate can play to keep the peace.

America's commitment to global security will never waver. But in a world in which threats are more diffuse, and missions more complex, America cannot act alone. America alone cannot secure the peace. This is true in Afghanistan. This is true in failed states like Somalia, where terrorism and piracy is [sic] joined by famine and human suffering. And sadly, it will continue to be true in unstable regions for years to come.

The leaders and soldiers of NATO countries, and other friends and allies, demonstrate this truth through the capacity and courage they've shown in Afghanistan. But in many countries, there is a disconnect between the efforts of those who serve and the ambivalence of the broader public. I understand why war is not popular, but I also know this: The belief that peace is desirable is rarely enough to achieve it. Peace requires responsibility. Peace entails sacrifice. That's why NATO continues to be indispensable. That's why we must strengthen U.N. and regional peacekeeping, and not leave the task to a few countries. That's why we honor those who return home from peacekeeping and training abroad to Oslo and Rome; to Ottawa and Sydney; to Dhaka and Kigali—we honor them not as makers of war, but of wagers—but as wagers of peace.

Let me make one final point about the use of force. Even as we make difficult decisions about going to war, we must also think clearly about how we fight it. The Nobel Committee recognized this truth in awarding its first prize for peace to Henry Dunant—the founder of the Red Cross, and a driving force behind the Geneva Conventions.

Where force is necessary, we have a moral and strategic interest in binding ourselves to certain rules of conduct. And even as we confront a vicious adversary that abides by no rules, I believe the United States of America must remain a standard bearer in the conduct of war. That is what makes us different from those whom we fight. That is a source of our strength. That is why I prohibited torture. That is why I ordered the prison at Guantanamo Bay closed. And that is why I have reaffirmed America's commitment to abide by the Geneva Conventions. We lose ourselves when we compromise the very ideals that we fight to defend. [Applause] And we honor—we honor those ideals by upholding them not when it's easy, but when it is hard.

I have spoken at some length to the question that must weigh on our minds and our hearts as we choose to wage war. But let me now turn to our effort to avoid such tragic choices, and speak of three ways that we can build a just and lasting peace.

First, in dealing with those nations that break rules and laws, I believe that we must develop alternatives to violence that are tough enough to actually change behavior—for if we want a lasting peace, then the words of the international community must mean something. Those regimes that break the rules must be held accountable. Sanctions must exact a real price. Intransigence must be met with increased pressure—and such pressure exists only when the world stands together as one.

One urgent example is the effort to prevent the spread of nuclear weapons, and to seek a world without them. In the middle of the last century, nations agreed to be bound by a treaty whose bargain is clear: All will have access to peaceful nuclear power; those without nuclear weapons will forsake them; and those with nuclear weapons will work towards disarmament. I am committed to upholding this treaty. It is a centerpiece of my foreign policy. And I'm working with President Medvedev to reduce America and Russia's nuclear stockpiles.

But it is also incumbent upon all of us to insist that nations like Iran and North Korea do not game the system. Those who claim to respect international law cannot avert their eyes when those laws are flouted. Those who care for their own security cannot ignore the danger of an arms race in the Middle East or East Asia. Those who seek peace cannot stand idly by as nations arm themselves for nuclear war.

The same principle applies to those who violate international laws by brutalizing their own people. When there is genocide in Darfur, systematic rape in Congo, repression in Burma—there must be consequences. Yes, there will be engagement; yes, there will be diplomacy—but there must be consequences when those things fail. And the closer we stand together, the less likely we will be faced with the choice between armed intervention and complicity in oppression.

This brings me to a second point—the nature of the peace that we seek. For peace is not merely the absence of visible conflict. Only a just peace based on the inherent rights and dignity of every individual can truly be lasting.

It was this insight that drove drafters of the Universal Declaration of Human Rights after the Second World War. In the wake of devastation, they recognized that if human rights are not protected, peace is a hollow promise.

And yet too often, these words are ignored. For some countries, the failure to uphold human rights is excused by the false suggestion that these are somehow Western principles, foreign to local cultures or stages of a nation's development. And within America, there has long been a tension between those who describe themselves as realists or idealists—a tension that suggests a stark choice between the narrow pursuit of interests or an endless campaign to impose our values around the world.

I reject these choices. I believe that peace is unstable where citizens are denied the right to speak freely or worship as they please; choose their own leaders or assemble without fear. Pent-up grievances fester, and the suppression of tribal and religious identity can lead to violence. We also know that the opposite is true. Only when Europe became free did it finally find peace. America has never fought a war against a democracy, and our closest friends are governments that protect the rights of their citizens. No matter how callously defined, neither America's interests—nor the world's—are served by the denial of human aspirations.

So even as we respect the unique culture and traditions of different countries, America will always be a voice for those aspirations that are universal. We will bear witness to the quiet dignity of reformers like Aung Sang Suu Kyi; to the bravery of Zimbabweans who cast their ballots in the face of beatings; to the hundreds of thousands who have marched silently through the streets of Iran. It is telling that the leaders of these governments fear the aspirations of their own people more than the power of any other nation. And it is the responsibility of all free people and free nations to make clear that these movements—these movements of hope and history—they have us on their side.

Let me also say this: The promotion of human rights cannot be about exhortation alone. At times, it must be coupled with painstaking diplomacy. I know that engagement with repressive regimes lacks the satisfying purity of indignation. But I also know that sanctions without outreach—condemnation without discussion—can carry forward only a crippling status quo. No repressive regime can move down a new path unless it has the choice of an open door.

In light of the Cultural Revolution's horrors, Nixon's meeting with Mao appeared inexcusable—and yet it surely helped set China on a path where millions of its citizens have been lifted from poverty and connected to open societies. Pope John Paul's engagement with Poland created space not just for the Catholic Church, but for labor leaders like Lech Walesa. Ronald Reagan's efforts on arms control and embrace of perestroika not only improved relations with the Soviet Union, but empowered dissidents throughout Eastern Europe. There's no simple formula here. But we must try as best we can to balance isolation and engagement, pressure and incentives, so that human rights and dignity are advanced over time.

Third, a just peace includes not only civil and political rights—it must encompass economic security and opportunity. For true peace is not just freedom from fear, but freedom from want.

It is undoubtedly true that development rarely takes root without security; it is also true that security does not exist where human beings do not have access to enough food, or clean water, or the medicine and shelter they need to survive. It does not exist where children can't aspire to a decent education or a job that supports a family. The absence of hope can rot a society from within.

And that's why helping farmers feed their own people—or nations educate their children and care for the sick—is not mere charity. It's also why the world must come together to confront climate change. There is little scientific dispute that if we do nothing, we will face more drought, more famine, more mass displacement—all of which will fuel more conflict for decades. For this reason, it is not merely scientists and environmental activists who call for swift and forceful action—it's military leaders in my own country and others who understand our common security hangs in the balance.

Agreements among nations. Strong institutions. Support for human rights. Investments in development. All these are vital ingredients in bringing about the evolution that President Kennedy spoke about. And yet, I do not believe that we will have the will, the determination, the staying power, to complete this work without something more—and that's the continued expansion of our moral imagination; an insistence that there's something irreducible that we all share.

As the world grows smaller, you might think it would be easier for human beings to recognize how similar we are; to understand that we're all basically seeking the same things; that we all hope for the chance to live out our lives with some measure of happiness and fulfillment for ourselves and our families.

And yet somehow, given the dizzying pace of globalization, the cultural leveling of modernity, it perhaps comes as no surprise that people fear the loss of what they cherish in their particular identities—their race, their tribe, and perhaps most powerfully their religion. In some places, this fear has led to conflict. At times, it even feels like we're moving backwards. We see it in the Middle East, as the conflict between Arabs and Jews seems to harden. We see it in nations that are torn asunder by tribal lines.

And most dangerously, we see it in the way that religion is used to justify the murder of innocents by those who have distorted and defiled the great religion of Islam, and who attacked my country from Afghanistan. These extremists are not the first to kill in the name of God; the cruelties of the Crusades are amply recorded. But they remind us that no Holy War can ever be a just war. For if you truly believe that you are carrying out divine will, then there is no need for restraint—no need to spare the pregnant mother, or the medic, or the Red Cross worker, or even a person of one's own faith. Such a warped view of religion is not just incompatible with the concept of peace, but I believe it's incompatible with the very purpose of faith—for the one rule that lies at the heart of every major religion is that we do unto others as we would have them do unto us.

Adhering to this law of love has always been the core struggle of human nature. For we are fallible. We make mistakes, and fall victim to the temptations of pride, and power, and sometimes evil. Even those of us with the best of intentions will at times fail to right the wrongs before us.

But we do not have to think that human nature is perfect for us to still believe that the human condition can be perfected. We do not have to live in an idealized world to still reach for those ideals that will make it a better place. The nonviolence practiced by men like Gandhi and King may not have been practical or possible in every circumstance, but the love that they preached—their fundamental faith in human progress —that must always be the North Star that guides us on our journey.

For if we lose that faith—if we dismiss it as silly or naïve; if we divorce it from the decisions that we make on issues of war and peace—then we lose what's best about humanity. We lose our sense of possibility. We lose our moral compass.

Like generations have before us, we must reject that future. As Dr. King said at this occasion so many years ago, "I refuse to accept despair as the final response to the ambiguities of history. I refuse to accept the idea that the 'isness' of man's present condition makes him morally incapable of reaching up for the eternal 'oughtness' that forever confronts him."

Let us reach for the world that ought to be—that spark of the divine that still stirs within each of our souls. [Applause]

Somewhere today, in the here and now, in the world as it is, a soldier sees he's outgunned, but stands firm to keep the peace. Somewhere today, in this world, a young protestor awaits the brutality of her government, but has the courage to march on. Somewhere today, a mother facing punishing poverty still takes the time to teach her child, scrapes together what few coins she has to send that child to school—because she believes that a cruel world still has a place for that child's dreams.

Let us live by their example. We can acknowledge that oppression will always be with us, and still strive for justice. We can admit the intractability of depravation, and still strive for dignity. Clear-eyed, we can understand that there will be war, and still strive for peace. We can do that—for that is the story of human progress; that's the hope of all the world; and at this moment of challenge, that must be our work here on Earth. Thank you very much. [Applause]

Notes

1   See Marvin G. Bauer, "Henry W. Grady," in *A History and Criticism of American Public Address*, Ed. W. Norwood Brigance (New York: McGraw Hill, 1943), volume one, pp. 387–406.

2   See "A Moral Victory," *Newsweek*, 17 October 1986: 30.

CHAPTER 2
Rational Argument

Rational argument is a powerful, but limited, strategy for appealing to an audience. Several works are included in this section to illustrate both the power and the limitations of the strategy. To reveal the functioning of rational argument, it is important to lay out the purpose of each work, the rhetorical advantages and barriers the rhetor faced, and the characteristics of the rhetoric itself. From this data, the critic should be able to build an argument for whether or not the rhetor did a good job of adapting his/her rhetoric to the situation.

MARTIN LINDSTROM, YOU LOVE YOUR iPHONE. LITERALLY

In an editorial Martin Lindstrom argues that many Americans are developing an addiction to new communication technologies, especially advanced phones. He claims that this addiction is reflected in chemical responses in the brain to the new technologies. He concludes that people should lessen their dependence on technologies and take steps to make direct personal connections with other people. Given the reliance of millions of Americans, especially among the young, on these technologies, his conclusion is controversial.

You Love Your iPhone. Literally.

Martin Lindstrom

With Apple widely expected to release its iPhone 5 on Tuesday, Apple addicts across the world are getting ready for their latest fix.

But should we really characterize the intense consumer devotion to the iPhone as an addiction? A recent experiment that I carried out using neuroimaging technology suggests that drug-related terms like "addiction" and "fix" aren't as scientifically accurate as a word we use to describe our most cherished personal relationships. That word is "love."

As a branding consultant, I have followed Apple from its early days as a cult brand to its position today as one of the most valuable, widely admired companies on earth. A few years back, I conducted an experiment to examine the similarities between some of the world's strongest brands and the world's greatest religions. Using functional magnetic resonance imaging (fMRI) tests, my team looked at subjects' brain activity as they viewed consumer images involving brands like Apple and Harley-Davidson and religious images like rosary beads and a photo of the pope. We found that the brain activity was uncannily similar when viewing both types of imagery.

This past summer, I gathered a group of 20 babies between the ages of 14 and 20 months. I handed each one a BlackBerry. No sooner had the babies grasped the phones than they swiped their little fingers across the screens as if they were iPhones, seemingly expecting the screens to come to life. It appears that a whole new generation is being primed to navigate the world of electronics in a ritualized, Apple-approved way.

Friends who have accidentally left home without their iPhones tell me they feel stressed-out, cut off and somehow un-whole. That sounds a lot like separation anxiety to me. Not long ago, I headed an effort to identify the 10 most powerful, affecting sounds in the world: I found that a vibrating phone came in third, behind only the Intel chime and the sound of a baby giggling. Phantom vibration syndrome is the term I use to describe our habit of scrambling for a cellphone we feel rippling in our pocket, only to find out we are mistaken. Similar to pressing an elevator button repeatedly in the belief that the elevator will descend sooner, we check our phones for e-mails and texts countless times a day, almost as if we can will others to text, call, e-mail or Skype us.

So are our smartphones addictive, medically speaking? Some psychologists suggest that using our iPhones and BlackBerrys may tap into the same associative learning pathways in the brain that make other compulsive behaviors—like gambling—so addictive. As with addiction to drugs or cigarettes or food, the chemical driver of this process is the feel-good neurotransmitter dopamine.

Earlier this year, I carried out an fMRI experiment to find out whether iPhones were really, truly addictive, no less so than alcohol, cocaine, shopping or video games. In conjunction with the San Diego-based firm MindSign Neuromarketing, I enlisted eight men and eight women between the ages of 18 and 25. Our 16 subjects were exposed separately to audio and to video of a ringing and vibrating iPhone.

In each instance, the results showed activation in *both* the audio and visual cortices of the subjects' brains. In other words, when they were exposed to the video, our subjects' brains didn't just see the vibrating iPhone, they "heard" it, too; and when they were exposed to the audio, they also "saw" it. This powerful cross-sensory phenomenon is known as synesthesia.

But most striking of all was the flurry of activation in the insular cortex of the brain, which is associated with feelings of love and compassion. The subjects' brains responded to the sound of their phones as they would respond to the presence or proximity of a girlfriend, boyfriend or family member.

In short, the subjects didn't demonstrate the classic brain-based signs of addiction. Instead, they *loved* their iPhones.

As we embrace new technology that does everything but kiss us on the mouth, we risk cutting ourselves off from human interaction. For many, the iPhone has become a best friend, partner, lifeline, companion and, yes, even a Valentine. The man or woman we love most may be seated across from us in a romantic Paris bistro, but his or her 8GB, 16GB or 32GB rival lies in wait inside our pockets and purses.

My best advice? Shut off your iPhone, order some good Champagne and find love and compassion the old-fashioned way.

Martin Lindstrom is the author of "Brandwashed: Tricks Companies Use to Manipulate Our Minds and Persuade Us to Buy."

JULIÁN CASTRO, "ON THE U.S./MEXICO BORDER"

In a statement criticizing Trump Administration immigration policy, former San Antonio Mayor Secretary of Housing, and candidate for the Democratic nomination for president, Julián Castro, described how his family arrived in the United States. In so doing, he made a powerful statement combining rational argument, narrative, and an appeal to basic American values.

On the U.S./Mexico Border
Julián Castro

Last night in Texas, President Donald Trump once again created a circus of fear and paranoia around our border, telling lies to suit his political purposes.

It made me think about the path my own family took to arrive in the U.S., through a border crossing at Eagle Pass, Texas. That's where my grandmother, Victoria Castro, entered the U.S. as a seven-year-old orphan from Mexico. She then came to live with her nearest relatives on the west side of San Antonio. In San Antonio, she raised my mother as a single parent, and my mother raised my brother and me as a single parent. Eagle Pass is where our family started in America, so I visited a border crossing there to record a short video.

Eagle Pass, along with El Paso, McAllen and many other communities along the border, is one of the safest cities for its size in the United States today. The facts tell us that apprehensions at the southern border are at some of their lowest levels since the early 1970s, and that it was like this long before any walls were built.

Walls do not create real security. Walls create separation and division.

Just two generations after my grandmother came across this border, one of her grandsons, my brother Joaquin, is a member of Congress, and I'm running for President of the United States. Our nation has always been a country of immigrants, folks who have made a profound and positive difference to our nation's progress. That's true today, and if we get this right, it will be true tomorrow. We can have a nation of laws and a nation of immigrants, and a greater America because of that.

Don't believe Trump's lies—we don't have to choose between border security and being compassionate. We can have both. Join me in restoring the promise of America.

Thank you.

The impeachment trial of President Clinton in the Senate in the winter of 1999 was one of the most dramatic moments in recent American political history. In the following statement, Wisconsin Representative James Sensenbrenner built what he believed was a strong case for the removal of the President from office. It is important to consider the arguments (and other strategies) that Sensenbrenner used and also to consider why his arguments ultimately lost out.

The Rule of Law Should Apply to Everyone

James Sensenbrenner

When this trial began four long weeks ago, we said that what was on trial was the truth and the rule of law. That has not changed despite the lengthy legal arguments you have heard. The truth is still the truth, and a lie is still a lie, and the rule of law should apply to everyone, no matter what excuses are made by the President's defenders.

The news media characterizes the managers as 13 angry men. They are right in that we are angry, but they are dead wrong about what we are angry about. We have not spent long hours poring through the evidence, sacrificed time with our families, and subjected ourselves to intense political criticism to further a political vendetta.

We have done so because of our love for this country and respect for the office of the Presidency, regardless of who may hold it. We have done so because of our devotion to the rule of law, and our fear that if the President does not suffer the legal and constitutional consequences of his actions, the impact of allowing the President to stand above the law will be felt for generations to come.

The Almanac of American Politics has called me a stickler for ethics.

To that I plead guilty as charged because laws not enforced are open invitations for more serious and more criminal behavior. This trial was not caused by Kenneth Starr, who only did his duty under a law which President Clinton himself signed.

It was not caused by the House Judiciary Committee's review of the independent counsel's mountain of evidence; nor was it caused by the House of Representatives approving two articles of impeachment; nor by the Senate conducting a trial mandated by the Constitution. Regardless of what some may say, this constitutional crisis was caused by William Jefferson Clinton and by no one else.

President Clinton's actions, and his actions alone, have caused the national agenda for the past year to be almost exclusively concentrated on those actions and what consequences the President, and the President alone, must suffer for them.

This trial is not about the President's affair with Monica Lewinsky. It is about the perjury and obstruction of justice he committed during the course of the civil rights lawsuit filed against him and the subsequent independent counsel investigation authorized by Attorney General Janet Reno.

The President has repeatedly apologized for his affair, but he has never, never apologized for the consequences of the perjury and obstruction of justice he has committed. Perhaps those decisions were based upon a Dick Morris public opinion poll which told the President that the American people would forgive his adultery but not his perjury. Perhaps it was for another reason.

Whatever the White House's motivations were, the fact remains that the President's apologies and the statements of his surrogate contritionists have been carefully crafted for the President to continue to evade and, yes, avoid responsibility for his deceiving the courts to prevent them from administering justice. . . .

To keep a President in office, whose gross misconduct and criminal actions are a well-established fact, will weaken the authority of the Presidency, undermine the rule of law, and cheapen those words, which have made America different from most other nations in the earth; "equal justice under law."

For the sake of our country and for future generations, please find the President guilty of perjury and obstruction of justice when you cast your votes.

Alexandria Ocasio-Cortez of New York was the surprise winner first of a primary battle and then of a seat in the House of Representatives in the 2018 election. Her advocacy for progressive policies made her one of the most popular and controversial young Democrats in the House of Representatives. In this speech, she used the life of one of her constituents to make an argument about national immigration policy.

First Speech of Representative Ocasio-Cortez

Alexandria Ocasio-Cortez

Madam Speaker, today I rise to tell the story of one of my constituents, Yahey Obeid. Mr. Obeid was born in Yemen and came to the United States when he was eight years old. His childhood dream was to become a pilot, and he knew and felt that in the United States, all things are possible and his dream could come true. Mr. Obeid's dream did come true. He has been a Federal employee for 14 years, has two children, and a mortgage for his home in the Morris Park neighborhood of the Bronx. He studied hard, got his pilot's license, and is now an air traffic controller supervisor at John F. Kennedy International Airport in New York City. I spoke with Mr. Obeid today over the phone. He and air traffic controllers like him across the country missed their first paycheck this past week. He was telling me about how stressful his job is. Every single day, air traffic controllers have thousands of people's lives in their hands. With weather changes, flight delays, staffing complexities, and a myriad of other issues, their days almost never go exactly to plan. His job is to find solutions, analyze and adapt in real time to keep people safe in one of the busiest airspaces in the United States and the world. It is terrifying to think that almost every single air traffic controller in the United States is currently distracted at work because they don't know when their next paycheck is coming. Federal workers' jobs are stressful enough. The rise in New York City's cost of living is stressful enough. The fact that Mr. Obeid's family cannot be reunified due to fears over the Muslim ban is stressful enough. His several- thousand-dollar-a-month Bronx mortgage is stressful enough. The anti-immigrant sentiment of this administration is stressful enough. The truth of this shutdown is that it is actually not about a wall, it is not about the border, and it is certainly not about the well-being of everyday Americans. The truth is this shutdown is about the erosion of American democracy and the subversion of our most basic governmental norms. It is not normal to hold 800,000 workers' paychecks hostage. It is not normal to shut down the government when we don't get what we want. It is not normal for public servants to run away and hide from the public that they serve. And it is certainly not normal to starve the people we serve for a proposal that is wildly unpopular among the American people. Each and every Member of this body has a responsibility to this Nation and to everyone in the United States of America, whether they voted for us or not. This President shares in that responsibility as well, which means he has a responsibility to my constituent, Mr. Obeid. President Trump has a responsibility to all air traffic controllers, FDA inspectors, TSA workers, and he has a responsibility to maintain the basic functioning of the United States Government.

Alexandria Ocasio-Cortez, "First Speech of Representative Ocasio-Cortez," Congressional Record, *January 16, 2019, H668-H669*

CHAPTER 3
Narrative Rhetoric

Narrative is one of the most powerful forms of rhetoric. Several samples of narrative rhetoric are included to illustrate the principles that shape narrative. In analyzing these works, the critic should focus on the defining characteristics of narrative form and function. It is helpful to lay out the characters, plot, setting, and theme for each story and then consider the degree to which the story fulfills the functions served by narrative. At that point, the work of narrative can be evaluated using the internal evaluation method. The critic should identify the purpose, rhetorical barriers (and advantages), as well as the strategies, including any non-narrative strategies that are part of the rhetoric, and then ask whether the strategies overcome the barriers.

CHERRIES FOR MY GRANDMA

In "Cherries for My Grandma," Geoffrey Canada uses the power of narrative to explain the life circumstances faced by extremely poor Americans. Writing at the same time that many politicians were proposing major cuts in welfare and other social programs, Canada attempts to humanize the poor in order to build a case for continued support for anti-poverty programs.

Cherries for My Grandma
Geoffrey Canada

America has won a great victory as the Soviet Union has turned toward democracy and turned its nuclear missiles away from our shores. But we have shown little of the grace and compassion at home that this victory should have produced. We have turned from a cold war with the Soviet Union to a cold war with poor Americans, mostly poor women and children. I have heard much debate about the poor, much of it threatening and angry. There is so much this country needs to understand and to do about poverty.

I grew up poor in the Bronx. My mother raised my three brothers and me by herself. When she couldn't find work, we went on welfare. When she could find work, it was in jobs that paid women—especially black women—so little money that we couldn't tell the difference between welfare and work except that our mother wasn't home when she was working.

People talk about poverty and the poor like it's so easy to not be poor. But I know a different story. It takes great sacrifice and talent to work your way out of poverty. My mother used to make all of her own clothes. You couldn't raise four boys on her salary and afford to buy dresses to wear to work. When we were young, she used to make our clothes, cut our hair and make toys for us out of cereal boxes. All her life she sacrificed for us. She put off getting her college degree and her master's degree until we were grown and on our own.

And you know what? We hated being poor. We loved our mother but we ruined her Christmas every year with our tears of disappointment and not getting exactly what we wanted. I couldn't help but be angry when my shoes had holes in them and there was no money to buy new ones. And I couldn't help but stare angrily when I needed money to go on a school trip and there wasn't any money to be had.

And while there was much love in our family, being poor strained our loving bonds. We had to blame someone, and my mother was the only target. And here she was giving up all she had for us, going without lunch, without movies and nights out, walking 10 blocks to the train because she couldn't afford to pay the 15 cents extra to take the bus. And she would come home to four boys with their hands out, angry because we wanted something, needed something she could not give.

There are some Americans who think poverty stems from a lack of values and determination. But you can work hard all your life, have impeccable values and still be poor. My grandfather was the pastor of Mount Pleasant Baptist Church in Harlem.

My grandmother was a Christian woman. They were hard-working, moral people. They were poor.

I lived with my grandparents during my high school years. My grandmother worked all her life: caring for other people's children, selling baked goods or Avon products, doing whatever she could do to help bring money into the house. She was a beautiful woman, kind and intelligent. She was determined to save my soul.

I was a wild and reckless adolescent whose soul was indeed in peril. And I fell in love with my grandmother. A deep love that any of us would develop if an angel came into our lives. The more time I spent with her, the more I loved her. She cooled my hot temper and anger over being poor, and she showed me there was dignity even in poverty.

In all the years I knew her, she was never able to afford material things that others took for granted. She worked very hard but never could afford anything of luxury. She taught me how one could enjoy a deep spiritual love of life that was not tied to material things. This is a tough lesson to teach in a country that places so much value on materialism.

But each summer my grandmother and I would conspire to indulge her one vice: cherries. She loved cherries. Two or three times a week when my grandfather was at work, I would walk the mile to the supermarket and buy half a pound of cherries. My grandmother and I would eat them secretly because my grandfather would have had a fit if he'd known we spent an extra dollar a week on them.

My summers with my grandmother were measured by how good the cherries were that year. It was our little secret. And I was amazed at how much she loved cherries, and how expensive cherries were. Later when I went off to Bowdoin College in Brunswick, Me., I would sit in my room and think about how much my mother and grandmother had sacrificed for me to be in college.

I would fantasize about how when I graduated and got a good job, the first thing I would buy with my first check in August would be a whole crate of cherries. It would have to be August because our cherry summers taught us that August cherries were the sweetest. I would dream of wrapping the crate up in gift paper, putting a bow on it and presenting it to Grandma. And many a night I would go to sleep in the cold winter Maine nights warmed by the vision of my grandmother's excitement when I brought her this small treasure.

Grandma died during my sophomore year. I never got to give her all the cherries she could eat. And if you want my opinion, the summer of 1971, the last summer she was alive, was really the last great summer for cherries.

Poverty is tough on families in many ways. It's not quite as simple to get out of as people make out. We must be careful to make sure we build ladders so children and their families can climb out of poverty. It's not an easy climb. You can climb all your life and never make it out.

Grandma, who sacrificed so much for all of us, I just want to say I know that in all I've been acknowledged for, I still haven't reached the level of love and compassion that you tried to teach me. I think you accomplished your goal: you saved my soul. And I hope they let me bring gifts to Heaven. You'll know what's in the box.

TESTIMONY OF ANNA DOYLE AND TESTIMONY OF LISA HERDAHL

One of the most contentious issues of the present day concerns the proper boundaries (if any) that should exist between government and religion. One site where this issue is often worked out is in the public schools. In the following two statements, Anna Doyle and Lisa Herdahl tell personal narratives about the experience of their families in the public schools. Doyle believes that schools discriminate against Christians. Herdahl focuses on religious harassment that her children received at school.

Testimony of Anna Doyle

My name is Anna Doyle and these are two of my six children, Rebecca and Kathryn. This was their first year in the public school, as they had previously been home-schooled. We live in a suburban community, and my husband felt that since we had to pay so much in property taxes, the children ought to be able to go to the schools, and so at his urging, I enrolled them this year.

The first difficulty encountered by my youngest daughter, Kathryn, happened early in the year, when the teacher told the children to "bring in your favorite book". Kathryn chose to bring a book called "Jesus My Love", which had come with her Home-school program the previous year, and which she loved so much that she used to bring it to bed with her. That

From Hearing before the Subcommittee on the Constitution of the Committee on the Judiciary House of Representatives 104 Congress, July 23, 1996.

afternoon, Kathryn came home in tears. Absolutely overwhelmed, she told me that her teacher had told her that her book was "against the law". She threw the book on the kitchen table and ran into her room, crying.

After calming her down, I called the teacher. She admitted that this was what she had said to Kathryn, but she thought that Katie knew she meant only that "it was against the law to read this book for sharing time. Of course Kathryn can *have* a book like this, but she can't share it with her friends in school. I used the words 'against the law' because I wanted to make sure that Katie knew that I don't personally have anything against this book." I didn't argue with the teacher at this time, because I didn't want to be in an adversarial relationship with her, for Katie's sake. I explained to Katie that her teacher was mistaken about what she said, and we prayed for her. Then I told Katie that "if the law ever says that you can't do something that you know God wants you to do, you have to do what makes God happy, even if you go to jail, or get punished for it. We obey the law in all things, except if the law tries to tell us not to serve God."

Shortly thereafter, another incident occurred which was similar in nature. Kathryn has a Rosary which I made for her out of nylon cord. She would wear it around her neck when she went to school. Two of the other children in the classroom had admired it, and Kathryn had told them I would make them one, too. When she brought them into school, the teacher took them away and told Katie that the "principal said that it's not allowed" to give these to your friends in school. She returned them to Katie at the end of the day, and told her that she needed to leave them home from now on. I called the principal to try to discuss this with him, but he never called me back. At that point, I contacted the Rutherford Institute, because I didn't want my daughter to continually have her faith challenged in this way. The Rutherford Institute sent me a letter, and a legal memorandum which outlined the rights enjoyed by my daughter as a student. I brought these to the principal's office, and discussed the situation with him. He backpedaled on his decision to allow Kathryn to give the Rosaries to her two friends who had asked her for them.

In early December, a friend of mine, Abigail Tardiff, made us an Advent card which was to be used as a family activity. My children loved it and wanted to bring them to school to share with their friends, just as children will bring Christmas and "Holiday" greeting cards. My older daughter, Rebecca, gave one to each student in her class, and she gave one to her teacher. The cards were signed by Rebecca,

so it was clear that they came from a student, and not from the school. The teacher went around the room and took the cards away from all the students, telling them that they could not have these in school because they were religious in nature. Rebecca came home angry and upset, feeling embarrassed about the situation. When I went to talk to the teacher, she referred me to the principal. I pointed out to him that he allows the students to pass out Christmas cards, and Valentine's day cards, and he told me that if I challenged him, he would ban both, and not allow any sharing from the home at all. He said that these Advent cards were "blatantly religious," and that he wasn't going to allow them to be distributed in his school. He said that he had discussed it with the Superintendent of Schools, and he felt confident that he was within his legal rights to prohibit any materials from home, and that he would do so rather than allow these cards to be distributed. Because I didn't want the children to lose their right to share Christmas cards and Valentine's day cards, I dropped the matter.

My son, Matthew, who is 12, is a special needs student. He suffers from a neurological condition called "Tourette's Syndrome", and receives Special Education. His teacher wanted to have as a behavior goal in Matthew's IEP (individual education plan) that "Matthew would learn to refrain from discussing religion in school." Later in the year, as part of the 6th grade health curriculum, Matthew's class participated in a program called "Project Focus," in which a Sensei from a Martial Arts center came to the school for seven consecutive weeks and taught the children Eastern Meditation techniques. At the end of the program, the school was going to give the children each a "Yin-Yang" symbol on a keychain. This is the symbol for the Eastern Religion of Taoism. The school was paying for both the instructor, and the Yin-Yangs as part of the regular instructional program. It would seem that only Judeo-Christian symbols are prohibited in the school.

Another incident occurred later in the year. My son Joshua, who is Rebecca's twin brother, had been told by his teacher to write a report on "anyone from American History." He chose to do his report on St. Isaac Jogues. When he brought the report to school, his teacher told him to write a new report on another person. I went to the school the next day and asked her why she wouldn't allow him to give his report. She said, "You know I can't let him read that report to the class—it is religious in nature. Please have Joshua write a report on someone 'normal'." I pressed the point with her, and because my son was standing next to me in tears, she relented, and allowed him to read his report. I know that this particular teacher happens to be a Christian, and does not have any personal bias against religion. She just believes, from having worked in the public school for some time, that one is prohibited from any religious expression in the schools, and she is fearful of the consequences if she were to allow it. This attitude was also expressed to me by Rebecca's teacher—that she was afraid of what might happen if she had allowed the children to have the Advent cards.

This seems to be the prevailing attitude in the public schools—that there is something shameful about religion. The term "religious" is used in a perjorative sense. Any expression of religious beliefs from the children is censored. The children learn from this to keep their faith hidden, and in doing so, they lose their faith. My children will not be returning to the public school next year, because if they did, we would continually be in conflict with the school, which might teach my children not to respect legitimate authority, and the children will internalize this prohibition against sharing their faith in public. Even after only one year in this kind of an environment, there are already signs in my children that they feel afraid to talk about God in public—it is clear to me that they have been made to feel ashamed of their religion and embarrassed for trying to express it. I was always taught that in America we enjoy freedom of religion, but from what I have seen this year in the schools, we are plagued by 'freedom' *from* religion.

Testimony of Lisa Herdahl

Hi. My name is Lisa Herdahl, and I have come to Washington today at the request of the committee to speak to you firsthand about the religious harassment that families like mine, who live in communities where they are in the religious minority, suffer when the separation of church and state has been breached.

For two years my family has been harassed and stigmatized because we live in a community in which our religious beliefs and practices differ from those of the majority of the people in our community and because of what happens in our public school.

In October 1993, my husband, my six children, and I moved down from Wisconsin to a small community in Ecru, MS, of less than 500 people, so that my husband could find work and my children could be near their grandparents. I enrolled my five oldest children in North Pontotoc Attendance Center, a public school that serves kindergarten through 12, and the only public school in our community. At the time that I enrolled my children in the school, I learned of vocal prayers that were being broadcast over the school intercom and recited in the classrooms during the day and that the students at the school attended religious Bible instruction as part of their official studies. In fact, I heard the prayer myself over the intercom when I registered my children in school. I stated that I did not want my children to attend the Bible classes or to participate in the prayers.

I am a Christian and I am raising my children to be Christians, and I believe that it is my job as a parent, not the job of a public school, to teach my children about religion and prayer. Religion is something that my children learn at home and in church, and I do not want and did not want the public schools telling my children when to pray and how to pray.

Because prayers were being broadcast over the school intercom as classes were beginning in the morning, my children could not avoid them. I was particularly concerned because the intercom prayers were in the name of Jesus. That is directly contrary to my family's religious beliefs because I teach my children to pray directly to God. My ability as a parent to teach my children to pray and our religious freedom were being undermined.

Because I requested that my children not participate in the religious instruction at school, my children have been ridiculed and harassed by teachers and classmates and falsely called devil worshipers and atheists. For example, my son David was leaving his elementary classroom before Bible class, and one of his classmates asked to leave with him. His teacher said words to the effect that, "David doesn't believe in God. People who believe in God go to Bible class—those who don't, don't go to Bible class." David was later harassed by other children who falsely accused him of not believing in God.

Another time, when my son Jason was seven years old and in second grade, his teacher placed headphones on his ears during the prayers in the morning. After the teacher put the headphones on Jason's head, his classmates responded by calling him football head and baseball head. Jason, who is now eight, has continued to be called names by his classmates, thumped on the head and grabbed by his ears, and it is no wonder that sometimes he does not want to go to school.

There are many other examples, as well. When the religious Bible classes take place, my elementary

From Hearings before the Committee on the Judiciary United States Senate 104 Congress, 1997.

school children leave the room and sit in another class, sometimes with older children and sometimes with younger children, or go into the hall for the full class period and are teased and ostracized as well. One of my sons told me that a friend of his said that he couldn't play with him anymore because if he did my son's friend would get beaten up.

Once one of my children asked if the people at the school and the town who were making things so hard for us were Christians. I said that they were. He replied that, in that case, he didn't want to be a Christian because he didn't want to be like the people in the town. I did my best to explain, but as a parent it is very hard to explain these differences.

I had many conversations with school officials to request the school stop the Bible classes and the prayers. I went to the assistant principal. I went to the principal. I went to the superintendent. I was just told that this was the way things were done in Pontotoc, and this is the way they had always been done. I even went to the Pontotoc school board last September. They said they would look into my concerns, but I never have received any response from them.

In order to protect my children, I had no choice but to file a lawsuit in Federal Court to stop the school's unconstitutional practices. As a result, the harassment of my family even got worse. Signs appeared all over the town in support of the school practices. I have been called atheist and worse names. I, personally, have received death threats in the mail, and my family has received bomb threats. For several months I was afraid to even start my car in the morning, and my husband did all of the shopping for the family. I was afraid to go to the stores.

Fortunately, the first amendment protected us in court. In response to a request for a preliminary injunction from my attorneys from People for the American Way and the ACLU's of Mississippi, the Federal Court in Mississippi issued a decision finding that the prayers over the intercom and in the classrooms were unconstitutional. The judge said that even if the prayers could be considered, as the school called them, student-initiated, they were still unconstitutional because they had the school district's seal of approval and because they constituted Government sponsorship of religion and the students were captive audiences during the prayers. The judge ordered the school to stop allowing the intercom and classroom prayers, and there will be a trial next March on the remaining issues, including the Bible classes.

My family's experience demonstrates clearly that the public schools are certainly not hostile to religious practices, as some people suggest. I have heard from families all over the country, many of whom face similar violations of their religious freedom. The pressures these families face to accept religious oppression is, in my opinion, far greater than the pressure against those who push for Government-sponsored prayer. Many of these families are afraid to come forward. I know their fear. People warned me not to complain about the organized prayer in the Pontotoc schools. They warned me of the danger and the ridicule that we would face. I stood up for what I believe is right, but many families live in fear of coming forward. Even in Pontotoc County, I have heard from people who agree with me privately but are afraid to say so publicly.

My family believes deeply in God, and our religious faith is important to us, but because our religious beliefs are different from others in our community and because of the organized religious practices in our public school, we have been harassed and stigmatized. It has been difficult for my family, but we have drawn even closer together, and my children are learning an important lesson about standing up for what they believe in and the real religious liberty. I hope our experience will help other families who are concerned about religious liberty as well. Thank you.

TESTIMONY OF MICHAEL J. FOX

Michael J. Fox is an actor who is known for his work in both film and television. He also is a victim of Parkinson's disease. In testimony before a United States Senate committee, he combined his personal narrative with argument and other strategies to argue for increased funding for research on Parkinson's disease.

Testimony of Michael J. Fox

Mr. Chairman and members of the subcommittee, thank you for inviting me to testify today about the need for greater Federal investment in Parkinson's research.

Some, or perhaps all, of you, most of you, are familiar with me from my work in film and television. What I wish to speak to you about today has little or nothing to do with celebrity save for this brief reference. When I first spoke publicly about my eight years experience as a person with Parkinson's,

From Hearing before a Subcommittee of the Committee on Appropriations United States Senate 106 Congress, March 22, 2000.

many were surprised, in part, because of my age. Although 30 percent of all Parkinson's patients are under 50, and 20 percent are under 40, that number is growing.

I had hidden my symptoms and struggles very well, through increasing amounts of medication, through surgery, and by employing the hundreds of little tricks and techniques a person with Parkinson's learns to mask his or her condition for as long as possible. While the changes in my life were profound and progressive, I kept them to myself for a number of reasons—fear, denial for sure, but I also felt that it was important for me to quietly just soldier on.

When I did share my story, the response was overwhelming and deeply inspiring. I heard from thousands of Americans affected by Parkinson's, writing and calling to offer encouragement and to tell me of their experience. They spoke of pain, frustration, fear, and hope. Always hope.

What I understood very clearly is that the time for quietly soldiering on is through. The war against Parkinson's is a winnable war, and I have resolved to play a role in that victory. What celebrity has given me is the opportunity to raise the visibility of Parkinson's Disease and focus attention on the desperate need for more research dollars. While I am able, for the time being, to continue doing what I love best, others are not so fortunate.

These are doctors, teachers, policemen, nurses, and, as you had indicated earlier, legislators, and parents who are no longer able to work to provide for their families or to live out their dreams. The one million Americans living with Parkinson's want to beat this disease. So do the millions more Americans who have family members suffering from Parkinson's. But it will not happen until Congress adequately funds Parkinson's research.

For many people with Parkinson's, managing their disease is a full-time job. It is a constant balancing act. Too little medicine causes tremors and stiffness. Too much medicine produces uncontrollable movement and slurring. And far too often, Parkinson's patients wait and wait—as I am right now—for the medicines to kick in.

New investigational therapies have helped some people like me control symptoms but, in the end, we all face the same reality—the medicine stops working. For people living with Parkinson's, the status quo is not good enough. As I began to understand what research might promise for the future, I became hopeful that I would not face the terrible suffering so many with Parkinson's endure. But I was shocked and frustrated to learn the amount of funding for Parkinson's research is so meager.

Compared to the amount of Federal funding going to other diseases, research funding for Parkinson's lags far behind. In a country with a $15 billion investment in medical research, we can and must do better.

At present, Parkinson's is inadequately funded, no matter how one cares to spend it. Meager funding means a continued lack of effective treatments, slower progress in understanding the cause of the disease, and little chance that a cure will come in time.

I applaud the steps you are taking to fulfill the promise of the Udall Parkinson's Research Act. But, we must be clear, we are not there yet.

If, however, an adequate investment is made, there is much to be hopeful for. We have a tremendous opportunity to close the gap for Parkinson's. We are learning more and more about this disease. The scientific community believes that with a significant investment into Parkinson's research, new discoveries and improved treatment strategies are close at hand. Many have called Parkinson's the most curable neurological disorder and the one expected to produce a breakthrough first.

Scientists tell me that a cure is possible—some say even by the end of the next decade—if the research dollars match the research opportunity.

Mr. Chairman, you and the members of the subcommittee have done so much to increase the investment in medical research in this country. I thank you for your vision. Most people do not know just how important this research is until they or someone in their family faces a serious illness. I know I did not.

The Parkinson's community strongly supports your efforts to double medical research funding. At the same time, I implore you to do more for people with Parkinson's. Take up Parkinson's as if your life depended on it. Increase funding for Parkinson's research by $75 million over the current levels for the coming fiscal year. Make this a down payment for a fully funded Parkinson's research agenda. It will make Parkinson's nothing more than a footnote in medical textbooks.

I would like to close on a personal note. Today you will hear from, or have already heard from, more than a few experts in the fields of science, bookkeeping, and other areas. I am an expert on only one—what it is like to be a young man, husband and father, with Parkinson's Disease.

With the help of daily medications and selective exertion, I can still perform my job, in my case, in a very public arena. I can still help out with the daily tasks and rituals involved in home life. But I do not kid myself—that will change. Physical and mental exhaustion will become more and more of a factor, as will increased rigidity, tremor and dyskinesia.

I can expect, in my forties, to face challenges most will not expect until their seventies or eighties, if ever. But with your help, and if we all do everything we can to eradicate this disease, in my fifties, I will be dancing at my children's weddings, and mine will be one of millions of happy stories.

Thank you for your time and attention.

JULIÁN CASTRO, PRESIDENTIAL ANNOUNCEMENT SPEECH

In the previous chapter, a short statement by Castro was analyzed to consider how argument can be combined with narrative and value-laden appeals. In the speech announcing his run for the presidency, Castro used his life story to build a case that he could serve as an effective president who represented all of the people. Narrative has often been at the core of presidential campaigns. Abraham Lincoln was called the "rail splitter" as a way of showing that he was a common man. Like Lincoln and so many other political candidates, personal narrative was at the core of Castro's message. It is important to think about how narrative has evolved as a political and rhetorical strategy as the nation has embraced a much more diverse sense of identity than in previous times.

Presidential Announcement Speech
Julián Castro

"Good morning! And buenos dias! Thank you, Mom. I'm guessing some of you are here more for her than for me. So many journeys for me and for my family began right here, and today we begin another one. I'm lucky in this journey, to have an incredible partner with me—my wife Erica. And I have amazing inspiration: our daughter, Carina, and our little boy, Cristián.

I want to thank each and every one of you for joining us. What a great crowd! This place—the west side of San Antonio—is a special place for me.

This is the place my grandmother, Victoria, came to in 1922 when she immigrated from Mexico as a seven-year-old orphan. It's where she grew up, where she worked for years as a maid, a cook and a babysitter while raising my mother as a single parent. It's where my mother became an activist, working to improve the quality of life for her community. It's where she raised my brother, Joaquin, and me as a single parent. Joaquin and I were baptized just over there (pointing) and so were my children. It's here that I got a good public school education, and I had the honor of serving these neighborhoods as mayor of San Antonio.

This morning, I rode the number 68 bus with my brother down Guadalupe Street as we did so many times as kids. And this time I brought my daughter Carina. That was the same bus route that we used to take with my mother to get to school or to her work during the summer.

Look around, there are no frontrunners born here, but I've always believed that with big dreams and hard work, anything is possible. This is a community like so many other communities in our country. A community of good people. Humble people. People who show up for work early and stay late—oftentimes at more than one job—so they can provide for their family.

When they go to bed at night they say hopeful prayers—they want their children to do well, they want good health, they want the dignity that comes from a good job and the peace of mind that comes from being able to retire on their own terms.

This is a community built by immigrants—families from Mexico, yes. But also, from Germany and other countries. Families who came here to build a future. Who came here to serve our country at Fort Sam Houston, and Lackland Air Force Base, and Randolph.

Today, this community represents America's future—diverse, fast-growing, optimistic, a place where people of different backgrounds have come together to create something truly special. And I am proud to call myself a son of San Antonio.

Six years ago, I had the honor of standing before the Democratic National Convention. I said then that the American Dream is not a sprint or a marathon but a relay. My story wouldn't be possible without the strong women who came before me and passed me the baton. Because of their hard work, I have the opportunity to stand here today.

My family's story wouldn't be possible without a country that challenged itself to live up to the promise of America. That was the point of the American Dream: It wasn't supposed to be just a dream.

America was the place where dreams could become real. But right now, the relay isn't working.

Today we're falling backwards instead of moving forward. And the opportunities that made America, America are reaching fewer and fewer people.

Today, we're at risk of dropping the baton. And that's why we are here today. Because we're going to make sure that the promise of America is there for everyone.

You see, the lesson I learned from my mother so many years ago in this community is that when we want to see change in our community, we don't wait for it. We work for it.

When my grandmother got here almost a hundred years ago, I'm sure she never could have imagined that just two generations later, one of her grandsons would be serving as a member of the United States Congress and the other would be standing with you here today to say these words: I am a candidate for President of the United States of America.

Cuando mi abuela llegó aquí, hace ya casi cien años, estoy seguro de que nunca se imaginó que solo dos generaciones después, uno de sus nietos formaría parte del Congreso de los Estados Unidos, y que el otro estaría ante ustedes hoy diciendo las siguientes palabras: Yo soy candidato para Presidente de los Estados Unidos.

I'm running for president because it's time for new leadership. Because it's time for new energy. And it's time for a new commitment to make sure that the opportunities I've had are available for every American.

In the years to come, we must go forward as one nation, working toward one destiny. And that destiny is to be the smartest, the healthiest, the fairest, and the most prosperous nation on earth. Again, we must be the smartest, the healthiest, the fairest, and the most prosperous nation on earth. Demanding anything less is a failure of vision. Achieving anything less is a failure of leadership.

To be the smartest nation requires an early investment in our children's education.

As mayor of this city, I challenged the voters to raise the sales tax to expand high quality, full day pre-k for thousands of San Antonio four year olds.

At the time, some said it was unrealistic. Even impossible. Education wasn't my job, they said. And who's going to vote for a tax increase in Texas, anyway? But the future of this community was my job. So I put my faith in the people.

We called our initiative PrekSA, and we brought together business leaders with educators, parents and students to make the case. And in November of 2012 the voters of this city said, "Yes! We believe in investing in early childhood education."

So the next fall I found myself standing outside a Prek4SA early childhood center as the first group of young students arrived for their first day of school. They had their little backpacks on. A lot of them were excited. And some were crying. Truth be told, a lot more of the parents were crying.

Sure, there were tears of sadness—of seeing their little ones walking into school for the first time. But there also tears of joy—the joy of knowing a great pre-k education was the first step on the road to a brighter future.

Today, we live in a world in which brainpower is the new currency of success. If we want to compete—and we'd better—we need everyone's talent. We don't have a single person to waste.

Here in San Antonio, I made PreK4SA happen. As President, we'll make Prek 4 the USA happen—universal pre-kindergarten for all children whose parents want it, so that all of our nation's students can get a strong start. And we won't stop there.

We'll work to make the first two years of college, a certification program or an apprenticeship accessible and affordable, so millions more young people and people who are returning to school later in life can get the skills they need to get a good job without drowning in debt.

Now, to be the healthiest nation, we need a better health care system.

Not a health care system that bends to the will of Big Pharma and the big insurers, but a health care system built for the people who need it.

For as long as I knew her, my grandmother was diabetic. As she grew older and her condition got worse, she needed more and more treatment. Thank God there was Medicare there for her. It should be there for everybody. It's time for Medicare for All–universal health care for every American.

To be the fairest nation, we have to reform and reimagine our justice system. All over this nation, for far too many people of color, any interaction with the police can become fatal.

If police in Charleston can arrest Dylann Roof after he murdered nine people worshipping at Bible study without hurting him, then don't tell me that Michael Brown, and Tamir Rice, and Aiyana Jones, and Eric Garner, and Jason Pero, and Stephon Clark, and Sandra Bland shouldn't still be alive today too.

We're going to keep saying their names and those of too many others just like them who were victims of state violence. We're going to keep saying that Black Lives Matter, while working toward a justice system where it's true.

You know what else is true? For far too many poor people who can't afford bail, an accusation alone can swiftly turn into a jail sentence. In our country, "innocent until proven guilty" shouldn't just be reserved for the wealthy few who can afford high priced lawyers. It should apply to every American.

We must also reform our immigration system, so that keeping families together—instead of tearing them apart—is our policy. Just a couple days ago, President Trump visited McAllen Texas—just south of here—after claiming that we're facing an 'invasion' at our border. He called it a national security crisis.

Well, there is a crisis today—it's a crisis of leadership. Donald Trump has failed to uphold the values of our great nation.

Yes, there are serious issues that need to be addressed in our broken immigration system—but seeking asylum is a legal right.

And the cruel policies of this administration are doing real and lasting harm. One of the things that I remember most about my grandmother is how she would talk to me about how she came to this country as a child separated from her dying mother. Even as a seventy-year-old woman, when she remembered those moments, she would cry like the seven-year-old girl she was when it happened, sobbing that she never got to say goodbye.

Yes, we must have border security, but there is a smart and humane way to do it. And there is no way in hell that caging children is keeping us safe. We say no to building a wall and say yes to building community. We say no to scapegoating immigrants, and yes to Dreamers, yes to keeping families together, and yes to finally passing comprehensive immigration reform.

If we all work together, we can build a nation more prosperous not only for those already doing well, but for everyone.

We can raise the minimum wage, so people don't have to work two or three jobs to support a family.

We can protect a woman's right to make her own decisions about her body, because for women, access to reproductive healthcare is an economic issue.

We can protect the right of workers to organize in an economy that is quickly changing and leaving too many families behind.

We can protect people from discrimination no matter who they love or how they identify.

And we'll work to make sure every American has a decent, safe, affordable place to live.

As housing secretary, I visited 100 different communities—big and small—across our country, from downtown Los Angeles to rural Wisconsin and the Pine Ridge Reservation. This much is clear: we have a housing crisis in this country.

Today, too many families are spending more than half of their income on rent. And that means more families are doubling up, sleeping on the couches of relatives or even on the streets. But you know what? You hardly ever hear about it. That's going to change. We will invest in housing that's affordable to the middle class and to the poor. And I know we can turn things around.

In the Obama administration we made ending homelessness a priority—starting with veteran homelessness. By the time we were done, we'd cut veteran homelessness almost in half. In the years to come, we can do that and more.

The biggest threat to our prosperity in the 21st century is climate change.

Don't let anybody tell you that we have to choose between growing our economy and protecting our planet. We can fight climate change and create great jobs—and we don't have a moment to waste. Scientists tell us that, if we don't get serious right now, the consequences will be tragic.

So we won't wait. As President, my first executive order will recommit the United States to the Paris Climate Accord. We're gonna say no to subsidizing big oil and say yes to passing a Green New Deal.

So, those are just some of the ways we're going to become the smartest, healthiest, fairest, and most prosperous nation on earth—it is our blueprint for 21st century opportunity.

And so you know that this is always—and only—about you: I won't be accepting a dime of PAC money in this campaign. And as President, we will work to overturn Citizens United—to get big money out of politics.

That's why I'm running. And that's what I'm running for. And I'll have a lot more to say about my plans in the days to come.

Throughout our nation's history, even in its darkest days, there have always been patriots who came together to do the hard work to get us closer to our nation's highest ideals—those who fought to abolish slavery, suffragists who organized for a woman's right to vote, a generation that sat in at lunch counters and marched across the Edmund Pettus bridge, the activists at Stonewall, and this generation that is Marching for Our Lives—people who have challenged us to perfect our union.

You and I, we stand on their shoulders, generations of men and women who made beds and made sacrifices, who fought in wars and fought discrimination, who picked crops and stood in picket lines.

They didn't wait. They made our nation what it is today. And now it's our turn to take that baton and to make our nation better than ever. I'm asking you to join me.

You give me your support, and I give you my word: I will spend every day working hard to make sure you can get a good job, find a decent place to live, have good health care when you get sick and that your children and grandchildren can reach their dreams, no matter who you are or where you come from.

We have always been at our best when we're united by something bigger. And in this journey, in the days to come, together we will show that hope can be bigger than fear. That light can be bigger than darkness, and that truth can be bigger than lies.

And as long as we work for it, tomorrow will always be better than today.

So, let's get to work. Vamonos!"

CHAPTER 4
Credibility Strategies

Some level of personal credibility is a necessary condition in effective rhetorical action. Credibility also can be developed in a work in order to motivate an audience to take action. And in rare cases, an individual may possess so much credibility that we accept a judgment simply based on his/her word. These sample works are included in this section to test the power of credibility. The critic should go through the process of internal evaluation by first identifying the purpose of the rhetoric, then considering the rhetorical barriers (and advantages) facing the rhetor, and then identifying the strategies in the rhetoric. At that point, the critic can compare the strategies to the barriers in order to test whether they were sufficient to achieve the purpose.

TESTIMONY OF RICHARD GERE

Richard Gere is not only a famous actor, but also an activist on behalf of Tibet. In testimony before Congress, Gere combined an appeal to credibility with other strategies to argue for supporting those who oppose the domination of Tibet by the People's Republic of China.

Testimony of Richard Gere

Thank you, Mr. Chairman, for the opportunity to appear before the Committee and to speak on the importance of U.S. refugee assistance to the Tibetan refugees and the substantial needs of that growing community. I am deeply honored to follow Assistant Secretary Julia Taft and to be included here with these fine men and women who are committed in their public lives to serving the needs of the desperate and disenfranchised. In a very real way, they are taking on the moral responsibility of our nation. I have been an activist for the cause of Tibet for many, many years and have been privileged to testify before this Committee and its Senate counterpart on the status of Tibet and His Holiness the Dalai Lama's efforts to find a lasting peace. In all this time, I am saddened to say, that conditions in Tibet have worsened and, as reported by the State Department this month, "tight controls on fundamental freedoms continued and in some cases intensified." I have visited Tibet and have seen at first hand the repressive conditions that lead Tibetan refugees to flee. I would urge you all to go and see for yourselves the degradation of the Tibetan people and culture and experience the suffocating presence of China's control system. Congressman Frank Wolf described the repression he found in Tibet as more brutal than he witnessed in Soviet Russia or Communist Romania—a repression applied with what Senator Daniel Patrick Moynihan has called "Stalinoid dementia." Anyone familiar with the issue of Tibet, as I believe this Committee is, understands that systematic human rights abuses, intensified control, cultural assimilation and resource exploitation have fundamentally changed the Tibetan way of life. To the extent that Tibetans can survive within these foreign and repressive Chinese-imposed paradigms, they remain in Tibet or they flee. What we are seeing this winter, is an increase in Tibetan refugees arriving in Nepal and India, and particularly an increase in the number of monks and nuns and children. I was in Kathmandu, Nepal for two weeks during the month of December. There is a transit camp of sorts there—a barefloored dormitory, a processing office, a small room where a single nurse administers inoculations to little ones and cleans and dresses the rotting flesh of frostbite victims. It is at once a wonderful and sorrowful place, a mixed bag of hope and despair. That it exists at all, is a result of Congressional initiative and State Department funding, and for that I am extremely grateful. I understand the building of a large dormitory with kitchen is near completion to relieve overcrowding and provide a semblance of privacy to monks and nuns, young children, and to separate men and women. After watching the crowd of new arrivals swell every day, I doubt that its purpose will be fully achieved this

Richard Gere's testimony before Subcommittee on International Operations and Human Rights of the Committee on International Relations of the House of Representatives was presented on February 24, 1988.

winter. There is an extraordinary Tibetan woman at the transit camp. Her name is Tsering Llamo. I bring her to your attention for two reasons. First, as a former Fulbright scholar, she represents a program, authorized by this Committee, that has returned to the Tibetan exile community a skilled cadre of young people, and she now serves magnificently in the U.S.-funded Tibetan refugee assistance program. Secondly, Tsering Llamo is asking for a proper clinic and funding for a visiting doctor. By the time they reach Kathmandu, Tibetan refugees are malnourished, exhausted and often traumatized. Many have been in flight from two to six months before reaching the Tibet-Nepal border. Descending from the Tibetan plateau, these refugees have few immunities to protect them from diseases that are rampant in Nepal and India. Many arrive with dysentery, scabies, and worms. In winter, about 75 percent of escapees cross the Himalayas by fording a 19,000 foot pass. They must cross in one day or risk death from exposure. Severe frostbite is common. Reports of torture among Tibetan refugees are alarmingly common. A paper issued last fall by Physicians for Human Rights found "highly credible" personal accounts of torture at the hands of Chinese authorities by more than one in every seven Tibetan refugees interviewed. Many of those tortured were children or young adults. According to the doctor's report, "the abuse which these torture victims suffered resulted in significant physical and psychological consequences." Though she may try, these maladies are more than Tsering Llamo can handle alone. Mr. Chairman, I thank you again for the invitation to speak before the Committee. I have purposefully made my remarks brief, but commend to you my colleagues at the International Campaign for Tibet for more detailed information on the plight of Tibetan refugees. I would like to end my remarks by calling on the U.S. Government to increase its funding for overseas protection programs. As it is the world over, the need for refugee assistance for Tibetans in India and Nepal is not going down, it is going up. And we can expect the refugee flow to increase as China continues its clamp down on freedoms. I urge the United States not to reduce or "flat out" its contributions to this account, but to provide abundant assistance where it is so desperately needed. I understand that reduction in resources has caused understaffing of the UNHCR's protection division. I can tell you unequivocaly that the UNHCR Tibetan refugee program in Kathmandu has saved lives and lessened the torment of Tibetans at the hands of bandits and border guards. UNHCR protection is vital to the border handling and safe transit of this refugee group through Nepal. Furthermore, as China does not seem willing to moderate its behavior in Tibet, the need may arise for many more Tibetans to leave their country. The generosity of India and Nepal may not be sufficient to handle their numbers so I sincerely hope that, should that occasion arise, the United States will open its borders to them. As an elder Tibetan refugee so eloquently pleaded, "We are facing difficulties of immense burden... full of prayers, I implore that this may reach the heart of a benevolent person." Finally, I would like to announce a program launched today by the International Campaign for Tibet and WITNESS of the Lawyers Committee for Human Rights, to provide interactive documentation of the 1998 winter exodus of refugees from Tibet. This program can be accessed on (www.savetibet.org) and will feature photographs of Tibetan refugees and their stories. Beginning with His Holiness the Dalai Lama's flight in 1959, over 140,000 Tibetans have been driven from their homeland. I invite you to bear witness to this tragic exodus as it continues today.

GEORGE W. BUSH, PRESIDENT DISCUSSES HURRICANE RELIEF IN ADDRESS TO THE NATION

Hurricane Katrina not only devastated Louisiana and Mississippi, but the slow Federal response to the disaster led many to conclude that President George W. Bush had not done an effective job as a leader in responding to the crisis. In an address in New Orleans shortly after the hurricane, President Bush attempted to rebuild his credibility and demonstrate that his administration was taking strong action to confront the problem.

President Discusses Hurricane Relief in Address to the Nation
George W. Bush

THE PRESIDENT: Good evening. I'm speaking to you from the city of New Orleans—nearly empty, still partly under water, and waiting for life and hope to return. Eastward from Lake Pontchartrain, across the Mississippi coast, to Alabama into Florida, millions of lives were changed in a day by a cruel and wasteful storm.

In the aftermath, we have seen fellow citizens left stunned and uprooted, searching for loved ones, and grieving for the dead, and looking for meaning in a tragedy that seems so blind and random. We've also witnessed the kind of desperation no citizen of this great and generous nation should ever have to know—fellow Americans calling out for food and water, vulnerable people left at the mercy of criminals who had no mercy, and the bodies of the dead lying uncovered and untended in the street.

These days of sorrow and outrage have also been marked by acts of courage and kindness that make all Americans proud. Coast Guard and other personnel rescued tens of thousands of people from flooded neighborhoods. Religious congregations and families have welcomed strangers as brothers and sisters and neighbors. In the community of Chalmette, when two men tried to break into a home, the owner invited them to stay—and took in 15 other people who had no place to go. At Tulane Hospital for Children, doctors and nurses did not eat for days so patients could have food, and eventually carried the patients on their backs up eight flights of stairs to helicopters.

Many first responders were victims themselves, wounded healers, with a sense of duty greater than their own suffering. When I met Steve Scott of the Biloxi Fire Department, he and his colleagues were conducting a house-to-house search for survivors. Steve told me this: "I lost my house and I lost my cars, but I still got my family ... and I still got my spirit."

Across the Gulf Coast, among people who have lost much, and suffered much, and given to the limit of their power, we are seeing that same spirit—a core of strength that survives all hurt, a faith in God no storm can take away, and a powerful American determination to clear the ruins and build better than before.

Tonight so many victims of the hurricane and the flood are far from home and friends and familiar things. You need to know that our whole nation cares about you, and in the journey ahead you're not alone. To all who carry a burden of loss, I extend the deepest sympathy of our country. To every person who has served and sacrificed in this emergency, I offer the gratitude of our country. And tonight I also offer this pledge of the American people: Throughout the area hit by the hurricane, we will do what it takes, we will stay as long as it takes, to help citizens rebuild their communities and their lives. And all who question the future of the Crescent City need to know there is no way to imagine America without New Orleans, and this great city will rise again.

The work of rescue is largely finished; the work of recovery is moving forward. In nearly all of Mississippi, electric power has been restored. Trade is starting to return to the Port of New Orleans, and agricultural shipments are moving down the Mississippi River. All major gasoline pipelines are now in operation, preventing the supply disruptions that many feared. The breaks in the levees have been closed, the pumps are running, and the water here in New Orleans is receding by the hour. Environmental officials are on the ground, taking water samples, identifying and dealing with hazardous debris, and working to get drinking water and waste water treatment systems operating again. And some very sad duties are being carried out by professionals who gather the dead, treat them with respect, and prepare them for their rest.

In the task of recovery and rebuilding, some of the hardest work is still ahead, and it will require the creative skill and generosity of a united country.

Our first commitment is to meet the immediate needs of those who had to flee their homes and leave all their possessions behind. For these Americans, every night brings uncertainty, every day requires new courage, and in the months to come will bring more than their fair share of struggles.

The Department of Homeland Security is registering evacuees who are now in shelters and churches, or private homes, whether in the Gulf region or far away. I have signed an order providing immediate assistance to people from the disaster area. As of today, more than 500,000 evacuee families have gotten emergency help to pay for food, clothing, and other essentials. Evacuees who have not yet registered should contact FEMA or the Red Cross. We need to know who you are, because many of you will be eligible for broader assistance in the future. Many families were separated during the evacuation, and we are working to help you reunite. Please call this number: 1-877-568-3317—that's 1-877-568-3317—and we will work to bring your family back together, and pay for your travel to reach them.

In addition, we're taking steps to ensure that evacuees do not have to travel great distances or navigate bureaucracies to get the benefits that are there for them. The Department of Health and Human Services has sent more than 1,500 health professionals, along with over 50 tons of medical supplies—including vaccines and antibiotics and medicines for people with chronic conditions such as diabetes. The Social Security Administration is delivering checks. The Department of Labor is helping displaced persons apply for temporary jobs and unemployment benefits. And the Postal Service is registering new addresses so that people can get their mail.

To carry out the first stages of the relief effort and begin rebuilding at once, I have asked for, and the

Congress has provided, more than $60 billion. This is an unprecedented response to an unprecedented crisis, which demonstrates the compassion and resolve of our nation.

Our second commitment is to help the citizens of the Gulf Coast to overcome this disaster, put their lives back together, and rebuild their communities. Along this coast, for mile after mile, the wind and water swept the land clean. In Mississippi, many thousands of houses were damaged or destroyed. In New Orleans and surrounding parishes, more than a quarter-million houses are no longer safe to live in. Hundreds of thousands of people from across this region will need to find longer-term housing.

Our goal is to get people out of the shelters by the middle of October. So we're providing direct assistance to evacuees that allows them to rent apartments, and many already are moving into places of their own. A number of states have taken in evacuees and shown them great compassion—admitting children to school, and providing health care. So I will work with the Congress to ensure that states are reimbursed for these extra expenses.

In the disaster area, and in cities that have received huge numbers of displaced people, we're beginning to bring in mobile homes and trailers for temporary use. To relieve the burden on local health care facilities in the region, we're sending extra doctors and nurses to these areas. We're also providing money that can be used to cover overtime pay for police and fire departments while the cities and towns rebuild.

Near New Orleans, and Biloxi, and other cities, housing is urgently needed for police and firefighters, other service providers, and the many workers who are going to rebuild these cities. Right now, many are sleeping on ships we have brought to the Port of New Orleans—and more ships are on their way to the region. And we'll provide mobile homes, and supply them with basic services, as close to construction areas as possible, so the rebuilding process can go forward as quickly as possible.

And the federal government will undertake a close partnership with the states of Louisiana and Mississippi, the city of New Orleans, and other Gulf Coast cities, so they can rebuild in a sensible, well-planned way. Federal funds will cover the great majority of the costs of repairing public infrastructure in the disaster zone, from roads and bridges to schools and water systems. Our goal is to get the work done quickly. And taxpayers expect this work to be done honestly and wisely—so we'll have a team of inspectors general reviewing all expenditures.

In the rebuilding process, there will be many important decisions and many details to resolve, yet we're moving forward according to some clear principles. The federal government will be fully engaged in the mission, but Governor Barbour, Governor Blanco, Mayor Nagin, and other state and local leaders will have the primary role in planning for their own future. Clearly, communities will need to move decisively to change zoning laws and building codes, in order to avoid a repeat of what we've seen. And in the work of rebuilding, as many jobs as possible should go to the men and women who live in Louisiana, Mississippi, and Alabama.

Our third commitment is this: When communities are rebuilt, they must be even better and stronger than before the storm. Within the Gulf region are some of the most beautiful and historic places in America. As all of us saw on television, there's also some deep, persistent poverty in this region, as well. That poverty has roots in a history of racial discrimination, which cut off generations from the opportunity of America. We have a duty to confront this poverty with bold action. So let us restore all that we have cherished from yesterday, and let us rise above the legacy of inequality. When the streets are rebuilt, there should be many new businesses, including minority-owned businesses, along those streets. When the houses are rebuilt, more families should own, not rent, those houses. When the regional economy revives, local people should be prepared for the jobs being created.

Americans want the Gulf Coast not just to survive, but to thrive; not just to cope, but to overcome. We want evacuees to come home, for the best of reasons—because they have a real chance at a better life in a place they love.

When one resident of this city who lost his home was asked by a reporter if he would relocate, he said, "Naw, I will rebuild—but I will build higher." That is our vision for the future, in this city and beyond: We'll not just rebuild, we'll build higher and better. To meet this goal, I will listen to good ideas from Congress, and state and local officials, and the private sector. I believe we should start with three initiatives that the Congress should pass.

Tonight I propose the creation of a Gulf Opportunity Zone, encompassing the region of the disaster in Louisiana and Mississippi and Alabama. Within this zone, we should provide immediate incentives for job-creating investment, tax relief for small businesses, incentives to companies that create jobs, and loans and loan guarantees for small businesses, including minority-owned enterprises, to get them up and running again. It is entrepreneurship that creates jobs and opportunity; it is entrepreneurship that helps break the cycle of poverty; and we will take the side of entrepreneurs as they lead the economic revival of the Gulf region.

I propose the creation of Worker Recovery Accounts to help those evacuees who need extra help finding work. Under this plan, the federal government would provide accounts of up to $5,000, which these evacuees could draw upon for job training and education to help them get a good job, and for child care expenses during their job search.

And to help lower-income citizens in the hurricane region build new and better lives, I also propose that Congress pass an Urban Homesteading Act. Under this approach, we will identify property in the region owned by the federal government, and provide building sites to low-income citizens free of charge, through a lottery. In return, they would pledge to build on the lot, with either a mortgage or help from a charitable organization like Habitat for Humanity. Home ownership is one of the great strengths of any community, and it must be a central part of our vision for the revival of this region.

In the long run, the New Orleans area has a particular challenge, because much of the city lies below sea level. The people who call it home need to have reassurance that their lives will be safer in the years to come. Protecting a city that sits lower than the water around it is not easy, but it can, and has been done. City and parish officials in New Orleans, and state officials in Louisiana will have a large part in the engineering decisions to come. And the Army Corps of Engineers will work at their side to make the flood protection system stronger than it has ever been.

The work that has begun in the Gulf Coast region will be one of the largest reconstruction efforts the world has ever seen. When that job is done, all Americans will have something to be very proud of—and all Americans are needed in this common effort. It is the armies of compassion—charities and houses of worship, and idealistic men and women—that give our reconstruction effort its humanity. They offer to those who hurt a friendly face, an arm around the shoulder, and the reassurance that in hard times, they can count on someone who cares. By land, by sea, and by air, good people wanting to make a difference deployed to the Gulf Coast, and they've been working around the clock ever since.

The cash needed to support the armies of compassion is great, and Americans have given generously. For example, the private fundraising effort led by former Presidents Bush and Clinton has already received pledges of more than $100 million. Some of that money is going to the Governors to be used

for immediate needs within their states. A portion will also be sent to local houses of worship to help reimburse them for the expense of helping others. This evening the need is still urgent, and I ask the American people to continue donating to the Salvation Army, the Red Cross, other good charities, and religious congregations in the region.

It's also essential for the many organizations of our country to reach out to your fellow citizens in the Gulf area. So I've asked USA Freedom Corps to create an information clearinghouse, available at usafreedomcorps.gov, so that families anywhere in the country can find opportunities to help families in the region, or a school can support a school. And I challenge existing organizations—churches, and Scout troops, or labor union locals to get in touch with their counterparts in Mississippi, Louisiana, or Alabama, and learn what they can do to help. In this great national enterprise, important work can be done by everyone, and everyone should find their role and do their part.

The government of this nation will do its part, as well. Our cities must have clear and up-to-date plans for responding to natural disasters, and disease outbreaks, or a terrorist attack, for evacuating large numbers of people in an emergency, and for providing the food and water and security they would need. In a time of terror threats and weapons of mass destruction, the danger to our citizens reaches much wider than a fault line or a flood plain. I consider detailed emergency planning to be a national security priority, and therefore, I've ordered the Department of Homeland Security to undertake an immediate review, in cooperation with local counterparts, of emergency plans in every major city in America.

I also want to know all the facts about the government response to Hurricane Katrina. The storm involved a massive flood, a major supply and security operation, and an evacuation order affecting more than a million people. It was not a normal hurricane—and the normal disaster relief system was not equal to it. Many of the men and women of the Coast Guard, the Federal Emergency Management Agency, the United States military, the National Guard, Homeland Security, and state and local governments performed skillfully under the worst conditions. Yet the system, at every level of government, was not well-coordinated, and was overwhelmed in the first few days. It is now clear that a challenge on this scale requires greater federal authority and a broader role for the armed forces—the institution of our government most capable of massive logistical operations on a moment's notice.

Four years after the frightening experience of September the 11th, Americans have every right to expect a more effective response in a time of emergency. When the federal government fails to meet such an obligation, I, as President, am responsible for the problem, and for the solution. So I've ordered every Cabinet Secretary to participate in a comprehensive review of the government response to the hurricane. This government will learn the lessons of Hurricane Katrina. We're going to review every action and make necessary changes, so that we are better prepared for any challenge of nature, or act of evil men, that could threaten our people.

The United States Congress also has an important oversight function to perform. Congress is preparing an investigation, and I will work with members of both parties to make sure this effort is thorough.

In the life of this nation, we have often been reminded that nature is an awesome force, and that all life is fragile. We're the heirs of men and women who lived through those first terrible winters at Jamestown and Plymouth, who rebuilt Chicago after a great fire, and San Francisco after a great earthquake, who reclaimed the prairie from the Dust Bowl of the 1930s. Every time, the people of this land have come back from fire, flood, and storm to build anew—and to build better than what we had before. Americans have never left our destiny to the whims of nature—and we will not start now.

These trials have also reminded us that we are often stronger than we know—with the help of grace and one another. They remind us of a hope beyond all pain and death, a God who welcomes the lost to a house not made with hands. And they remind us that we're tied together in this life, in this nation—and that the despair of any touches us all.

I know that when you sit on the steps of a porch where a home once stood, or sleep on a cot in a crowded shelter, it is hard to imagine a bright future. But that future will come. The streets of Biloxi and Gulfport will again be filled with lovely homes and the sound of children playing. The churches of Alabama will have their broken steeples mended and their congregations whole. And here in New Orleans, the street cars will once again rumble down St. Charles, and the passionate soul of a great city will return.

In this place, there's a custom for the funerals of jazz musicians. The funeral procession parades slowly through the streets, followed by a band playing a mournful dirge as it moves to the cemetery. Once the casket has been laid in place, the band breaks into a joyful "second line"—symbolizing the triumph of the spirit over death. Tonight the Gulf Coast is still coming through the dirge—yet we will live to see the second line.

Thank you, and may God bless America.

REPRESENTATIVE PRAMILA JAYAPAL, "FAMILY SEPARATION CRISIS"

Representative Jayapal used a speech in the House of Representatives to attack the immigration policies of the Trump Administration. She focused on a policy that had separated the children of undocumented immigrants from their parents. In the speech, she cited her own experience visiting immigrants who had been separated from their children in combination with argument, narrative, and value appeals to back up her position.

Family Separation Crisis
Pramila Jayapal

One year ago, I became the first Member of Congress to go into a Federal prison where hundreds of men and women, mothers and fathers, had been separated from their children and were being held in the prison system, in the Federal prison just south of my district.

I cannot, even today, 365 days later, forget the stories that these mothers and fathers told me. They told me about how immigration agents said to them, "Your families don't exist anymore," and that they would never see their children again.

At the time that I saw them, it was already three to four weeks after they had been separated, and the majority of those parents had no idea where their children were.

In fact, that morning, some of them had been handed slips that supposedly had the names of their children written on those slips of paper. One woman came over to me crying and she said: These are not my children.

That slip that supposedly had the names of her children did not match her actual children.

Can you imagine? I just think, as a mother, and for all the mothers and fathers out there, as a parent, can you imagine being separated from your child, in some cases children as young as six months, later

Representative Pramila Jayapal, "Family Separation Crisis," Congressional Record, May 9, 2019, H3663

we found out three months old, babies, who were torn off the breasts of their mothers?

These moms described immigration agents tearing them from their children without the opportunity to say good-bye. Some of them told me that when they went to go to the bathroom, they were told their children would still be there. When they came back, their children were gone. But they could hear them in the very next room crying for them, screaming for their parents, and these mothers were not able to go.

They told me how immigration agents put them in line with their children, and they would send the parents in one direction and the children in another direction.

One of the mothers told me how she left Guatemala with her 8- and 12-year- old children. Her husband is in prison. He was put in prison for raping a young child around the same age as her daughter. He was just about to come out of prison, and she was afraid that he would come out of prison and then go after their child, rape her daughter.

Another woman from El Salvador told me how she got a protection order against her ex-husband, who is a police officer, but the protection order was meaningless. He continued to antagonize her family, so she left.

Many of these mothers told me how they had left one or two of their children behind because they wanted to try to save one. It was too difficult to bring small children on the long journey that they were taking—the incredible sacrifice as a parent of trying to save one child.

One mother told me that she had three children. The first was shot and killed by gang members. The second was shot and paralyzed by gang members. She left the paralyzed child at home because she knew that he would not be able to make the journey. She took the final child. She tried to bring that child to safety.

After everything these mothers experienced— the trauma in their home countries, the cruel separation from their children—the treatment that they experienced in immigration custody was just outrageous. Immigration agents told them that they were "filthy." They used that word.

Immigration agents laughed at these mothers when they cried about losing their children. And these mothers told me how they were detained in cells that were so cold that they called them "the ice box" because it was so cold.

Many of these mothers described being put there after crossing the Rio Grande River; and they were still wet, and they were put into these freezer boxes, these ice boxes, without blankets, without sleeping mats. Some mothers described how they went without water for five days.

After public outcry and pressure from elected officials, the government set up a number for parents to call to get information on their children, but some of the parents that I spoke to in Texas said that the number didn't work or that ICE wouldn't allow them to speak to their children.

One mother mentioned that she repeatedly tried to call her child to try to locate her child, but the number would not go through.

One mother told me that, when she requested to talk to her child, the ICE agents would get mad; and agents mentioned that, in some instances, families would have to pay for these phone calls.

And this isn't just anecdotal. The DHS inspector general's September 2018 report found mixed results among parents attempting to call their children and that important information about how to contact separated children was not always available....

I cannot imagine that this is the country that we call the greatest country in the world. I cannot imagine that my country that I am proud of, that I serve here as a Member of Congress for would do this to children.

And this administration has consistently demonized and vilified immigrants, but this policy of cruel family separation is hard to even describe, hard to imagine that it is happening in our borders.

CHAPTER 5
Aesthetic Strategies

Aesthetic strategies are generally used as support for other rhetorical strategies. For example, parallel structure, antithesis, and labeling might be used to add interest to and reinforce an argument. However, in some cases, aesthetic strategies may function as primary means of persuasion in a dispute.

Several samples of aesthetic strategies are included. In relation to each of them, the critic first should identify the aesthetic strategies present in the rhetoric. At that point, the critic should conduct an internal evaluation of each work by moving through the stages of purpose identification, isolation of rhetorical barriers and advantages, consideration of strategies, and on-balance comparison of the strategies to the barriers.

ICONIC CIVIL RIGHTS PHOTO

Pictures are said to be worth a thousand words, but in fact they often are difficult to interpret without words. In this case, the words on the signs combine with the image from the March on Washington in 1963. The caption from the National Archives for this picture reads: "On August 28, 1963 America saw one of the largest marches on Washington in support of civil rights. Called the March on Washington for Jobs and Freedom the protest was organized by a group of civil rights, labor, and religious organizations, under the theme 'jobs, and freedom.' Around 250,000 people took part in the protest which ended with Martin Luther King, Jr. giving his famous I Have a Dream speech." It is important to consider how the combination of words and images continues to send an important message today about the continuing need to battle for economic justice and civil rights for all.

Leaders at the Head of the Civil Rights March on Washington, D.C. on August 28, 1963. Source: National Archives, Record Group 306, of the U.S. Information Agency, 1900–2003.

BARACK OBAMA, "EULOGY FOR REV. CLEMENTA PINCKNEY"

President Obama was known not only for the eloquence of his policy and campaign speeches, but for his ability to speak movingly on ceremonial occasions, such as the eulogy. During his presidency, he presented several moving eulogies following mass shootings. In his highly acclaimed eulogy for Pinckney, Obama had to confront the aftermath of a mass shooting at a Black church in Charleston, South Carolina by a white supremacists which resulted in the death of Reverend Pinckney and several others. Obama relied on language strategies to fulfill the functions of the eulogy and help the audience move forward.

Eulogy for
Rev. Clementa Pinckney
Barack Obama

Giving all praise and honor to God.

The Bible calls us to hope. To persevere, and have faith in things not seen.

"They were still living by faith when they died," Scripture tells us. "They did not receive the things promised; they only saw them and welcomed them from a distance, admitting that they were foreigners and strangers on Earth."

We are here today to remember a man of God who lived by faith. A man who believed in things not seen. A man who believed there were better days ahead, off in the distance. A man of service who persevered, knowing full well he would not receive all those things he was promised, because he believed his efforts would deliver a better life for those who followed.

To Jennifer, his beloved wife; to Eliana and Malana, his beautiful, wonderful daughters; to the Mother Emanuel family and the people of Charleston, the people of South Carolina.

I cannot claim to have the good fortune to know Reverend Pinckney well. But I did have the pleasure of knowing him and meeting him here in South Carolina, back when we were both a little bit younger. Back when I didn't have visible grey hair. The first thing I noticed was his graciousness, his smile, his reassuring baritone, his deceptive sense of humor— all qualities that helped him wear so effortlessly a heavy burden of expectation.

Friends of his remarked this week that when Clementa Pinckney entered a room, it was like the future arrived; that even from a young age, folks knew he was special. Anointed. He was the progeny of a long line of the faithful—a family of preachers who spread God's word, a family of protesters who sowed change to expand voting rights and desegregate the South. Clem heard their instruction, and he did not forsake their teaching.

He was in the pulpit by 13, pastor by 18, public servant by 23. He did not exhibit any of the cockiness of youth, nor youth's insecurities; instead, he set an example worthy of his position, wise beyond his years, in his speech, in his conduct, in his love, faith, and purity.

As a senator, he represented a sprawling swath of the Lowcountry, a place that has long been one of the most neglected in America. A place still wracked by poverty and inadequate schools; a place where children can still go hungry and the sick can go without treatment. A place that needed somebody like Clem.

His position in the minority party meant the odds of winning more resources for his constituents were often long. His calls for greater equity were too often unheeded, the votes he cast were sometimes lonely. But he never gave up. He stayed true to his convictions. He would not grow discouraged. After a full day at the capitol, he'd climb into his car and head to the church to draw sustenance from his family, from his ministry, from the community that loved and needed him. There he would fortify his faith, and imagine what might be.

Reverend Pinckney embodied a politics that was neither mean, nor small. He conducted himself quietly, and kindly, and diligently. He encouraged progress not by pushing his ideas alone, but by seeking out your ideas, partnering with you to make things happen. He was full of empathy and fellow feeling, able to walk in somebody else's shoes and see through their eyes. No wonder one of his senate colleagues remembered Senator Pinckney as "the most gentle of the 46 of us—the best of the 46 of us."

Clem was often asked why he chose to be a pastor and a public servant. But the person who asked probably didn't know the history of the AME church. As our brothers and sisters in the AME church know, we don't make those distinctions. "Our calling,"

Barack Obama, "Eulogy for Rev. Clementa Pinckney," June 26, 2015

Clem once said, "is not just within the walls of the congregation, but...the life and community in which our congregation resides."

He embodied the idea that our Christian faith demands deeds and not just words; that the "sweet hour of prayer" actually lasts the whole week long— that to put our faith in action is more than individual salvation, it's about our collective salvation; that to feed the hungry and clothe the naked and house the homeless is not just a call for isolated charity but the imperative of a just society.

What a good man. Sometimes I think that's the best thing to hope for when you're eulogized—after all the words and recitations and resumes are read, to just say someone was a good man.

You don't have to be of high station to be a good man. Preacher by 13. Pastor by 18. Public servant by 23. What a life Clementa Pinckney lived. What an example he set. What a model for his faith. And then to lose him at 41—slain in his sanctuary with eight wonderful members of his flock, each at different stages in life but bound together by a common commitment to God.

Cynthia Hurd. Susie Jackson. Ethel Lance. DePayne Middleton-Doctor. Tywanza Sanders. Daniel L. Simmons. Sharonda Coleman-Singleton. Myra Thompson. Good people. Decent people. God-fearing people. People so full of life and so full of kindness. People who ran the race, who persevered. People of great faith.

To the families of the fallen, the nation shares in your grief. Our pain cuts that much deeper because it happened in a church. The church is and always has been the center of African-American life—a place to call our own in a too often hostile world, a sanctuary from so many hardships.

Over the course of centuries, black churches served as "hush harbors" where slaves could worship in safety; praise houses where their free descendants could gather and shout hallelujah—rest stops for the weary along the Underground Railroad; bunkers for the foot soldiers of the Civil Rights Movement. They have been, and continue to be, community centers where we organize for jobs and justice; places of scholarship and network; places where children are loved and fed and kept out of harm's way, and told that they are beautiful and smart—and taught that they matter. That's what happens in church.

That's what the black church means. Our beating heart. The place where our dignity as a people is inviolate. When there's no better example of this tradition than Mother Emanuel—a church built by blacks

seeking liberty, burned to the ground because its founder sought to end slavery, only to rise up again, a Phoenix from these ashes.

When there were laws banning all-black church gatherings, services happened here anyway, in defiance of unjust laws. When there was a righteous movement to dismantle Jim Crow, Dr. Martin Luther King, Jr. preached from its pulpit, and marches began from its steps. A sacred place, this church. Not just for blacks, not just for Christians, but for every American who cares about the steady expansion— of human rights and human dignity in this country; a foundation stone for liberty and justice for all. That's what the church meant.

We do not know whether the killer of Reverend Pinckney and eight others knew all of this history. But he surely sensed the meaning of his violent act. It was an act that drew on a long history of bombs and arson and shots fired at churches, not random, but as a means of control, a way to terrorize and oppress. An act that he imagined would incite fear and recrimination; violence and suspicion. An act that he presumed would deepen divisions that trace back to our nation's original sin.

Oh, but God works in mysterious ways. God has different ideas.

He didn't know he was being used by God. Blinded by hatred, the alleged killer could not see the grace surrounding Reverend Pinckney and that Bible study group—the light of love that shone as they opened the church doors and invited a stranger to join in their prayer circle. The alleged killer could have never anticipated the way the families of the fallen would respond when they saw him in court— in the midst of unspeakable grief, with words of forgiveness. He couldn't imagine that.

The alleged killer could not imagine how the city of Charleston, under the good and wise leadership of Mayor Riley—how the state of South Carolina, how the United States of America would respond— not merely with revulsion at his evil act, but with big-hearted generosity and, more importantly, with a thoughtful introspection and self-examination that we so rarely see in public life.

Blinded by hatred, he failed to comprehend what Reverend Pinckney so well understood—the power of God's grace.

This whole week, I've been reflecting on this idea of grace. The grace of the families who lost loved ones. The grace that Reverend Pinckney would preach about in his sermons. The grace described in one of my favorite hymnals—the one we all know: Amazing grace, how sweet the sound that saved a wretch like me. I once was lost, but now I'm found; was blind but now I see.

According to the Christian tradition, grace is not earned. Grace is not merited. It's not something we deserve. Rather, grace is the free and benevolent favor of God—as manifested in the salvation of sinners and the bestowal of blessings. Grace.

As a nation, out of this terrible tragedy, God has visited grace upon us, for he has allowed us to see where we've been blind. He has given us the chance, where we've been lost, to find our best selves. We may not have earned it, this grace, with our rancor and complacency, and short-sightedness and fear of each other—but we got it all the same. He gave it to us anyway. He's once more given us grace. But it is up to us now to make the most of it, to receive it with gratitude, and to prove ourselves worthy of this gift.

For too long, we were blind to the pain that the Confederate flag stirred in too many of our citizens. It's true, a flag did not cause these murders. But as people from all walks of life, Republicans and Democrats, now acknowledge—including Governor Haley, whose recent eloquence on the subject is worthy of praise—as we all have to acknowledge, the flag has always represented more than just ancestral pride. For many, black and white, that flag was a reminder of systemic oppression and racial subjugation. We see that now.

Removing the flag from this state's capitol would not be an act of political correctness; it would not be an insult to the valor of Confederate soldiers. It would simply be an acknowledgment that the cause for which they fought—the cause of slavery—was wrong—the imposition of Jim Crow after the Civil War, the resistance to civil rights for all people was wrong. It would be one step in an honest accounting of America's history; a modest but meaningful balm for so many unhealed wounds. It would be an expression of the amazing changes that have transformed this state and this country for the better, because of the work of so many people of goodwill, people of all races striving to form a more perfect union. By taking down that flag, we express God's grace.

But I don't think God wants us to stop there. For too long, we've been blind to the way past injustices continue to shape the present. Perhaps we see that now. Perhaps this tragedy causes us to ask some tough questions about how we can permit so many of our children to languish in poverty, or attend dilapidated schools, or grow up without prospects for a job or for a career.

Perhaps it causes us to examine what we're doing to cause some of our children to hate. Perhaps it softens hearts towards those lost young men, tens and tens of thousands caught up in the criminal justice system—and leads us to make sure that that system is not infected with bias; that we embrace changes in how we train and equip our police so that the bonds of trust between law enforcement and the communities they serve make us all safer and more secure.

Maybe we now realize the way racial bias can infect us even when we don't realize it, so that we're guarding against not just racial slurs, but we're also guarding against the subtle impulse to call Johnny back for a job interview but not Jamal. So that we search our hearts when we consider laws to make it harder for some of our fellow citizens to vote. By recognizing our common humanity by treating every child as important, regardless of the color of their skin or the station into which they were born, and to do what's necessary to make opportunity real for every American—by doing that, we express God's grace.

For too long, we've been blind to the unique mayhem that gun violence inflicts upon this nation. Sporadically, our eyes are open: When eight of our brothers and sisters are cut down in a church basement, 12 in a movie theater, 26 in an elementary school. But I hope we also see the 30 precious lives cut short by gun violence in this country every single day; the countless more whose lives are forever changed—the survivors crippled, the children traumatized and fearful every day as they walk to school, the husband who will never feel his wife's warm touch, the entire communities whose grief overflows every time they have to watch what happened to them happen to some other place.

The vast majority of Americans—the majority of gun owners—want to do something about this. We see that now. And I'm convinced that by acknowledging the pain and loss of others, even as we respect the traditions and ways of life that make up this beloved country—by making the moral choice to change, we express God's grace.

We don't earn grace. We're all sinners. We don't deserve it. But God gives it to us anyway. And we choose how to receive it. It's our decision how to honor it.

None of us can or should expect a transformation in race relations overnight. Every time something like this happens, somebody says we have to have a conversation about race. We talk a lot about race. There's no shortcut. And we don't need more talk. None of us should believe that a handful of gun safety measures will prevent every tragedy. It will not. People of goodwill will continue to debate the merits of various policies, as our democracy requires—this is a big, raucous place, America is. And there are good people on both sides of these debates. Whatever solutions we find will necessarily be incomplete.

But it would be a betrayal of everything Reverend Pinckney stood for, I believe, if we allowed ourselves to slip into a comfortable silence again. Once the eulogies have been delivered, once the TV cameras move on, to go back to business as usual—that's what we so often do to avoid uncomfortable truths about the prejudice that still infects our society. To settle for symbolic gestures without following up with the hard work of more lasting change—that's how we lose our way again.

It would be a refutation of the forgiveness expressed by those families if we merely slipped into old habits, whereby those who disagree with us are not merely wrong but bad; where we shout instead of listen; where we barricade ourselves behind preconceived notions or well-practiced cynicism.

Reverend Pinckney once said, "Across the South, we have a deep appreciation of history—we haven't always had a deep appreciation of each other's history." What is true in the South is true for America. Clem understood that justice grows out of recognition of ourselves in each other. That my liberty depends on you being free, too. That history can't be a sword to justify injustice, or a shield against progress, but must be a manual for how to avoid repeating the mistakes of the past—how to break the cycle. A roadway toward a better world. He knew that the path of grace involves an open mind—but, more importantly, an open heart.

That's what I've felt this week—an open heart. That, more than any particular policy or analysis, is what's called upon right now, I think—what a friend of mine, the writer Marilyn Robinson, calls "that reservoir of goodness, beyond, and of another kind, that we are able to do each other in the ordinary cause of things."

That reservoir of goodness. If we can find that grace, anything is possible. If we can tap that grace, everything can change.

Amazing grace. Amazing grace.

(Begins to sing)—Amazing grace—how sweet the sound, that saved a wretch like me; I once was lost, but now I'm found; was blind but now I see.

Clementa Pinckney found that grace.

Cynthia Hurd found that grace.

Susie Jackson found that grace.

Ethel Lance found that grace.

DePayne Middleton-Doctor found that grace.

Tywanza Sanders found that grace.

Daniel L. Simmons, Sr. found that grace.

Sharonda Coleman-Singleton found that grace.

Myra Thompson found that grace.

Through the example of their lives, they've now passed it on to us. May we find ourselves worthy of that precious and extraordinary gift, as long as our lives endure. May grace now lead them home. May God continue to shed His grace on the United States of America.

HOW DOES YOUR INCOME "STACK UP"?

In How Does Your Income "Stack Up"? a liberal advocacy group uses visual argument to claim that current taxation policy favors the rich. While the argument they make is a common one, the use of visual materials and other aesthetic strategies to support it, makes their approach unique. It is important to consider whether the visual material will make the overall claim more persuasive than it otherwise would be.

How Does Your Income "Stack Up"?

Picture your annual income as a stack of $100 bills.

Do you make $25,000? Your stack of $100 bills is 1 inch high.

Do you make $100,000? Your stack of $100 bills is 4 inches high.

Do you make $1 million? Your stack of $100 bills is 3.3 feet high.

Do you make $1 billion? Your stack of $100 bills is over ½ mile high!

The U.S. Income distribution is not a "Bell Curve"...it is an "L-Curve"!

On the scale of the football field graph shown here the bottom 99% of the population measure their incomes in inches. The top 1% measure their incomes as stacks of $100 bills feet or even miles high! The total wealth of the few people in the vertical spike equals the total wealth of the rest of the population combined.

The L-Curve raises many questions. Why does the wealth (which we all help produce) go so disproportionately to the few at the top? Why, in a prosperous economy, is there so much poverty? Why has the lion's share of the growth in recent economic booms, gone almost exclusively to those in the vertical spike while wages have stagnated?

Politically speaking, the L-Curve raises even more questions. Concentration of **wealth** produces concentration of **power** that is fundamentally incompatible with democracy. Why does our government give tax cuts to those on the vertical spike that result in cuts in services for the rest of us? The horizontal spike has the votes, but the vertical spike has the influence! They own the media. Your TV set is their pipeline into your brain! They set the agenda and the terms of debate. Furthermore, by the time you enter the voting booth all the "serious" candidates have been filtered and pre-selected by their ability to raise funds from those on the vertical spike. Those who can't attract big money are marginalized.

The only way to make the government *for* the people is to make it of the people and *by* the people. That means we, the people, must wake up. We must wake up our neighbors! We must learn to talk to each other directly. We must bypass the media culture and rebuild true community. Democracy does not start in the voting booth. It starts by *building a movement at the grass roots level* that values people over profits.

For more on the L-Curve and its implications, see: *www.lcurve.org*

The Income Distribution of the United States

(Visualized on the scale of a football field; income measured as stacks of $100 bills.)

The top of the graph varies from year to year. In Bill Gates' best year he increased his net worth by $50 billion ... a 30 mile high stack of $100 bills!

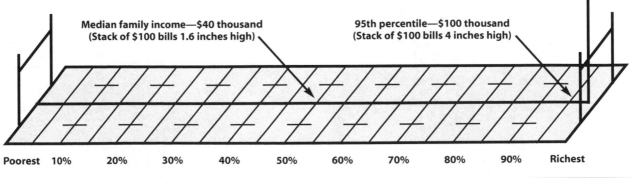

Median family income—$40 thousand
(Stack of $100 bills 1.6 inches high)

95th percentile—$100 thousand
(Stack of $100 bills 4 inches high)

Poorest 10%   20%   30%   40%   50%   60%   70%   80%   90%   Richest

Representative Adam Schiff, a Democrat from California, used language strategies to add emphasis to his arguments and value appeals concerning actions by the Trump campaign in the 2016 campaign.

Statement of House Judiciary Chairman
Adam Schiff

My colleagues might think it's okay that the Russians offered dirt on the Democratic candidate for president as part of what's described as the Russian government's effort to help the Trump campaign. You might think that's okay. My colleagues might think it's okay that when that was offered to the son of the president, who had a pivotal role in the campaign, that the president's son did not call the FBI, he did not adamantly refuse that foreign help—no, instead that son said he would "love" the help with the Russians.

You might think it was okay that he took that meeting. You might think it's okay that Paul Manafort, the campaign chair, someone with great experience running campaigns, also took that meeting. You might think it's okay that the president's son-in-law also took that meeting. You might think it's okay that they concealed it from the public. You might think it's okay that their only disappointment after that meeting was that the dirt they received on Hillary Clinton wasn't better. You might think it's okay. I don't.

You might think it's okay that, when it was discovered a year later that they had lied about that meeting and said it was about adoptions, you might think it's okay that the president is reported to have helped dictate that lie. You might think it's okay. I don't.

You might think it's okay that the campaign chairman of a presidential campaign would offer information about that campaign to a Russian oligarch in exchange for money or debt forgiveness. You might think that's okay. I don't. You might think it's okay that that campaign chairman offered polling data, campaign polling data, to someone linked to Russian intelligence. I don't think that's okay.

You might think it's okay if that the president himself called on Russia to hack his opponent's emails, if they were listening. You might think it's okay that, later that day, the Russians in fact attempted to hack a server affiliated with that campaign. I don't think that's okay.

You might think that it's okay that the president's son-in-law sought to establish a secret back-channel of communication with Russians through a Russian diplomatic facility. I don't think that's okay.

You might think it's okay that an associate of the president made direct contact with the GRU through Guccifer 2.0 and WikiLeaks, that is considered a hostile intelligence agency. You might think it's okay that a senior campaign official was instructed to reach that associate and find out what that hostile intelligence agency had to say, in terms of dirt on his opponent.

You might think it's okay that the national security adviser-designate secretly conferred with a Russian ambassador about undermining U.S. sanctions, and you might think it's okay he lied about it to the FBI.

You might say that's all okay. You might say that's just what you need to do to win. But I don't think it's okay. I think it's immoral, I think it's unethical, I think it's unpatriotic and, yes, I think it's corrupt, and evidence of collusion.

Now, I have always said that whether this amounts to proof of conspiracy was another matter. Whether the special counsel could prove beyond a reasonable doubt the proof of that crime was up to the special counsel and that I would accept his decision, and I do. He is a good and honorable man and he is a good prosecutor.

But I do not think that conduct, criminal or not, is okay. And the day we do think that's okay is the day we will look back and say, that is the day America lost its way.

And I'll tell you one more thing that is apropos of the hearing today. I don't think it's okay that during a presidential campaign Mr. Trump sought the Kremin's help to consummate a real estate deal in Moscow that would make him a fortune. According to the special counsel, hundreds of millions of dollars. I don't think it's okay that he concealed it from the public. I don't think it's okay he advocated a new and more favorable policy towards the Russians, even as he was seeking the Russian's help, the Kremlin's help, to make money.

I don't think it's okay that his attorney lied to our committee. There is a different word for that than collusion and it's called compromise. And that's the subject of our hearing today.

CHAPTER 6
Strategies for Producing an Emotional Response

Rhetoric that merely appeals to our intellect is unlikely to get us off the couch. To motivate people to take action, it is necessary to energize both their "heads" and their "hearts." And if you really want to energize people, you also energize their glands to produce passion or anger. Several works of rhetoric are included to illustrate the way that sub-strategies can be used to tap emotional responses.

In relation to each of these works, an internal evaluation should reveal how it functions. The first step is to identify the purpose served by the rhetoric. After identifying the rhetorical barriers/advantages that the rhetor faces, the critic then should focus on strategies. Once again, the final evaluation requires a comparison of the strategies to the barriers in order to check to see if the purpose has been fulfilled.

REMARKS TO THE CONVOCATION OF THE CHURCH OF GOD IN CHRIST IN MEMPHIS

In "Remarks to the Convocation of the Church of God in Christ in Memphis," President Bill Clinton used the site of the final speech of Martin Luther King, Jr., to make a major address concerning problems facing African-Americans. In so doing, Clinton faced the risk that he could offend his audience. He also drew on his close personal relationship with many leaders in the Black community. In the address, Clinton assumes the voice of King, by telling the audience what King would say if he were there. Clinton also relies on a host of other strategies. It is important to consider whether Clinton's use of King's voice in combination with other strategies was effective.

Remarks to the Convocation of the Church of God in Christ in Memphis
William J. Clinton

Thank you. Please sit down. Bishop Ford, Mrs. Mason, Bishop Owens, and Bishop Anderson; my bishops, Bishop Walker and Bishop Lindsey. Now, if you haven't had Bishop Lindey's barbecue, you haven't had barbecue. And if you haven't heard Bishop Walker attack one of my opponents, you have never heard a political speech. *[Laughter]*

I am glad to be here. You have touched my heart. You brought tears to my eyes and joy to my spirit. Last year I was over with you at the convention center. Two years ago your bishops came to Arkansas, and we laid a plaque at The Point in Little Rock, Arkansas, at 8th and Gaines, where Bishop Mason received the inspiration for the name of this great church. Bishop Brooks said from his pulpit that I would be elected President when most people

thought I wouldn't survive. I thank him, and I thank your faith, and I thank your works, for without you I would not be here today as your President.

Many have spoken eloquently and well, and many have been introduced. I want to thank my good friend Governor McWherter and my friend Mayor Herenton for being with me today, my friend Congressman Harold Ford, we are glad to be in his congressional district. I would like to, if I might, introduce just three other people who are Members of the Congress. They have come here with me, and without them it's hard for me to do much for you. The President proposes and the Congress disposes. Sometimes they dispose of what I propose, but I'm happy to say that according to a recent report in Washington, notwithstanding what you may have heard, this Congress has given me a higher percentage of my proposals than any first-year President since President Eisenhower. And I thank them for that. Let me introduce my good friend, a visitor to Tennessee, Congressman Bill Jefferson from New Orleans, Louisiana. Please stand up. *[Applause]* And an early supporter of my campaign, Congressman Bob Clement from

Presented November 13, 1993.

Tennessee, known to many of you. And a young man who's going to be coming back to the people of Tennessee and asking them to give him a promotion next year, Congressman Jim Cooper from Tennessee, and a good friend. Please welcome him.

You know, in the last 10 months, I've been called a lot of things, but nobody's called me a bishop yet. *[Laughter]* When I was about nine years old, my beloved and now departed grandmother, who was a very wise woman, looked at me and she said, "You know, I believe you could be a preacher if you were just a little better boy." *[Laughter]*

The proverb says, "A happy heart doeth good like medicine, but a broken spirit dryeth the bone." This is a happy place, and I'm happy to be here. I thank you for your spirit.

By the grace of God and your help, last year I was elected President of this great country. I never dreamed that I would ever have a chance to come to his hallowed place where Martin Luther King gave his last sermon. I ask you to think today about the purpose for which I ran and the purpose for which so many of you worked to put me in this great office. I have worked hard to keep faith with our common efforts; to restore the economy; to reverse the politics of helping only those at the top of our totem pole and not the hard-working middle class or the poor; to bring our people together across racial and regional and political lines; to make a strength out of our diversity instead of letting it tear us apart; to reward work and family and community and try to move us forward into the 21st century. I have tried to keep faith.

Thirteen percent of all my Presidential appointments are African-Americans, and there are five African-Americans in the Cabinet of the United States, $2^{1}/_{2}$ times as many as have ever served in this history of this great land. I have sought to advance the right to vote with the motor voter bill, supported so strongly by all the churches in our country. And next week it will be my great honor to sign the Restoration of Religious Freedoms Act, a bill supported widely by people across all religions and political philosophies to put back the real meaning of the Constitution, to give you and every other American the freedom to do what is most important in your life, to worship God as your spirit leads you.

I say to you, my fellow Americans, we have made a good beginning. Inflation is down. Interest rates are down. The deficit is down. Investment is up. Millions of Americans, including, I bet, some people in this room, have refinanced their homes or their business loans just in the last year. And in the last

10 months, this economy has produced more jobs in the private sector than in the previous four years.

We have passed a law called the family leave law, which says you can't be fired if you take a little time off when a baby is born or a parent is sick. We know that most Americans have to work, but you ought not to have to give up being a good parent just to take a job. If you can't succeed as a worker and a parent, this country can't make it.

We have radically reformed the college loan program, as I promised, to lower the cost of college loans and broaden the availability of it and make the repayment terms easier. And we have passed the national service law that will give in three years, three years from now, 100,000 young Americans a chance to serve their communities at home, to repair the frayed bonds of community, to build up the needs of people at the grassroots, and at the same time, earn some money to pay for a college education. It is a wonderful idea.

On April 15th, when people pay their taxes, somewhere between 15 million and 18 million working families on modest incomes, families with children and incomes of under $23,000, will get a tax cut, not a tax increase, in the most important effort to ensure that we reward work and family in the last 20 years. Fifty million American parents and their children will be advantaged by putting the Tax Code back on the side of working American parents for a change.

Under the leadership of the First Lady, we have produced a comprehensive plan to guarantee health care security to all Americans. How can we expect the American people to work and to live with all the changes in the global economy, where the average 18-year-old will change work seven times in a lifetime, unless we can simply say we have joined the ranks of all the other advanced countries around the world; you can have decent health care that's always there, that can never be taken away. It is time we did that, long past time. I ask you to help us achieve that.

But we have so much more to do. You and I know that most people are still working harder for the same or lower wages, that many people are afraid that their job will go away. We have to provide the education and training our people need, not just for our children but for our adults, too. If we cannot close this country up to the forces of change sweeping throughout the world, we have to at least guarantee people the security of being employable. They have to be able to get a new job if they're going to have to get a new job. We don't do that today, and we must, and we intend to proceed until that is done.

We have a guarantee that there will be some investment in those areas of our country, in the inner cities and in the destitute rural areas in the Mississippi Delta, of my home State and this State and Louisiana and Mississippi and other places like it throughout America. It's all very well to train people, but if they don't have a job, they can be trained for nothing. We must get investment to those places where the people are dying for work.

And finally, let me say, we must find people who will buy what we have to produce. We are the most productive people on Earth. That makes us proud. But what that means is that every year one person can produce more in the same amount of time. Now, if fewer and fewer people can produce more and more things, and yet you want to create more jobs and raise people's incomes, you have to have more customers for what it is you're making. And that is why I have worked so hard to sell more American products around the world, why I have asked that we be able to sell billions of dollars of computers we used, not to sell to foreign countries and foreign interests, to put our people to work.

Why? Next week I am going all the way to Washington State to meet with the President of China and the Prime Minister of Japan and the heads of 13 other Asian countries, the fastest growing part of the world, to say, "We want to be your partners. We will buy your goods, but we want you to buy ours too, if you please." That is why.

That is why I have worked so hard for this North American trade agreement that Congressman Ford endorsed today and Congressman Jefferson endorsed and Congressman Cooper and Congressman Clement, because we know that Americans can compete and win only if people will buy what it is we have to sell. There are 90 million people in Mexico. Seventy cents of every dollar they spend on foreign goods, they spend on American goods. People worry fairly about people shutting down plants in America and going not just to Mexico but to any place where the labor is cheap. It has happened.

What I want to say to you, my fellow Americans, is nothing in this agreement makes that more likely. That has happened already. It may happen again. What we need to do is keep the jobs here by finding customers there. That's what this agreement does. It gives us a chance to create opportunity for people. I have friends in this audience, people who are ministers from my State, fathers and sons, people—I've looked out all over this vast crowd and I see people I've known for years. They know. I spent my whole life working to create jobs. I would never knowingly do anything that would take a job away from the American people. This agreement will make more jobs. Now, we can also leave it if it doesn't work in six months. But if we don't take it, we'll lose it forever. We need to take it, because we have to do better.

But I guess what I really want to say to you today, my fellow Americans, is that we can do all of this and still fail unless we meet the great crisis of the spirit that is gripping America today.

When I leave you, Congressman Ford and I are going to a Baptist church near here to a town meeting he's having on health care and violence. I tell you, unless we do something about crime and violence and drugs that is ravaging the community, we will not be able to repair this country.

If Martin Luther King, who said, "Like Moses, I am on the mountaintop, and I can see the promised land, but I'm not going to be able to get there with you, but we will get there." If he were to reappear by my side today and give us a report card on the last 25 years, what would he say? You did a good job, he would say, voting and electing people who formerly were not electable because of the color of their skin. You have more political power, and that is good. You did a good job, he would say, letting people who have the ability to do so live wherever they want to live, go wherever they want to go in this great country. You did a good job, he would say, elevating people of color into the ranks of the United States Armed Forces to the very top or into the very top of our Government. You did a very good job, he would say. He would say, you did a good job creating a black middle class of people who really are doing well, and the middle class is growing more among African-Americans than among non-African-Americans. You do a good job. You did a good job in opening opportunity.

But he would say, I did not live and die to see the American family destroyed. I did not live and die to see 13-year-old boys get automatic weapons and gun down nine-year-olds just for the kick of it. I did not live and die to see young people destroy their own lives with drugs and then build fortunes destroying the lives of others. That is not what I came here to do. I fought for freedom, he would say, but not for the freedom of people to kill each other with reckless abandon, not for the freedom of children to have children and the fathers of the children walk away from them and abandon them as if they don't amount to anything. I fought for people to have the right to work but not to have whole communities and people abandoned. This is not what I lived and died for.

My fellow Americans, he would say, I fought to stop white people from being so filled with hate that they would wreak violence on black people. I did not fight for the right of black people to murder other black people with reckless abandon.

The other day the Mayor of Baltimore, a dear friend of mine, told me a story of visiting the family of a young man who had been killed—18 years old—on Halloween. He always went out with little bitty kids so they could trick-or-treat safely. And across the street from where they were walking on Halloween, a 14-year-old boy gave a 13-year-old boy a gun and dared him to shoot the 18-year-old boy, and he shot him dead. And the Mayor had to visit the family.

In Washington, DC, where I live, your Nation's Capital, the symbol of freedom throughout the world, look how that freedom is being exercised. The other night a man came along the street and grabbed a one-year-old child and put the child in his car. The child may have been the child of the man. And two people were after him, and they chased him in the car, and they just kept shooting with reckless abandon, knowing that baby was in the car. And they shot the man dead, and a bullet went through his body into the baby's body, and blew the little bootie off the child's foot.

The other day on the front page of our paper, the Nation's Capital, are we talking about world peace or world conflict? No, big article on the front page of the Washington Post about an 11-year-old child planning her funeral: "These are the hymns I want sung. This is the dress I want to wear. I know I'm not going to live very long." The freedom to die before you're a teenager is not what Martin Luther King lived and died for.

More than 37,000 people die from gunshot wounds in this country every year. Gunfire is the leading cause of death in young men. And now that we've all gotten so cool that everybody can get a semiautomatic weapon, a person now is three times more likely to die than 15 years ago, because they're likely to have three bullets in them. One hundred and sixty thousand children stay home from school every day because they are scared they will be hurt in their school.

The other day I was in California at a town meeting, and a handsome young man stood up and said, "Mr. President, my brother and I, we don't belong to gangs. We don't have guns. We don't do drugs. We want to go to school. We want to be professionals. We want to work hard. We want to do well. We want to have families. And we changed our school because the school we were in was so dangerous. So when we showed up to the new school to register, my brother and I were standing in line and somebody ran into the school and started shooting a gun. My brother was shot down standing right in front of me at the safer school." The freedom to do that kind of thing is not what Martin Luther King lived and died for. It's not what people gathered in the hallowed church for the night before he was assassinated in April of 1968. If you had told anybody who was here in that church on that night that we would abuse our freedom in that way, they would have found it hard to believe. And I tell you it is our moral duty to turn it around.

And now I think finally we have a chance. Finally I think, we have a chance. We have a pastor here from New Haven, Connecticut. I was in his church with Reverend Jackson when I was running for President on a snowy day in Connecticut to mourn the death of children who had been killed in that city. And afterward we walked down the street for more than a mile in the snow. Then, the American people were not ready. People would say, "Oh, this is a terrible thing, but what can we do about it."

Now when we read that foreign visitors come to our shores and are killed randomly in our fine State of Florida, when we see our children planning their funeral, when the American people are finally coming to grips with the accumulated wave of crime and violence and the breakdown of family and community and the increase in drugs and the decrease in jobs. I think finally we may be ready to do something about it. And there is something for each of us to do. There are changes we can make from the outside in, that's the job of the President and the Congress and the Governors and the Mayors and the social service agencies. Then there's some changes we're going to have to make from the inside out, or the others won't matter. That's what the magnificent song was about, wasn't it? Sometimes there are no answers from the outside in; sometimes all the answers have to come from the values and the stirrings and the voices that speak to us from within.

So we are beginning. We are trying to pass a bill to make our people safer, to put another 100,000 police officers on the street, to provide boot camps instead of prisons for young people who can still be rescued, to provide more safety in our schools, to restrict the availability of these awful assault weapons, to pass the Brady bill and at least require people to have their criminal background checked before they get a gun, and to say, if you're not old enough to vote and you're not old enough to go to war, you ought not to own a handgun, and you ought not to use one unless you're on a target range.

We want to pass a health care bill that will make drug treatment available for everyone. We have to have drug treatment and education available to everyone and especially those who are in prison who are coming out. We have a drug czar now in Lee Brown, who was the police chief of Atlanta, of Houston, of New York, who understands these things. And when the Congress comes back next year we will be moving forward on that.

We need this crime bill now. We ought to give it to the American people for Christmas. And we need to move forward on all these other fronts. But I say to you, my fellow Americans, we need some other things as well. I do not believe we can repair the basic fabric of society until people who are willing to work have work. Work organizes life. It gives structure and discipline to life. It gives meaning and self-esteem to people who are parents. It gives a role model to children.

The famous African-American sociologist William Julius Wilson, has written a stunning book called "The Truly Disadvantaged," in which he chronicles in breathtaking terms how the inner cities of our country have crumbled as work has disappeared. And we must find a way, through public and private sources, to enhance the attractiveness of the American people who live there to get investment there. We cannot, I submit to you, repair the American community and restore the American family until we provide the structure, the value, the discipline, and the reward that work gives.

I read a wonderful speech the other day given at Howard University in a lecture series funded by Bill and Camille Cosby, in which the speaker said, I grew up in Anacostia years ago. Even then it was all black, and it was a very poor neighborhood. But you know, when I was a child in Anacostia, 100 percent African-American neighborhood, a very poor neighborhood, we had a crime rate that was lower than the average of the crime rate of our city. Why? Because we had coherent families. We had coherent communities. The people who filled the church on Sunday lived in the same place they went to church. The guy that owned the drugstore lived down the street. The person that owned the grocery store lived in our community. We were whole." And I say to you, we have to make our people whole again. This church has stood for that. Why do you think you have five million members in this country? Because people know you are filled with the spirit of God to do the right thing in this life by them.

So I say to you, we have to make a partnership, all the Government Agencies, all the business folks,

but where there are no families, where there is no order, where there is no hope, where we are reducing the size of our armed services because we have won the cold war, who will be there to give structure, discipline, and love to these children? You must do that. And we must help you.

Scripture says, you are the salt of the Earth and the light of the world. That if your light shines before men they will give glory to the Father in heaven. That is what we must do. That is what we must do. How would we explain it to Martin Luther King if he showed up today and said, yes, we won the cold war. Yes, the biggest threat that all of us grew up under, communism and nuclear war, communism gone, nuclear war receding. Yes, we developed all these miraculous technologies. Yes, we all have got a VCR in our home. It's interesting. Yes, we get 50 channels on the cable. Yes, without regard to race, if you work hard and play by the rules, you can get into a service academy or a good college, you'll do just great. How would we explain to him all these kids getting killed and killing each other? How would we justify the things that we permit that no other country in the world would permit? How could we explain that we gave people the freedom to succeed, and we created conditions in which millions abuse that freedom to destroy the things that make life worth living and life itself? We cannot.

And so I say to you today, my fellow Americans, you gave me this job, and we're making progress on the things you hired me to do. But unless we deal with the ravages of crime and drugs and violence and unless we recognize that it's due to the breakdown of the family, the community, and the disappearance of jobs, and unless we say some of this cannot be done by Government, because we have to reach deep inside to the values, the spirit, the soul, and the truth of human nature, none of the other things we seek to do will ever take us where we need to go.

So in this pulpit, on this day, let me ask all of you in your heart to say we will honor the life and the work of Martin Luther King, we will honor the meaning of our church, we will somehow by God's grace, we will turn this around. We will give these children a future. We will take away their guns and give them books. We will take away their despair and give them hope. We will rebuild the families and the neighborhoods and the communities. We won't make all the work that has gone on here benefit just a few. We will do it together by the grace of God.

Thank you.

HEART SAVERS ADVERTISEMENT

Heart Savers, a health advocacy group, has paid for a number of advertisements that are designed to educate the American people about the dangers associated with a high-fat diet. In this particular advertisement, they focus on the milk industry and the popular milk advertising campaign showing well-known people sporting a milk mustache. Clearly, Heart Savers realizes that rational argumentative strategies will not be sufficient to achieve their aim of decreasing fat consumption by convincing people to drink skim milk. It is important to consider the variety of sub-strategies that they use for producing an emotional reaction.

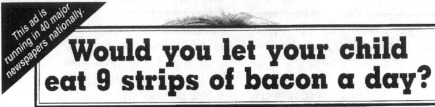

This ad is running in 40 major newspapers nationally.

Would you let your child eat 9 strips of bacon a day?

"My family just switched from 2% to skim milk.
We'll all be healthier and I'll lose weight !"

DRINK SKIM MILK!
It has all the nutrients of whole & 2% milk, but no fat.

It has all the calcium of whole & 2% milk, but fewer calories.

DON'T DRINK 2% MILK!
It is *not* low fat!
(It does not meet the FDA definition)
It has 3 grams of saturated fat per 8 oz. serving.

Time, Newsweek and Life Magazines refused to publish this ad. All three are running ads in the Milk Industry's multi-million dollar national ad campaign.

Would you let your child eat 9 strips of bacon a day?
3 glasses of 2% milk have 9 grams of saturated fat, the same amount as 9 strips of cooked bacon!

A PUBLIC SERVICE OF

NHSA

National **Heart Savers** Association
9140 West Dodge Road
Omaha, Nebraska 68114

PHIL SOKOLOF, President

Reprinted by permission of National Heart Savers Association

TESTIMONY OF TAMMY WATTS

No issue produces sharper conflict or greater emotional reaction than abortion. The values of life and personal autonomy are so basic that people tend to feel very strongly about them and find it difficult to reach compromise positions when the values are in conflict. In recent years, much debate about abortion has focused on late-term abortions, which are sometimes called "partial birth abortions." In testimony before a United States House of Representatives Committee, Tammy Watts used a personal narrative to argue that in some cases late-term abortions are needed for medical reasons. Watts' testimony uses personal narrative (and argument) to tap into basic values and needs at the heart of the abortion dispute.

Testimony of Tammy Watts

Good morning. My name is Tammy Watts. I would like to thank the subcommittee for inviting me here today. My story is one of heartbreak, one of tragedy, but also one of compassion.

When I found out I was pregnant on October 10, 1994, it was a great day, because on the same day, my nephew, Tanner James Gilbert was born. We were doubly blessed. My husband and I ran through the whole variety of emotions, scared, happy, excited, the whole thing. We immediately started making our plans. We talked about names, what kind of baby's room we wanted, would it be a boy or girl. We told everyone we knew, and I was only three weeks pregnant at the time.

It was not an easy pregnancy. Almost as soon as my pregnancy was confirmed, I started getting really sick. I had severe morning sickness, and so I took some time off of work to get through that stage. As the pregnancy progressed, I had some spotting, which is common, but my doctor said to take disability leave from work and take things one month at a time.

During that leave, I had a chance to spend a lot of time with my newborn nephew, Tanner, and his mom Melanie, my sister-in-law. I watched him grow day by day, sharing all the news with my husband. We made our plans, excited by watching Tanner grow, thinking, "This is what our baby is going to be like."

Then I had more trouble in January. My husband and I had gone out to dinner, came back and were watching TV when I started having contractions. They lasted for about a half an hour and then they stopped. But then the doctor told me that I should stay out of work for the rest of my pregnancy. I was very disappointed that I couldn't share my pregnancy with the people at work, let them watch me grow. But our excitement just kept growing, and we made our normal plans, everything that prospective parents do.

I had had a couple of earlier ultrasounds which turned out fine. I took the alphafetoprotein test, which is supposed to show fetal anomalies, anything like what we later found out we had. Mine came back clean.

In March, I went in for a routine seven-month ultrasound. They were saying this looks good, this looks good. Then suddenly, they got really quiet. The doctor said, "This is something I did not expect to see." My heart dropped. He said he was not sure what it was, and after about a solid hour of ultrasound, he and another doctor decided to send me to a perinatologist. That was also when they told us we were going to have a girl. They said, "Don't worry. It's probably nothing. It can even be the machine."

So we went home. We were a little bit frightened so we called some family members. My husband's parents were away and wanted to come home, but we told them to wait. The next day the perinatologist did ultrasound for about two hours, and said he thought the ultrasound showed a condition in which the intestines grow on the outside of the body, something that is easily corrected with surgery after birth. But just to make sure, he made an appointment for me in San Francisco with a specialist.

After another intense ultrasound with the specialist, the doctors met with us along with a genetic counselor. They absolutely did not beat around the bush. They told me, "Your daughter has no eyes. Six fingers and six toes, and enlarged kidneys which were already failing. The mass on the outside of her stomach involves her bowel and bladder, and her heart and other major organs are also affected." This is part of a syndrome called trisomy-13, where on the 13th gene there's an extra chromosome. They told me, "Almost everything in life, if you've got more of it, it's great, except for this. This is one of the most devastating syndromes, and your child will not live."

My mother-in-law collapsed to her knees. What do you do? What do you say? I remember just looking out the window. I couldn't look at anybody. So

From Hearing before the Subcommittee on the Constitution of the Committee on the Judiciary House of Representatives, 104 Congress, June 15, 1995.

my mother-in-law asked, "Do we go on? Does she have to go on?" The doctor said, no, that there was a place in Los Angeles that could help if we could not cope with carrying the pregnancy to term. The genetic counselor explained exactly how the procedure would be done if we chose to end the pregnancy, and we made an appointment for the next day.

I had a choice. I could have carried this pregnancy to term, knowing that everything was wrong. I could have gone on for two more months doing everything that an expectant mother does, but knowing my baby was going to die, and would probably suffer a great deal before dying. My husband and I would have to endure that knowledge and watch that suffering. We could never have survived that, and so we made the choice together, my husband and I, to terminate this pregnancy.

We came home, packed, and called the rest of our families. At this point, there wasn't a person in the world who didn't know how excited we were about this baby. My sister-in-law and best friend divided up our phone book and called everyone. I didn't want to have to tell anyone. I just wanted it to be over with.

On Thursday morning, we started the procedure. It was over about 6 p.m. Friday night. The doctor, nurses, and counselors were absolutely wonderful. While I was going through the most horrible experience of my life, they had more compassion than I have ever felt from anybody. We had wanted this baby so much. We named her Mackenzie. Just because we had to end the pregnancy didn't mean we didn't want to say goodbye. Thanks to the type of procedure that Dr. McMahon uses in terminating these pregnancies, we got to hold her and be with her and love her and have pictures for a couple of hours, which was wonderful and heartbreaking all at once. They had her wrapped in a blanket. We spent some time with her, said our goodbyes, and went back to the hotel.

Before we went home, I had a checkup with Dr. McMahon and everything was fine. He said, "I'm going to tell you two things. First, I never want to see you again. I mean that in a good way. Second, my job isn't done with you yet until I get the news that you have had a healthy baby." He gave me hope that this tragedy was not the end, that we could have children just as we had planned.

I remember getting on the plane, and as soon as it took off, we began crying because we were leaving our child behind. The really hard part started when I got home. I had to go through my milk coming in and everything you go through if you have a child.

I don't know how to explain the heartache. There are no words. There's nothing I can tell you, express or show you, that would allow you to feel what I feel. If you think about the worst thing that has happened to you in your life and multiply it by a million, maybe then you might be close. You do what you can. I couldn't deal with anybody, couldn't see anybody, especially my nephews. It was too heartbreaking. People came to see me, and I don't remember them being there.

Eventually, I came around to being able to see and talk to people. I am a whole new person, a whole different person. Things that used to be important now seem silly. My family and my friends are everything to me. My belief in God has strengthened. I never blamed God for this. I am a good Christian woman. However, I did question.

Through a lot of prayer and talk with my pastor, I have come to realize that everything happens for a reason, and Mackenzie's life had meaning. I knew it would come to pass some day that I would find out why it happened, and I think it is for this reason. I am supposed to be here to talk to you and say, you can't take this away from women and families. You can't. It is so important that we be able to make these decisions, because we are the only ones who can.

We made another painful decision shortly after the procedure. Dr. McMahon said, "This will be very difficult, but I have to ask you. Given the anomalies Mackenzie had so vast and different, there is a program at Cedars-Sinai which is trying to find out the causes for why this happens. They would like to accept her into this program." I said, "I know what that means, autopsies and the whole realm of testing." But we decided how can we not do this? If I can keep one family from going through what we went through, it would make her life have more meaning. So they are doing the testing now. Because Dr. McMahon does the procedure the way he does, it made the testing possible.

I can tell you one thing after our experience, I know more than ever that there is no way to judge what someone else is going through. Until you have walked a mile in my shoes, don't pretend to know what this was like for me. I don't pretend to know what someone else is going through. Everybody has got a reason for doing what they have to do. Nobody should be forced into having to make the wrong decision. That's what you'll be doing if you pass this legislation. Let doctors be free to treat their patients in the way they think is best, like my doctor did for me.

I understand this legislation would make my doctor a criminal. My doctor is the furthest thing from a criminal in the world. Many times I have called him my angel. They say there are angels walking around the world protecting us, and I know he is one. If I was not led to Dr. McMahon, I don't know how I would have lived through this. I can't imagine where we would be without him.

RONALD REAGAN, "ADDRESS TO MEMBERS OF THE BRITISH PARLIAMENT," JUNE 8, 1982

At Westminster, President Reagan argued that ultimately the Cold War was a battle of ideas that would be won by the liberal democracies of the West led by the United States. At the time, his view was seen as naïve and many thought that his Soviet policy was overly aggressive and risked war. Yet, in less than a decade his prediction would be proved correct as the Soviet Union collapsed and the Cold War ended. It is important to consider how Reagan marshalled rational argument, narrative, and value appeals in support of his position.

Address to Members of the British Parliament

Ronald Reagan

My Lord Chancellor, Mr. Speaker:

The journey of which this visit forms a part is a long one. Already it has taken me to two great cities of the West, Rome and Paris, and to the economic summit at Versailles. And there, once again, our sister democracies have proved that even in a time of severe economic strain, free peoples can work together freely and voluntarily to address problems as serious as inflation, unemployment, trade, and economic development in a spirit of cooperation and solidarity.

Other milestones lie ahead. Later this week, in Germany, we and our NATO allies will discuss measures for our joint defense and America's latest initiatives for a more peaceful, secure world through arms reductions.

Each stop of this trip is important, but among them all, this moment occupies a special place in my heart and in the hearts of my countrymen—a moment of kinship and homecoming in these hallowed halls.

Speaking for all Americans, I want to say how very much at home we feel in your house. Every American would, because this is, as we have been so eloquently told, one of democracy's shrines. Here the rights of free people and the processes of representation have been debated and refined.

It has been said that an institution is the lengthening shadow of a man. This institution is the lengthening shadow of all the men and women who have sat here and all those who have voted to send representatives here.

This is my second visit to Great Britain as President of the United States. My first opportunity to stand on British soil occurred almost a year and a half ago when your Prime Minister graciously hosted a diplomatic dinner at the British Embassy in Washington. Mrs. Thatcher said then that she hoped I was not distressed to find staring down at me from the grand staircase a portrait of His Royal Majesty King George III. She suggested it was best to let bygones be bygones, and in view of our two countries' remarkable friendship in succeeding years, she added that most Englishmen today would agree with Thomas Jefferson that "a little rebellion now and then is a very good thing." [Laughter]

Well, from here I will go to Bonn and then Berlin, where there stands a grim symbol of power untamed. The Berlin Wall, that dreadful gray gash across the city, is in its third decade. It is the fitting signature of the regime that built it.

And a few hundred kilometers behind the Berlin Wall, there is another symbol. In the center of Warsaw, there is a sign that notes the distances to two capitals. In one direction it points toward Moscow. In the other it points toward Brussels, headquarters of Western Europe's tangible unity. The marker says that the distances from Warsaw to Moscow and Warsaw to Brussels are equal. The sign makes this point: Poland is not East or West. Poland is at the center of European civilization. It has contributed mightily to that civilization. It is doing so today by being magnificently unreconciled to oppression.

Poland's struggle to be Poland and to secure the basic rights we often take for granted demonstrates why we dare not take those rights for granted. Gladstone, defending the Reform Bill of 1866, declared, "You cannot fight against the future. Time is on our side." It was easier to believe in the march of democracy in Gladstone's day—in that high noon of Victorian optimism.

Ronald Reagan, "Address to Members of the British Parliament," June 8, 1982

We're approaching the end of a bloody century plagued by a terrible political invention—totalitarianism. Optimism comes less easily today, not because democracy is less vigorous, but because democracy's enemies have refined their instruments of repression. Yet optimism is in order, because day by day democracy is proving itself to be a not-at-all-fragile flower. From Stettin on the Baltic to Varna on the Black Sea, the regimes planted by totalitarianism have had more than 30 years to establish their legitimacy. But none—not one regime—has yet been able to risk free elections. Regimes planted by bayonets do not take root.

The strength of the Solidarity movement in Poland demonstrates the truth told in an underground joke in the Soviet Union. It is that the Soviet Union would remain a one-party nation even if an opposition party were permitted, because everyone would join the opposition party. [Laughter]

America's time as a player on the stage of world history has been brief. I think understanding this fact has always made you patient with your younger cousins—well, not always patient. I do recall that on one occasion, Sir Winston Churchill said in exasperation about one of our most distinguished diplomats: "He is the only case I know of a bull who carries his china shop with him." [Laughter]

But witty as Sir Winston was, he also had that special attribute of great statesmen—the gift of vision, the willingness to see the future based on the experience of the past. It is this sense of history, this understanding of the past that I want to talk with you about today, for it is in remembering what we share of the past that our two nations can make common cause for the future.

We have not inherited an easy world. If developments like the Industrial Revolution, which began here in England, and the gifts of science and technology have made life much easier for us, they have also made it more dangerous. There are threats now to our freedom, indeed to our very existence, that other generations could never even have imagined.

There is first the threat of global war. No President, no Congress, no Prime Minister, no Parliament can spend a day entirely free of this threat. And I don't have to tell you that in today's world the existence of nuclear weapons could mean, if not the extinction of mankind, then surely the end of civilization as we know it. That's why negotiations on intermediate-range nuclear forces now underway in Europe and the START talks—Strategic Arms Reduction Talks—which will begin later this month, are not just critical to American or Western policy; they are critical to mankind. Our commitment to early success in these negotiations is firm and unshakable, and our purpose is clear: reducing the risk of war by reducing the means of waging war on both sides.

At the same time there is a threat posed to human freedom by the enormous power of the modern state. History teaches the dangers of government that overreaches—political control taking precedence over free economic growth, secret police, mindless bureaucracy, all combining to stifle individual excellence and personal freedom.

Now, I'm aware that among us here and throughout Europe there is legitimate disagreement over the extent to which the public sector should play a role in a nation's economy and life. But on one point all of us are united—our abhorrence of dictatorship in all its forms, but most particularly totalitarianism and the terrible inhumanities it has caused in our time—the great purge, Auschwitz and Dachau, the Gulag, and Cambodia.

Historians looking back at our time will note the consistent restraint and peaceful intentions of the West. They will note that it was the democracies who refused to use the threat of their nuclear monopoly in the forties and early fifties for territorial or imperial gain. Had that nuclear monopoly been in the hands of the Communist world, the map of Europe—indeed, the world—would look very different today. And certainly they will note it was not the democracies that invaded Afghanistan or supressed Polish Solidarity or used chemical and toxin warfare in Afghanistan and Southeast Asia.

If history teaches anything it teaches self-delusion in the face of unpleasant facts is folly. We see around us today the marks of our terrible dilemma—predictions of doomsday, antinuclear demonstrations, an arms race in which the West must, for its own protection, be an unwilling participant. At the same time we see totalitarian forces in the world who seek subversion and conflict around the globe to further their barbarous assault on the human spirit. What, then, is our course? Must civilization perish in a hail of fiery atoms? Must freedom wither in a quiet, deadening accommodation with totalitarian evil?

Sir Winston Churchill refused to accept the inevitability of war or even that it was imminent. He said, "I do not believe that Soviet Russia desires war. What they desire is the fruits of war and the indefinite expansion of their power and doctrines. But what we have to consider here today while time remains is the permanent prevention of war and the establishment of conditions of freedom and democracy as rapidly as possible in all countries."

Well, this is precisely our mission today: to preserve freedom as well as peace. It may not be easy to see; but I believe we live now at a turning point.

In an ironic sense Karl Marx was right. We are witnessing today a great revolutionary crisis, a crisis where the demands of the economic order are conflicting directly with those of the political order. But the crisis is happening not in the free, non-Marxist West, but in the home of Marxist-Leninism, the Soviet Union. It is the Soviet Union that runs against the tide of history by denying human freedom and human dignity to its citizens. It also is in deep economic difficulty. The rate of growth in the national product has been steadily declining since the fifties and is less than half of what it was then.

The dimensions of this failure are astounding: A country which employs one-fifth of its population in agriculture is unable to feed its own people. Were it not for the private sector, the tiny private sector tolerated in Soviet agriculture, the country might be on the brink of famine. These private plots occupy a bare three percent of the arable land but account for nearly one-quarter of Soviet farm output and nearly one-third of meat products and vegetables. Overcentralized, with little or no incentives, year after year the Soviet system pours its best resource into the making of instruments of destruction. The constant shrinkage of economic growth combined with the growth of military production is putting a heavy strain on the Soviet people. What we see here is a political structure that no longer corresponds to its economic base, a society where productive forces are hampered by political ones.

The decay of the Soviet experiment should come as no surprise to us. Wherever the comparisons have been made between free and closed societies—West Germany and East Germany, Austria and Czechoslovakia, Malaysia and Vietnam—it is the democratic countries what are prosperous and responsive to the needs of their people. And one of the simple but overwhelming facts of our time is this: Of all the millions of refugees we've seen in the modern world, their flight is always away from, not toward the Communist world. Today on the NATO line, our military forces face east to prevent a possible invasion. On the other side of the line, the Soviet forces also face east to prevent their people from leaving.

The hard evidence of totalitarian rule has caused in mankind an uprising of the intellect and will. Whether it is the growth of the new schools of economics in America or England or the appearance of the so-called new philosophers in France, there is one unifying thread running through the intellectual work of these groups—rejection of the arbitrary power of the state, the refusal to subordinate the rights of the individual to the superstate, the realization that collectivism stifles all the best human impulses.

Since the exodus from Egypt, historians have written of those who sacrificed and struggled for freedom—the stand at Thermopylae, the revolt of Spartacus, the storming of the Bastille, the Warsaw uprising in World War II. More recently we've seen evidence of this same human impulse in one of the developing nations in Central America. For months and months the world news media covered the fighting in El Salvador. Day after day we were treated to stories and film slanted toward the brave freedom-fighters battling oppressive government forces in behalf of the silent, suffering people of that tortured country.

And then one day those silent, suffering people were offered a chance to vote, to choose the kind of government they wanted. Suddenly the freedom-fighters in the hills were exposed for what they really are—Cuban-backed guerrillas who want power for themselves, and their backers, not democracy for the people. They threatened death to any who voted, and destroyed hundreds of buses and trucks to keep the people from getting to the polling places. But on election day, the people of El Salvador, an unprecedented 1.4 million of them, braved ambush and gunfire, and trudged for miles to vote for freedom.

They stood for hours in the hot sun waiting for their turn to vote. Members of our Congress who went there as observers told me of a women who was wounded by rifle fire on the way to the polls, who refused to leave the line to have her wound treated until after she had voted. A grandmother, who had been told by the guerrillas she would be killed when she returned from the polls, and she told the guerrillas, "You can kill me, you can kill my family, kill my neighbors, but you can't kill us all." The real freedom-fighters of El Salvador turned out to be the people of that country—the young, the old, the in-between.

Strange, but in my own country there's been little if any news coverage of that war since the election. Now, perhaps they'll say it's—well, because there are newer struggles now.

On distant islands in the South Atlantic young men are fighting for Britain. And, yes, voices have been raised protesting their sacrifice for lumps of rock and earth so far away. But those young men aren't fighting for more real estate. They fight for a cause—for the belief that armed aggression must not be allowed to succeed, and the people must participate in the decisions of government—the decisions of government under the rule of law. If there had been firmer support for that principle some 45 years ago, perhaps our generation wouldn't have suffered the bloodletting of World War II.

In the Middle East now the guns sound once more, this time in Lebanon, a country that for too long has had to endure the tragedy of civil war, terrorism, and foreign intervention and occupation. The fighting in Lebanon on the part of all parties must stop, and Israel should bring its forces home. But this is not enough. We must all work to stamp out the scourge of terrorism that in the Middle East makes war an ever-present threat.

But beyond the troublespots lies a deeper, more positive pattern. Around the world today, the democratic revolution is gathering new strength. In India a critical test has been passed with the peaceful change of governing political parties. In Africa, Nigeria is moving into remarkable and unmistakable ways to build and strengthen its democratic institutions. In the Caribbean and Central America, 16 of 24 countries have freely elected governments. And in the United Nations, 8 of the 10 developing nations which have joined that body in the past five years are democracies.

In the Communist world as well, man's instinctive desire for freedom and self-determination surfaces again and again. To be sure, there are grim reminders of how brutally the police state attempts to snuff out this quest for self-rule—1953 in East Germany, 1956 in Hungary, 1968 in Czechoslovakia, 1981 in Poland. But the struggle continues in Poland. And we know that there are even those who strive and suffer for freedom within the confines of the Soviet Union itself. How we conduct ourselves here in the Western democracies will determine whether this trend continues.

No, democracy is not a fragile flower. Still it needs cultivating. If the rest of this century is to witness the gradual growth of freedom and democratic ideals, we must take actions to assist the campaign for democracy.

Some argue that we should encourage democratic change in right-wing dictatorships, but not in Communist regimes. Well, to accept this preposterous notion—as some well-meaning people have—is to invite the argument that once countries achieve a nuclear capability, they should be allowed an undisturbed reign of terror over their own citizens. We reject this course.

As for the Soviet view, Chairman Brezhnev repeatedly has stressed that the competition of ideas and systems must continue and that this is entirely consistent with relaxation of tensions and peace.

Well, we ask only that these systems begin by living up to their own constitutions, abiding by their own laws, and complying with the international obligations they have undertaken. We ask only for a process, a direction, a basic code of decency, not for an instant transformation.

We cannot ignore the fact that even without our encouragement there has been and will continue to be repeated explosions against repression and dictatorships. The Soviet Union itself is not immune to this reality. Any system is inherently unstable that has no peaceful means to legitimize its leaders. In such cases, the very repressiveness of the state ultimately drives people to resist it, if necessary, by force.

While we must be cautious about forcing the pace of change, we must not hesitate to declare our ultimate objectives and to take concrete actions to move toward them. We must be staunch in our conviction that freedom is not the sole prerogative of a lucky few, but the inalienable and universal right of all human beings. So states the United Nations Universal Declaration of Human Rights, which, among other things, guarantees free elections.

The objective I propose is quite simple to state: to foster the infrastructure of democracy, the system of a free press, unions, political parties, universities, which allows a people to choose their own way to develop their own culture, to reconcile their own differences through peaceful means.

This is not cultural imperialism, it is providing the means for genuine self-determination and protection for diversity. Democracy already flourishes in countries with very different cultures and historical experiences. It would be cultural condescension, or worse, to say that any people prefer dictatorship to democracy. Who would voluntarily choose not to have the right to vote, decide to purchase government propaganda handouts instead of independent newspapers, prefer government to worker-controlled unions, opt for land to be owned by the state instead of those who till it, want government repression of religious liberty, a single political party instead of a free choice, a rigid cultural orthodoxy instead of democratic tolerance and diversity?

Since 1917 the Soviet Union has given covert political training and assistance to Marxist-Leninists in many countries. Of course, it also has promoted the use of violence and subversion by these same forces. Over the past several decades, West European and other Social Democrats, Christian Democrats, and leaders have offered open assistance to fraternal, political, and social institutions to bring about peaceful and democratic progress. Appropriately, for a vigorous new democracy, the Federal Republic of Germany's political foundations have become a major force in this effort.

We in America now intend to take additional steps, as many of our allies have already done, toward realizing this same goal. The chairmen and other leaders of the national Republican and Democratic Party organizations are initiating a study with the bipartisan American political foundation to determine how the United States can best contribute as a nation to the global campaign for democracy now gathering force. They will have the cooperation of congressional leaders of both parties, along with representatives of business, labor, and other major institutions in our society. I look forward to receiving their recommendations and to working with these institutions and the Congress in the common task of strengthening democracy throughout the world.

It is time that we committed ourselves as a nation—in both the pubic and private sectors—to assisting democratic development.

We plan to consult with leaders of other nations as well. There is a proposal before the Council of Europe to invite parliamentarians from democratic countries to a meeting next year in Strasbourg. That prestigious gathering could consider ways to help democratic political movements.

This November in Washington there will take place an international meeting on free elections. And next spring there will be a conference of world authorities on constitutionalism and self-government hosted by the Chief Justice of the United States. Authorities from a number of developing and developed countries—judges, philosophers, and politicians with practical experience—have agreed to explore how to turn principle into practice and further the rule of law.

At the same time, we invite the Soviet Union to consider with us how the competition of ideas and values—which it is committed to support—can be conducted on a peaceful and reciprocal basis. For example, I am prepared to offer President Brezhnev an opportunity to speak to the American people on our television if he will allow me the same opportunity with the Soviet people. We also suggest that panels of our newsmen periodically appear on each other's television to discuss major events.

Now, I don't wish to sound overly optimistic, yet the Soviet Union is not immune from the reality of what is going on in the world. It has happened in the past—a small ruling elite either mistakenly attempts to ease domestic unrest through greater repression and foreign adventure, or it chooses a wiser course. It begins to allow its people a voice in their own destiny. Even if this latter process is not realized soon, I believe the renewed strength of the democratic movement, complemented by a global campaign for freedom, will strengthen the prospects for arms control and a world at peace.

I have discussed on other occasions, including my address on May 9th, the elements of Western policies toward the Soviet Union to safeguard our interests and protect the peace. What I am describing now is a plan and a hope for the long term—the march of freedom and democracy which will leave Marxism-Leninism on the ash-heap of history as it has left other tyrannies which stifle the freedom and muzzle the self-expression of the people. And that's why we must continue our efforts to strengthen NATO even as we move forward with our Zero-Option initiative in the negotiations on intermediate-range forces and our proposal for a one-third reduction in strategic ballistic missile warheads.

Our military strength is a prerequisite to peace, but let it be clear we maintain this strength in the hope it will never be used, for the ultimate determinant in the struggle that's now going on in the world will not be bombs and rockets, but a test of wills and ideas, a trial of spiritual resolve, the values we hold, the beliefs we cherish, the ideals to which we are dedicated.

The British people know that, given strong leadership, time and a little bit of hope, the forces of good ultimately rally and triumph over evil. Here among you is the cradle of self-government, the Mother of Parliaments. Here is the enduring greatness of the British contribution to mankind, the great civilized ideas: individual liberty, representative government, and the rule of law under God.

I've often wondered about the shyness of some of us in the West about standing for these ideals that have done so much to ease the plight of man and the hardships of our imperfect world. This reluctance to use those vast resources at our command reminds me of the elderly lady whose home was bombed in the Blitz. As the rescuers moved about, they found a bottle of brandy she'd stored behind the staircase, which was all that was left standing. And since she was barely conscious, one of the workers pulled the cork to give her a taste of it. She came around immediately and said, "Here now—there now, put it back. That's for emergencies." [Laughter]

Well, the emergency is upon us. Let us be shy no longer. Let us go to our strength. Let us offer hope. Let us tell the world that a new age is not only possible but probable.

During the dark days of the Second World War, when this island was incandescent with courage, Winston Churchill exclaimed about Britain's adversaries, "What kind of a people do they think we are?" Well, Britain's adversaries found out what extraordinary people the British are. But all the democracies paid a terrible price for allowing the dictators to underestimate us. We dare not make that mistake again. So, let us ask ourselves, "What kind of people do we think we are?" And let us answer, "Free people, worthy of freedom and determined not only to remain so but to help others gain their freedom as well."

Sir Winston led his people to great victory in war and then lost an election just as the fruits of victory were about to be enjoyed. But he left office honorably, and, as it turned out, temporarily, knowing that the liberty of his people was more important than the fate of any single leader. History recalls his greatness in ways no dictator will ever know. And he left us a message of hope for the future, as timely now as when he first uttered it, as opposition leader in the Commons nearly 27 years ago, when he said, "When we look back on all the perils through which we have passed and at the mighty foes that we have laid low and all the dark and deadly designs that we have frustrated, why should we fear for our future? We have," he said, "come safely through the worst."

Well, the task I've set forth will long outlive our own generation. But together, we too have come through the worst. Let us now begin a major effort to secure the best—a crusade for freedom that will engage the faith and fortitude of the next generation. For the sake of peace and justice, let us move toward a world in which all people are at last free to determine their own destiny.

Thank you.

CHAPTER 7
Confrontation and Social Movement Rhetoric

In confrontative rhetoric, the speaker/writer attacks or offends an external audience in order to create the preconditions for social change. Confrontation is sometimes needed to get the attention of the other side. It also may be needed to garner publicity and to convince an internal audience of movement supporters that change is, in fact, possible. On the other hand, confrontation is also an extremely dangerous strategy that risks producing backlash.

Confrontative rhetoric can be assessed via the internal process used to evaluate all rhetorical action. However, after identifying the purpose, rhetorical barriers (and advantages), and strategies, the critic should consider whether there was another alternative besides the use of confrontation. Because of the risks associated with the strategy, confrontation should always be used only on crucial issues and as a last resort.

Several works are included to illustrate confrontation as a strategy and also the risks associated with it.

AMNESTY INTERNATIONAL POSTCARD

Amnesty International (AI) is probably the most important human rights organization in the world. AI has been honored with the Nobel Peace Prize and has fought for the rights of innocent victims of oppression around the globe. The postcard is included to illustrate the danger associated with confrontation.

In analyzing the postcard, it is important to consider how AI used this small work of rhetoric to motivate an internal audience of AI members to continued effort (and contributions). Of course, the postcard also was aimed at persuading foreign leaders to end oppression. It is significant to consider the strategies that AI utilized in an attempt to achieve that aim and why they rejected confrontation as an appeal.

Minister of the Interior
Ismet Sezgin
Icisleri Bakanligi
0644, Ankara,
TURKEY

Place
40-cent
Stamp
Here

Dear Minister:

As a person concerned about the protection of basic human rights, I want to express my concerns about the degrading acts by police officers that are often used to terrorize innocent women in your country.

The brutal torture and sexual assault of Mediha Curabaz by local police in Adana is but one example of the type of violent, <u>unpunished</u> attacks that I am protesting.

I urge you to use the full power of your office to thoroughly investige all reports of rape, sexual abuse and other violations by any government officials of the human rights of women <u>and</u> to see that the guilty parties are brought to justice.

Sincerely,

_____

I'M MAD AS HELL, AND I'M NOT GOING TO TAKE IT ANYMORE

In "I'm Mad as Hell, and I'm Not Going to Take It Anymore," Jack Gargan uses strong language to attack this nation's political leaders for failing to cut the national debt or take other actions. Gargan uses strong language in relation to those he opposes, but does not attack his audience. It is important to consider how he mixes confrontative and adaptive strategies.

I'M MAD AS HELL AND I'M NOT GOING TO TAKE IT ANYMORE!

Hi, it's me again, Jack Gargan, the guy who—with the help of thousand of concerned Americans—ran 245 of these full-page ads in major newspapers across the country in the 1990 elections. If anything, I'm now even angrier at that self-serving, arrogant bunch of congressmen who care more about getting re-elected than they care about what is happening to our country.

Specifically, I'M FURIOUS that our national debt has increased another TRILLION dollars since my last ad. It's now over FOUR TRILLION DOLLARS! That is national economic suicide! YOUR congressman is buying votes with your children's money.

I'M ALARMED that it takes about 66% of all personal income taxes just to pay the yearly interest on this debt. Much of this interest is paid to foreign investors who use it to buy up the productive capacity of our nation. At the current rate of spending, in only three years it will take 100% of all personal income taxes just to pay the interest on our national debt! YOUR Congressman does not seem to be concerned about this (as proven in the next paragraph).

I'M ENRAGED that our spendthrift Congress has nearly doubled the rate of deficit spending in the past two years. Like drunken engineers on a runaway train, they have hit the accelerator instead of the brakes as we careen right toward the precipice of economic disaster. You and your family are passengers on that train! YOUR Congressman is the engineer.

I'M OUTRAGED that Congressmen can bounce more checks than most of us write, and never pay a penalty. They run our country with the same callous recklessness.

I'M ANGERED at a greedy Congress whose perks would put a maharajah to shame. Then, like sneak-thieves, voted themselves an undeserved pay raise in the middle of the night. How come YOUR Congressman won't co-sponsor a bill to repeal that obscene pay-raise?

I'M APPALLED at their arrogance. They totally ignore the wishes of their constituents while pandering to their special interest friends.

I'M CONTEMPTUOUS of their hypocritical, self-serving, inept, spineless character they so brazenly displayed in the Judge Thomas fiasco.

I'M INCENSED that "the Keating Five" has become the "Keating None." All of them off scot-free while you and I pay for a scam which cost more than World War II! I don't hear YOUR Congressman demanding justice.

I'M GRIEVED that to this day not a single member of Congress has taken up my publicly disavow the Republican/Democrat deal which—in exchange for a "Yes" vote on the payraise—put a gag on challengers from either party bringing up the issue of that pay-grab during the 1990 election campaign. Apparently YOUR Congressman condones this outrageous conspiracy.

I'M SHOCKED that the Congress of the United States continues to steal money from the Social Security trust fund to cover up their overspending. You don't see YOUR Congressman raising a cry of alarm, do you?

I'M IRATE that they lie to us whenever it serves their purpose and "cook the books" on revenues and expenses to keep the deficit from being fully revealed. If we ran our business that way, we'd be in jail!

Finally (only because I'm running out of adjectives, not congressional abuses), I'M STILL WAITING for any incumbent Congressman to accept my long-standing challenge to meet me "any time, any place" to debate the issue of why he/she is worth keeping in office. Or, send me your "champion" to defend all of you! Your silence condemns you all! How come YOUR Congressman has not accepted this challenge??

The problem is the system. We send a lot of good people to Washington, only to have them utterly corrupted by the system. "To get along, you gotta go along." This good ol' boy/seniority system is killing our nation. The answer is to break it up with a clean sweep. Replace those corrupted people with new ones who are responsive to us, not special interests. Then, so the new gang does not become as corrupt as the old, immediately sponsor legislation to eliminate deficit spending and limit congressional terms (preferably one six-year term), House and Senate, then GO HOME and live under the laws you passed for the rest of us. Maybe then the real problems of this nation will be addressed. What have we got to lose? Collectively, we can't possibly do any worse.

It's also time to wake up, America! It's not everyone else's congressman who is to blame. IT'S OUR OWN! If we had a law where we would all vote on the Congressman in the next district, you'd really see some turnover! Think about this: Our founding fathers put their own lives and fortune at risk for the welfare of the nation. Today's Congressman risks the welfare of the nation for their own personal fortune.

In spite of starting my campaign too little, too late last election, it still had an enormous impact on the outcome: an incredible 12% average difference in the vote spread of every congressman who had any opposition at all! In the words of Ron Brown, Democratic Committee Chariman: "I think the real result was to change the political landscape of America." Political analysts described it as "a turning point in recent political history." The stunning results of recent primary selections bear out those prophecies.

Our biggest problem last election was a lack of viable candidates running against incumbents. Almost 20% had no opposition at all! To solve that problem I have been running "HELP WANTED: CONGRESSMEN AND WOMEN" ads all over the country in cooperation with The Coalition to End the Permanent Congress. I am pleased to report that hundreds of qualified people responded. You will now have a good challenger running against the incumbent in most congressional districts.

We are having an impact on congressional elections far out of proportion to our modest resources. I have run this nationwide campaign for 2 1/2 years on less money than usually spent by just one congressional incumbent. You can be assured that your contribution, no matter how small or large, is gratefully accepted and carefully spent.

I need your help to run this ad in major papers in every congressional district in the nation (they cost from a few thousand dollars up to $100,000 per page, averaging $10,000 to $20,000 per page for most major papers). For those who cannot afford a contribution due to the depression, your vote is even more important. Be sure you and all your family and friends are registered to vote, and exercise that right.

ILHAN OMAR, "WE MUST APPLY OUR UNIVERSAL VALUES TO ALL NATIONS. ONLY THEN WILL WE ACHIEVE PEACE," *WASHINGTON POST*, MARCH 17, 2019

Ilhan Omar is a Democratic representative of Minnesota in the House of Representatives. In this Op Ed, she criticizes American foreign policy for not supporting human rights throughout the world. Representative Omar focuses on U.S. support for governments in the Middle East that repress their own people. In particular, she criticizes U.S. policy for uncritically supporting Israel and not adequately supporting the rights of Palestinians. Some criticized previous statements critiquing Israeli policy by Ilhan Omar as expressing anti-Semitic views. It is important to consider how she challenged her audience by claiming that her views reflected a commitment to "universal values."

We Must Apply Our Universal Values to All Nations. Only Then Will We Achieve Peace
Ilhan Omar

Since I began my first term in Congress, I have sought to speak openly and honestly about the scale of the issues our country faces—whether it is ending the crippling burden of student debt, tackling the existential threat of climate change or making sure no one in one of the richest countries in the world dies from lack of health care. As a survivor of war and a refugee, I have also sought to have an honest conversation about U.S. foreign policy, militarism and our role in the world.

This question of how the United States engages in conflict abroad is deeply personal to me. I fled my home country of Somalia when I was eight years old from a conflict that the United States later engaged in. I spent the next four years in a refugee camp in Kenya, where I experienced and witnessed unspeakable suffering from those who, like me, had lost everything because of war.

I saw firsthand the devastating toll of war. And I dreamed of one day coming to the United States of America—a land that promised peace and opportunity regardless of one's faith or ethnicity. But I also saw how America's image in the world is undermined when we don't live up to those values. And I witnessed how our continuous involvement in foreign conflicts—even those undertaken with the best of intentions—can damage our own reputation abroad.

I believe in an inclusive foreign policy—one that centers on human rights, justice and peace as the pillars of America's engagement in the world, one that brings our troops home and truly makes military action a last resort. This is a vision that centers on the experiences of the people directly affected by conflict, that takes into account the long-term effects of U.S. engagement in war and that is sincere about our values regardless of short-term political convenience.

This means reorienting our foreign affairs to focus on diplomacy and economic and cultural engagement. At a time when we spend more on our military than the next seven countries combined, our global armed presence is often the most immediate contact people in the developing world have with the United States. National security experts across the political spectrum agree that we don't need nearly 800 military bases outside the United States to keep our country safe.

Valuing human rights also means applying the same standards to our friends and our enemies. We do not have the credibility to support those fighting for human rights in Venezuela, Cuba and Nicaragua if we do not also support those fighting for human rights in Honduras, Guatemala and Brazil. Our criticisms of oppression and regional instability caused by Iran are not legitimate if we do not hold Egypt, the United Arab Emirates and Bahrain to the same standards.

And we cannot continue to turn a blind eye to repression in Saudi Arabia—a country that is consistently ranked among the worst of the worst human rights offenders. Whether it is the murder of dissenters such as Jamal Khashoggi or war crimes against civilian populations in Yemen, we must hold all of

Ilhan Omar, "We must apply our universal values to all nations. Only then will we achieve peace," March 17, 2019

our allies to the same international standards as our enemies.

This vision also applies to the Israeli-Palestinian conflict. U.S. support for Israel has a long history. The founding of Israel 70 years ago was built on the Jewish people's connection to their historical homeland, as well as the urgency of establishing a nation in the wake of the horror of the Holocaust and the centuries of anti-Semitic oppression leading up to it. Many of the founders of Israel were themselves refugees who survived indescribable horrors.

We must acknowledge that this is also the historical homeland of Palestinians. And without a state, the Palestinian people live in a state of permanent refugeehood and displacement. This, too, is a refugee crisis, and they, too, deserve freedom and dignity.

A balanced, inclusive approach to the conflict recognizes the shared desire for security and freedom of both peoples. I support a two-state solution, with internationally recognized borders, which allows for both Israelis and Palestinians to have their own sanctuaries and self-determination. This has been official bipartisan U.S. policy across two decades and has been supported by each of the most recent Israeli and Palestinian leaders, as well as the consensus of the Israeli security establishment. As Jim Mattis, who later was President Trump's defense

secretary, said in 2011, "The current situation between those two peoples is unsustainable."

Working toward peace in the region also means holding everyone involved accountable for actions that undermine the path to peace—because without justice, there can never be a lasting peace. When I criticize certain Israeli government actions in Gaza or settlements in the West Bank, it is because I believe these actions not only threaten the possibility of peace in the region—they also threaten the United States' own national security interests.

My goal in speaking out at all times has been to encourage both sides to move toward a peaceful two-state solution. We need to reinsert this call back into the public debate with urgency. Both parties must come to the table for a final peace deal; violence will not bring us any closer to that day.

Peace and respect for human rights: These are universal values. They are what drove Americans to organize and protest for equal rights and civil rights. They are what motivated nonviolent movements from South Africa to South Asia to the American South. These are the values that propelled me to get involved in public life, and I know they are the values that drove Minnesotans to give a Somali American refugee a chance at representing them in Congress.

Let us apply these universal values to all nations. Only then will our world achieve peace.

PEOPLE FOR THE ETHICAL TREATMENT OF ANIMALS—LOVE US, DON'T EAT US AND STATEMENT WHY DOES PETA USE CONTROVERSIAL TACTICS?

People for the Ethical Treatment of Animals (PETA] is an advocacy group opposed to all forms of animal mistreatment. Consequently, PETA advocates that all people should become vegetarians and avoid supporting any industry that in PETA's view mistreats animals. Their views are controversial and implementation of them would produce vast changes in society.

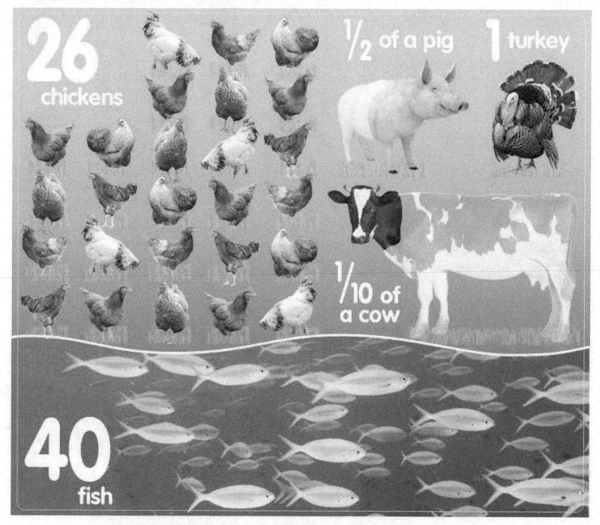

Courtesy of PETA (www.PETA.org)

CHAPTER 8
Generic Rhetoric

This chapter contains a number of works to illustrate the system of generic analysis that was developed in chapter ten of *Analyzing Rhetoric: A Handbook for the Informed Citizen in a New Millennium*. The first section of the chapter contains several eulogies that can be tested with the evaluation system for eulogies. The next section focuses on Inaugural Addresses by John F. Kennedy, Jimmy Carter, Ronald Reagan, Barrack Obama, Donald Trump, and Nelson Mandela. The third main section focuses on Farewell Addresses and includes speeches by Dwight Eisenhower, Ronald Reagan, Bill Clinton and Barack Obama. The final section of the chapter focuses on apologia. An apologia is a speech of self-defense where the issue is not a question of policy, but the reputation of an individual. Three examples of apologia are included: President Reagan's speech concerning the Tower Commission report on the Iran Contra crisis, President Clinton's "Map Room" address concerning the Monica Lewinski scandal, and a statement from Senator Al Franken concerning sexual allegations.

EULOGIES FOR PRESIDENT RICHARD NIXON

Former President Richard Nixon died in April 1994. Nixon, who was Vice-President of the United States under Dwight Eisenhower, was elected President in 1968 and re-elected in 1972. His term in office has been praised as a time of great innovation, especially in domestic policy. Nixon's term as President also was marked by the eventual end of the Vietnam war and a major foreign policy initiative that finally led the United States to recognize the Peoples Republic of China. However, Nixon is most remembered for the Watergate scandal. What began as a small-time break-in at the Democratic National Committee, ultimately became a major coverup and national crisis. Eventually, Nixon realized that he must either resign from the presidency or be impeached and removed from office. He chose resignation. After his resignation, Nixon gradually rebuilt his reputation, largely with a series of books discussing foreign policy challenges facing the United States.

Three eulogies from the funeral for Richard Nixon are included. Nixon's former Secretary of State and National Security Advisor, Henry Kissinger, spoke of Nixon's foreign policy accomplishments. Then Senate Majority Leader Robert Dole of Kansas described Nixon as the quintessential American and President Bill Clinton spoke on behalf of the entire nation.

Eulogies for Richard Nixon
Henry Kissinger, Robert Dole, and William J. Clinton

SECRETARY KISSINGER

During the final week of Richard Nixon's life, I often imagined how he would have reacted to the tide of concern, respect, admiration and affection evoked by his last great battle. His gruff pose of never paying attention to media comment would have been contradicted by a warm glow and the ever-so-subtle hint that another recital of the commentary would not be unwelcome. And without quite saying so, he would have conveyed that it would mean a lot to him if Julie and Tricia, David and Ed were told of his friends' pride in this culmination to an astonishing life.

When I learned the final news, by then so expected, yet so hard to accept, I felt a profound void. In the words of Shakespeare: "He was a man. Take him. For all in all, I shall not look upon his like again."

In the conduct of foreign policy, Richard Nixon was one of the seminal presidents. He came into office when the forces of history were moving America from a position of dominance to one of leadership. Dominance reflects strength. Leadership must be earned. And Richard Nixon earned that leadership role for his country with courage, dedication and skill.

Delivered April 27, 1994.

When Richard Nixon took his Oath of Office, 550,000 Americans were engaged in combat in a place as far away from the United States as it was possible to be. America had no contact with China, the world's most populous nation. No negotiations with the Soviet Union, the other nuclear superpower. Most Moslem countries had broken diplomatic relations with the United States, and Middle East diplomacy was stalemated. All of this in the midst of the most anguishing domestic crisis since the Civil War.

When Richard Nixon left office, an agreement to end the war in Vietnam had been concluded, and the main lines of all subsequent policy were established: permanent dialogue with China; readiness without illusion to ease tensions with the Soviet Union; a peace process in the Middle East; the beginning, via the European Security Conference, of establishing human rights as an international issue, weakening Soviet hold on Eastern Europe.

Richard Nixon's foreign policy goals were long-range. And he pursued them without regard to domestic political consequences. When he considered our nation's interests at stake, he dared confrontations, despite the imminence of elections and also in the midst of the worst crisis of his life. And he bore, if with some pain, the disapproval of longtime friends and allies over relaxing tensions with China and the Soviet Union. He drew strength from a conviction. He often expressed to me the price for doing things halfway is no less than for doing it completely. So we might as well do them properly. That's Richard Nixon's greatest accomplishment. It was as much moral as it was political—to lead from strength at a moment of apparent weakness, to husband the nation's resilience and, thus, to play the basis for victory in the Cold War.

Shy and withdrawn, Richard Nixon made himself succeed in the most gregarious of professions, and steeled himself to conspicuous acts of extraordinary courage. In the face of wrenching domestic controversy, he held fast to his basic theme that the greatest free nation in the world had a duty to lead, and no right to abdicate.

Richard Nixon would be so proud that President Clinton and all living former Presidents of the United States are here, symbolizing that his long and sometimes bitter journey had concluded in reconciliation.

I wish that in his final hours I could have told him about Brian McDonald who, during the Cambodian crisis, had been fasting on a bench in Lafayette Park, across from the White House until, as he said, "President Nixon redeemed his pledge to withdraw American forces from their anguished country in two months"—a promise which was, in fact, kept.

Across the chasm of the decades, Brian called me the day Richard Nixon fell ill and left a message: "When you talk to President Nixon, tell him that I'm praying for him."

So let us now say goodbye to our gallant friend. He stood on pinnacles that dissolved into the precipice. He achieved greatly and suffered deeply. But he never gave up. In his solitude, he envisaged a new international order that would reduce lingering enmities, strengthen historic friendships, and give new hope to mankind—a vision where dreams and possibilities conjoined.

Richard Nixon ended the war. And he advanced the vision of peace of his Quaker youth. He was devoted to his family. He loved his country. And he considered service his honor. It was a privilege to have been allowed to help him.

SENATOR DOLE

I believe the second half of the 20th Century will be known as the age of Nixon. Why was he the most durable public figure of our time? Not because he gave the most eloquent speeches, but because he provided the most effective leadership. Not because he won every battle, but because he always embodied the deepest feelings of the people he led.

One of his biographers said that Richard Nixon was one of us. And so he was. He was a boy who heard the train whistle in the night and dreamed of all the distant places that lay at the end of the track. How American. He was a grocer's son who got ahead by working harder and longer than everyone else. How American.

He was a student who met expenses by doing research at the law library for 35 cents an hour while sharing a run-down farmhouse without water or electricity. How American. He was the husband and father who said that the best memorial to his wife was her children. How American.

To tens of millions of his countrymen, Richard Nixon was an American hero, a hero who shared and honored their belief in working hard, worshiping God, loving their families and saluting the flag. He called them the silent majority. Like them, he valued accomplishment more than ideology. They wanted their government to do the decent thing, but not to bankrupt them in the process.

They wanted his protection in a dangerous world, but they also wanted creative statesmanship in achieving a genuine peace with honor. These were the people from whom he had come and who have come to Yorba Linda these past few days by the tens of thousands—no longer silent in the grief. The

American people love a fighter. And in Dick Nixon, they found a gallant one.

In a marvelous biography of her mother, Julie recalls an occasion where Pat Nixon expressed amazement at her husband's ability to persevere in the face of criticism, to which the President replied, "I just get up every morning to confound my enemies." It was what Richard Nixon did after he got up every morning that not just confounded his enemies, but turned them into admirers.

It is true that no one knew the world better than Richard Nixon. And as a result, the man who was born in a house his father built would go on to become this century's greatest architect of peace.

But we should also not underestimate President Nixon's domestic achievements. For it was Richard Nixon who ended the draft, strengthened environmental and nutritional programs, and committed the government to a war on cancer. He leapfrogged the conventional wisdom to propose revolutionary solutions to health care and welfare reform, anticipating by a full generation the debates now raging on Capitol Hill.

I remember the last time I saw him—at a luncheon held on the Capitol honoring the 25th anniversary of his first inaugural. Without a note, President Nixon stood and delivered a compelling speech, capturing the global scene as only he could and sharing his vision of America's future. When it was over, he was surrounded by Democrats and Republicans alike, each wanting just one more word of Nixonian counsel, one more insight into world affairs.

Afterward, the President rested in my office before leaving the Capitol, only he got very little rest—for the office was filled with young Hill staffers, members of the Capitol police and many, many others, all hoping to shake his hand, get an autograph or simply convey their special feelings for a man who truly was one of us.

Today our grief is shared by millions of people the world over, but is also mingled with intense pride in a great patriot who never gave up and who never gave in. To know the secret of Richard Nixon's relationship with the American people, you need only to listen to his own words: "You must never be satisfied with success." He told us, "and you should never be discouraged by failure. Failure can be sad, but the greatest sadness is not to try and fail, but to fail to try. In the end, what matters is that you have always lived life to the hilt."

Strong, brave, unafraid of controversy, unyielding in his convictions, living every day of his life to the hilt, the largest figure of our time whose influence will be timeless—that was Richard Nixon. How American. May God bless Richard Nixon and may God bless the United States.

PRESIDENT CLINTON

President Nixon opened his memoirs with a simple sentence: "I was born in a house my father built." Today, we can look back at this little house and still imagine a young boy sitting by the window of the attic he shared with his three brothers, looking out to a world he could then himself only imagine. From those humble roots, as from so many humble beginnings in this country, grew the force of a driving dream—a dream that led to the remarkable journey that ends here today where it all began. Beside the same tiny home, mail-ordered from back East, near this towering oak tree which, back then, was a mere seedling.

President Nixon's journey across the American landscape mirrored that of his entire nation in this remarkable century. His life was bound up with the striving of our whole people, with our crises and our triumphs.

When he became President, he took on challenges here at home on matters from cancer research to environmental protection, putting the power of the federal government where Republicans and Democrats had neglected to put it in the past: in foreign policy. He came to the presidency at a time in our history when Americans were tempted to say we had enough of the world. Instead, he knew we had to reach out to old friends and old enemies alike. He would not allow America to quit the world.

Remarkably, he wrote nine of his 10 books after he left the presidency, working his way back into the arena he so loved by writing and thinking, and engaging us in his dialogue.

For the past year, even in the final weeks of his life, he gave me his wise counsel, especially with regard to Russia. One thing in particular left a profound impression on me. Though this man was in his ninth decade, he had an incredibly sharp and vigorous and rigorous mind.

As a public man, he always seemed to believe the greatest sin was remaining passive in the face of challenges. And he never stopped living that creed. He gave of himself with intelligence and energy and devotion to duty. And his entire country owes him a debt of gratitude for that service. Oh, yes, he knew great controversy amid defeat as well as victory. He made mistakes: and, they, like his accomplishments are part of his life and record.

But the enduring lesson of Richard Nixon is that he never gave up being part of the action and passion of his times. He said many times that unless a person has a goal, a new mountain to climb, his spirit will die. Well based on our last phone conversation and the letter he wrote me just a month ago, I can say that his spirit was very much alive to the very end. That is a great tribute to him, to his wonderful wife, Pat, to his children and to his grandchildren whose love he so depended on and whose love he returned in full measure.

Today is a day for his family, his friends and his nation to remember President Nixon's life in totality. To them, let us say, may the day of judging President Nixon on anything less than his entire life and career come to close. May we heed his call to maintain the will and the wisdom to build on America's greatest gift—its freedom; to lead a world full of difficulty to the just and lasting peace he dreamed of.

As it is written in the words of a hymn I heard in my church last Sunday: "Grant that I may realize that the trifling of life creates differences, but that in the higher things, we are all one."

In the twilight of his life, President Nixon knew that lesson well. It is, I feel certain, a faith he would want us all to keep. And so, on behalf of all four former Presidents who are here—President Ford, President Carter, President Reagan, President Bush—and on behalf of a grateful nation, we bid farewell to Richard Milhous Nixon.

EULOGIES FOR PRESIDENT RONALD REAGAN

After a nearly ten year battle with Alzheimer's disease, former President Ronald Reagan died in June 2004. During his presidency, Reagan was widely admired by Republicans, conservative Democrats (the so-called Reagan Democrats), and many independents. Liberals sharply criticized Reagan for cutting social programs and for what they saw as a dangerous foreign policy. Many also argued that Reagan was a mere figurehead, an actor who was out of his depth in the presidency. Over time, however, attitudes shifted and even some liberals came to admire the former president. One factor was the end of the Cold War, a result for which some historians gave Reagan significant credit. Another factor was the release of various documents demonstrating that Reagan had been heavily involved in drafting speeches and other materials in his administration.

At Reagan's funeral, former President George H.W. Bush spoke of what he learned from Reagan when he served as Vice President under Reagan for eight years. Former Prime Minster of Great Britain Margaret Thatcher and former Prime Minister of Canada Brian Mulroney spoke of Reagan from the perspective of the nation's two closest allies.

Reagan Eulogies
George H.W. Bush, Brian Mulroney, and Margaret Thatcher

GEORGE H. W. BUSH, ON RONALD REAGAN

When Franklin Roosevelt died in 1945, The New York Times wrote, "Men will thank God 100 years from now that Franklin D. Roosevelt was in the White House."

It will not take 100 years to thank God for Ronald Reagan. But why? Why was he so admired? Why was he so beloved?

He was beloved, first, because of what he was. Politics can be cruel, uncivil. Our friend was strong and gentle.

Once he called America hopeful, big-hearted, idealistic, daring, decent and fair. That was America and, yes, our friend.

And next, Ronald Reagan was beloved because of what he believed. He believed in America so he made it his shining city on a hill. He believed in freedom so he acted on behalf of its values and ideals. He believed in tomorrow so The Great Communicator became The Great Liberator.

He talked of winning one for the Gipper and as president, through his relationship with Mikhail Gorbachev, with us today, the Gipper and, yes, Mikhail Gorbachev won one for peace around the world.

If Ronald Reagan created a better world for many millions it was because of the world someone else created for him.

Nancy was there for him always. Her love for him provided much of his strength, and their love together transformed all of us as we've seen—renewed seeing again here in the last few days.

And one of the many memories we all have of both of them is the comfort they provided during our national tragedies.

Whether it was the families of the crew of the Challenger shuttle or the USS Stark or the Marines killed in Beirut, we will never forget those images of the president and first lady embracing them and embracing us during times of sorrow.

So, Nancy, I want to say this to you: Today, America embraces you. We open up our arms. We seek to comfort you, to tell you of our admiration for your courage and your selfless caring.

And to the Reagan kids—it's OK for me to say that at 80—Michael, Ron, Patti, today all of our sympathy, all of our condolences to you all, and remember, too, your sister Maureen home safe now with her father.

As his vice president for eight years, I learned more from Ronald Reagan than from anyone I encountered in all my years of public life. I learned kindness; we all did. I also learned courage; the nation did.

Who can forget the horrible day in March 1981, he looked at the doctors in the emergency room and said, "I hope you're all Republicans."

And then I learned decency; the whole world did. Days after being shot, weak from wounds, he spilled water from a sink, and entering the hospital room aides saw him on his hands and knees wiping water from the floor. He worried that his nurse would get in trouble.

The Good Book says humility goes before honor, and our friend had both, and who could not cherish such a man?

And perhaps as important as anything, I learned a lot about humor, a lot about laughter. And, oh, how President Reagan loved a good story.

When asked, "How did your visit go with Bishop Tutu?" he replied, "So-so."

It was typical. It was wonderful.

And in leaving the White House, the very last day, he left in the yard outside the Oval Office door a little sign for the squirrels. He loved to feed those squirrels. And he left this sign that said, "Beware of the dog," and to no avail, because our dog Millie came in and beat the heck out of the squirrels.

But anyway, he also left me a note, at the top of which said, "Don't let the turkeys get you down."

Well, he certainly never let them get him down. And he fought hard for his beliefs. But he led from conviction, but never made an adversary into an enemy. He was never mean-spirited.

Reverend Billy Graham, who I refer to as the nation's pastor, is now hospitalized and regrets that he can't be here today. And I asked him for a Bible passage that might be appropriate. And he suggested this from Psalm 37: "The Lord delights in the way of the man whose steps he has made firm. Though he

stumble, he will not fall for the Lord upholds him with his hand."

And then this, too, from 37: "There is a future for the man of peace."

God bless you, Ronald Wilson Reagan and the nation you loved and led so well.

BRIAN MULRONEY, ON RONALD REAGAN

In the spring of 1987 President Reagan and I were driven into a large hangar at the Ottawa Airport, to await the arrival of Mrs. Reagan and my wife, Mila, prior to departure ceremonies for their return to Washington. We were alone except for the security details.

President Reagan's visit had been important, demanding and successful. Our discussions reflected the international agenda of the times: The nuclear threat posed by the Soviet Union and the missile deployment by NATO; pressures in the Warsaw pact, challenges resulting from the Berlin Wall and the ongoing separation of Germany; and bilateral and hemispheric free trade.

President Reagan had spoken to Parliament, handled complex files with skill and good humor—strongly impressing his Canadian hosts—and here we were, waiting for our wives.

When their car drove in a moment later, out stepped Nancy and Mila—looking like a million bucks. As they headed towards us, President Reagan beamed, threw his arm around my shoulder and said with a grin: "You know, Brian, for two Irishmen we sure married up."

In that visit—in that moment—one saw the quintessential Ronald Reagan—the leader we respected, the neighbor we admired and the friend we loved—a president of the United States of America whose truly remarkable life we celebrate in this magnificent cathedral today.

Presidents and prime ministers everywhere sometimes wonder how history will deal with them.

Some can even evince a touch of the insecurity of Thomas d'Arcy McGee, an Irish immigrant to Canada, who became a Father of our Confederation. In one of his poems, McGee, thinking of his birthplace, wrote poignantly:

"Am I remembered in Erin
I charge you, speak me true
Has my name a sound, a meaning
In the scenes my boyhood knew."

Ronald Reagan will not have to worry about Erin because they remember him well and affectionately there. Indeed they do: from Erin to Estonia, from

Maryland to Madagascar from Montreal to Monterey. Ronald Reagan does not enter history tentatively—he does so with certainty and panache. At home and on the world stage, his were not the pallid etchings of a timorous politician. They were the bold strokes of a confident and accomplished leader.

Some in the West during the early 1980s believed communism and democracy were equally valid and viable. This was the school of "moral equivalence." In contrast Ronald Reagan saw Soviet communism as a menace to be confronted in the genuine belief that its squalid underpinning would fall swiftly to the gathering winds of freedom. Provided, as he said, that NATO and the industrialized democracies stood firm and united. They did. And we know now who was right.

Ronald Reagan was a president who inspired his nation and transformed the world. He possessed a rare and prized gift called leadership—that ineffable and sometimes magical quality that sets some men and women apart so that millions will follow them as they conjure up grand visions and invite their countrymen to dream big and exciting dreams.

I always thought that President Reagan's understanding of the nobility of the presidency coincided with the American dream.

One day President Mitterrand in referring to President Reagan said: "Il a vraiment la notion de l'Etat." Rough translation: "He really has a sense of the State about him." The translation does not fully capture the profundity of the observation: what President Mitterrand meant was that there is a vast difference between the job of president and the role of president.

Ronald Reagan fulfilled both with elegance and ease, embodying himself that unusual alchemy of history, tradition, achievement, inspiration, conduct and national pride that define the special role the president of the United States must assume at home and around the world. "La notion de l'Etat"—no one understood it better than Ronald Reagan and no one more eloquently summoned his nation to high purpose or brought forth the majesty of the presidency and made it glow, better than the man who saw his country as a "shining city on a hill,"

May our common future and that of our great nations be guided by wise men and women who will remember always the golden achievements of the Reagan era and the success that can be theirs if the values of freedom and democracy are preserved, unsullied and undiminished, until the unfolding decades remember little else.

I have been truly blessed to have had a friend like Ronald Reagan. I am grateful that our paths crossed and that our lives touched. I shall always remember him with deepest admiration and affection and I shall always feel honored by the journey we traveled together in search of better and more peaceful tomorrows for all God's children, everywhere.

And so, in the presence of his beloved and indispensable Nancy, his children, family, friends and the American people he so deeply revered, I say "au revoir" today to a gifted leader, historic president and gracious human being. And I do so with a line from Yeats, who wrote:

"Think where man's glory most begins and ends and say—my glory was that I had such friends."

MARGARET THATCHER, ON RONALD REAGAN

We have lost a great president, a great American, and a great man. And I have lost a dear friend.

In his lifetime Ronald Reagan was such a cheerful and invigorating presence that it was easy to forget what daunting historic tasks he set himself. He sought to mend America's wounded spirit, to restore the strength of the free world, and to free the slaves of communism. These were causes hard to accomplish and heavy with risk.

Yet they were pursued with almost a lightness of spirit. For Ronald Reagan also embodied another great cause—what Arnold Bennett once called 'the great cause of cheering us all up.' His politics had a freshness and optimism that won converts from every class and every nation—and ultimately from the very heart of the evil empire.

Yet his humour often had a purpose beyond humour. In the terrible hours after the attempt on his life, his easy jokes gave reassurance to an anxious world. They were evidence that in the aftermath of terror and in the midst of hysteria, one great heart at least remained sane and jocular. They were truly grace under pressure.

And perhaps they signified grace of a deeper kind. Ronnie himself certainly believed that he had been given back his life for a purpose. As he told a priest after his recovery 'Whatever time I've got left now belongs to the Big Fella Upstairs.'

And surely it is hard to deny that Ronald Reagan's life was providential, when we look at what he achieved in the eight years that followed.

Others prophesied the decline of the West; he inspired America and its allies with renewed faith in their mission of freedom.

Others saw only limits to growth; he transformed a stagnant economy into an engine of opportunity.

Others hoped, at best, for an uneasy cohabitation with the Soviet Union; he won the Cold War—not only without firing a shot, but also by inviting enemies out of their fortress and turning them into friends.

I cannot imagine how any diplomat, or any dramatist, could improve on his words to Mikhail Gorbachev at the Geneva summit: "Let me tell you why it is we distrust you." Those words are candid and tough and they cannot have been easy to hear. But they are also a clear invitation to a new beginning and a new relationship that would be rooted in trust.

We live today in the world that Ronald Reagan began to reshape with those words. It is a very different world with different challenges and new dangers. All in all, however, it is one of greater freedom and prosperity, one more hopeful than the world he inherited on becoming president.

As Prime Minister, I worked closely with Ronald Reagan for eight of the most important years of all our lives. We talked regularly both before and after his presidency. And I have had time and cause to reflect on what made him a great president.

Ronald Reagan knew his own mind. He had firm principles—and, I believe, right ones. He expounded them clearly, he acted upon them decisively.

When the world threw problems at the White House, he was not baffled, or disorientated, or overwhelmed. He knew almost instinctively what to do.

When his aides were preparing option papers for his decision, they were able to cut out entire rafts of proposals that they knew "the Old Man" would never wear.

When his allies came under Soviet or domestic pressure, they could look confidently to Washington for firm leadership.

And when his enemies tested American resolve, they soon discovered that his resolve was firm and unyielding.

Yet his ideas, though clear, were never simplistic. He saw the many sides of truth.

Yes, he warned that the Soviet Union had an insatiable drive for military power and territorial expansion; but he also sensed it was being eaten away by systemic failures impossible to reform.

Yes, he did not shrink from denouncing Moscow's 'evil empire.' But he realised that a man of goodwill might nonetheless emerge from within its dark corridors.

So the President resisted Soviet expansion and pressed down on Soviet weakness at every point until the day came when communism began to collapse beneath the combined weight of these pressures and its own failures. And when a man of goodwill did emerge from the ruins, President Reagan stepped forward to shake his hand and to offer sincere cooperation.

Nothing was more typical of Ronald Reagan than that large-hearted magnanimity—and nothing was more American.

Therein lies perhaps the final explanation of his achievements. Ronald Reagan carried the American people with him in his great endeavours because there was perfect sympathy between them. He and they loved America and what it stands for—freedom and opportunity for ordinary people.

As an actor in Hollywood's golden age, he helped to make the American dream live for millions all over the globe. His own life was a fulfilment of that dream. He never succumbed to the embarrassment some people feel about an honest expression of love of country.

He was able to say "God Bless America" with equal fervour in public and in private. And so he was able to call confidently upon his fellow-countrymen to make sacrifices for America—and to make sacrifices for those who looked to America for hope and rescue.

With the lever of American patriotism, he lifted up the world. And so today the world—in Prague, in Budapest, in Warsaw, in Sofia, in Bucharest, in Kiev and in Moscow itself—the world mourns the passing of the Great Liberator and echoes his prayer "God Bless America."

Ronald Reagan's life was rich not only in public achievement, but also in private happiness. Indeed, his public achievements were rooted in his private happiness. The great turning point of his life was his meeting and marriage with Nancy.

On that we have the plain testimony of a loving and grateful husband: "Nancy came along and saved my soul." We share her grief today. But we also share her pride—and the grief and pride of Ronnie's children.

For the final years of his life, Ronnie's mind was clouded by illness. That cloud has now lifted. He is himself again—more himself than at any time on this earth. For we may be sure that the Big Fella Upstairs never forgets those who remember Him. And as the last journey of this faithful pilgrim took him beyond the sunset, and as heaven's morning broke, I like to think—in the words of Bunyan—that "all the trumpets sounded on the other side."

We here still move in twilight. But we have one beacon to guide us that Ronald Reagan never had. We have his example. Let us give thanks today for a life that achieved so much for all of God's children.

On January 12, 2011 President Barack Obama eulogized those who died and spoke movingly of the survivors of a tragic mass shooting in Tucson, Arizona. President Obama presented the speech in an attempt to fulfill the purposes served by all eulogies, but also to comment on the rise of violence and angry words in politics.

Remarks by the President at a Memorial Service for the Victims of the Shooting in Tucson, Arizona

THE PRESIDENT: Thank you. [*Applause*] Thank you very much. Please, please be seated. [*Applause*]

To the families of those we've lost; to all who called them friends; to the students of this university, the public servants who are gathered here, the people of Tucson, and the people of Arizona: I have come here tonight as an American who, like all Americans, kneels to pray with you today and will stand by you tomorrow. [*Applause*]

There is nothing I can say that will fill the sudden hole torn in your hearts. But know this: The hopes of a nation are here tonight. We mourn with you for the fallen. We join you in your grief. And we add our faith to yours that Representative Gabrielle Giffords and the other living victims of this tragedy will pull through. [*Applause*]

> Scripture tells us:
> There is a river whose streams make glad the city of God,
> the holy place where the Most High dwells.
> God is within her, she will not fall;
> God will help her at break of day.

On Saturday morning, Gabby, her staff, and many of her constituents gathered outside a supermarket to exercise their right to peaceful assembly and free speech. [*Applause*] They were fulfilling a central tenet of the democracy envisioned by our founders—representatives of the people answering questions to their constituents, so as to carry their concerns back to our nation's capital. Gabby called it "Congress on Your Corner"—just an updated version of government of and by and for the people. [*Applause*]

And that quintessentially American scene, that was the scene that was shattered by a gunman's bullets. And the six people who lost their lives on Saturday—they, too, represented what is best in us, what is best in America. [*Applause*]

Judge John Roll served our legal system for nearly 40 years. [*Applause*] A graduate of this university and a graduate of this law school—[*applause*]—Judge Roll was recommended for the federal bench by John McCain 20 years ago—[*applause*]—appointed by President George H.W. Bush and rose to become Arizona's chief federal judge. [*Applause*]

His colleagues described him as the hardest-working judge within the Ninth Circuit. He was on his way back from attending Mass, as he did every day, when he decided to stop by and say hi to his representative. John is survived by his loving wife, Maureen, his three sons and his five beautiful grandchildren. [*Applause*]

George and Dorothy Morris—"Dot" to her friends—were high school sweethearts who got married and had two daughters. They did everything together—traveling the open road in their RV, enjoying what their friends called a 50-year honeymoon. Saturday morning, they went by the Safeway to hear what their congresswoman had to say. When gunfire rang out, George, a former Marine, instinctively tried to shield his wife. [*Applause*] Both were shot. Dot passed away.

A New Jersey native, Phyllis Schneck retired to Tucson to beat the snow. But in the summer, she would return East, where her world revolved around her three children, her seven grandchildren, and two-year-old great-granddaughter. A gifted quilter, she'd often work under a favorite tree, or sometimes she'd sew aprons with the logos of the Jets and the Giants—[*laughter*]—to give out at the church where she volunteered. A Republican, she took a liking to Gabby, and wanted to get to know her better. [*Applause*]

Dorwan and Mavy Stoddard grew up in Tucson together—about 70 years ago. They moved apart and started their own respective families. But after both were widowed they found their way back here, to, as one of Mavy's daughters put it, "be boyfriend and girlfriend again." [*Laughter*]

When they weren't out on the road in their motor home, you could find them just up the road, helping folks in need at the Mountain Avenue Church of Christ. A retired construction worker, Dorwan spent his spare time fixing up the church along with his dog, Tux. His final act of selflessness was to dive on top of his wife, sacrificing his life for hers. [*Applause*]

Everything—everything—Gabe Zimmerman did, he did with passion. [*Applause*] But his true passion was helping people. As Gabby's outreach director, he made the cares of thousands of her constituents his own, seeing to it that seniors got the Medicare benefits that they had earned, that veterans got the medals and the care that they deserved, that government was working for ordinary folks. He died doing what he loved—talking with people and seeing how he could help. And Gabe is survived by his parents, Ross and Emily, his brother, Ben, and his fiancée, Kelly, who he planned to marry next year. [*Applause*]

And then there is nine-year-old Christina Taylor Green. Christina was an A student; she was a dancer; she was a gymnast; she was a swimmer. She decided that she wanted to be the first woman to play in the Major Leagues, and as the only girl on her Little League team, no one put it past her. [*Applause*]

She showed an appreciation for life uncommon for a girl her age. She'd remind her mother, "We are so blessed. We have the best life." And she'd pay those blessings back by participating in a charity that helped children who were less fortunate.

Our hearts are broken by their sudden passing. Our hearts are broken—and yet, our hearts also have reason for fullness. Our hearts are full of hope and thanks for the 13 Americans who survived the shooting, including the congresswoman many of them went to see on Saturday.

I have just come from the University Medical Center, just a mile from here, where our friend Gabby courageously fights to recover even as we speak. And I want to tell you—her husband Mark is here and he allows me to share this with you—right after we went to visit, a few minutes after we left her room and some of her colleagues in Congress were in the room, Gabby opened her eyes for the first time. [*Applause*] Gabby opened her eyes for the first time. [*Applause*]

Gabby opened her eyes. Gabby opened her eyes, so I can tell you she knows we are here. She knows we love her. And she knows that we are rooting for her through what is undoubtedly going to be a difficult journey. We are there for her. [*Applause*]

Our hearts are full of thanks for that good news, and our hearts are full of gratitude for those who saved others. We are grateful to Daniel Hernandez—[*applause*]—a volunteer in Gabby's office. [*Applause*]

And, Daniel, I'm sorry, you may deny it, but we've decided you are a hero because—[*applause*]—you ran through the chaos to minister to your boss, and tended to her wounds and helped keep her alive. [*Applause*]

We are grateful to the men who tackled the gunman as he stopped to reload. [*Applause*] Right over there. [*Applause*] We are grateful for petite Patricia Maisch, who wrestled away the killer's ammunition, and undoubtedly saved some lives. [*Applause*] And we are grateful for the doctors and nurses and first responders who worked wonders to heal those who'd been hurt. We are grateful to them. [*Applause*]

These men and women remind us that heroism is found not only on the fields of battle. They remind us that heroism does not require special training or physical strength. Heroism is here, in the hearts of so many of our fellow citizens, all around us, just waiting to be summoned—as it was on Saturday morning. Their actions, their selflessness poses a challenge to each of us. It raises a question of what, beyond prayers and expressions of concern, is required of us going forward. How can we honor the fallen? How can we be true to their memory?

You see, when a tragedy like this strikes, it is part of our nature to demand explanations—to try and impose some order on the chaos and make sense out of that which seems senseless. Already we've seen a national conversation commence, not only about the motivations behind these killings, but about everything from the merits of gun safety laws to the adequacy of our mental health system. And much of this process, of debating what might be done to prevent such tragedies in the future, is an essential ingredient in our exercise of self-government.

But at a time when our discourse has become so sharply polarized—at a time when we are far too eager to lay the blame for all that ails the world at the feet of those who happen to think differently than we do—it's important for us to pause for a moment and make sure that we're talking with each other in a way that heals, not in a way that wounds. [*Applause*]

Scripture tells us that there is evil in the world, and that terrible things happen for reasons that defy human understanding. In the words of Job, "When I looked for light, then came darkness." Bad things happen, and we have to guard against simple explanations in the aftermath.

For the truth is none of us can know exactly what triggered this vicious attack. None of us can know with any certainty what might have stopped these shots from being fired, or what thoughts lurked in the inner recesses of a violent man's mind. Yes, we have to examine all the facts behind this tragedy. We cannot and will not be passive in the face of such violence. We should be willing to challenge old assumptions in order to lessen the prospects of such violence in the future. [*Applause*] But what we cannot do is use this tragedy as one more occasion to turn on each other. [*Applause*] That we cannot do. [*Applause*] That we cannot do.

As we discuss these issues, let each of us do so with a good dose of humility. Rather than pointing fingers or assigning blame, let's use this occasion to expand our moral imaginations, to listen to each other more carefully, to sharpen our instincts for empathy and remind ourselves of all the ways that our hopes and dreams are bound together. [*Applause*]

After all, that's what most of us do when we lose somebody in our family—especially if the loss is unexpected. We're shaken out of our routines. We're forced to look inward. We reflect on the past: Did we spend enough time with an aging parent, we wonder. Did we express our gratitude for all the sacrifices that they made for us? Did we tell a spouse just how desperately we loved them, not just once in a while but every single day?

So sudden loss causes us to look backward—but it also forces us to look forward; to reflect on the present and the future, on the manner in which we live our lives and nurture our relationships with those who are still with us. [*Applause*]

We may ask ourselves if we've shown enough kindness and generosity and compassion to the people in our lives. Perhaps we question whether we're doing right by our children, or our community, whether our priorities are in order.

We recognize our own mortality, and we are reminded that in the fleeting time we have on this Earth, what matters is not wealth, or status, or power, or fame—but rather, how well we have loved—[*applause*]—and what small part we have played in making the lives of other people better. [*Applause*]

And that process—that process of reflection, of making sure we align our values with our actions—that, I believe, is what a tragedy like this requires.

For those who were harmed, those who were killed—they are part of our family, an American family 300 million strong. [*Applause*] We may not have known them personally, but surely we see ourselves in them. In George and Dot, in Dorwan and Mavy, we sense the abiding love we have for our own husbands, our own wives, our own life partners. Phyllis—she's our mom or our grandma; Gabe our brother or son. [*Applause*] In Judge Roll, we recognize not only a man who prized his family and doing his job well, but also a man who embodied America's fidelity to the law. [*Applause*]

And in Gabby—in Gabby, we see a reflection of our public-spiritedness; that desire to participate in that sometimes frustrating, sometimes contentious, but always necessary and never-ending process to form a more perfect union. [*Applause*]

And in Christina—in Christina we see all of our children. So curious, so trusting, so energetic, so full of magic. So deserving of our love. And so deserving of our good example.

If this tragedy prompts reflection and debate—as it should—let's make sure it's worthy of those we have lost. [*Applause*] Let's make sure it's not on the usual plane of politics and point-scoring and pettiness that drifts away in the next news cycle.

The loss of these wonderful people should make every one of us strive to be better. To be better in our private lives, to be better friends and neighbors and coworkers and parents. And if, as has been discussed in recent days, their death helps usher in more civility in our public discourse, let us remember it is not because a simple lack of civility caused this tragedy—it did not—but rather because only a more civil and honest public discourse can help us face up to the challenges of our nation in a way that would make them proud. [*Applause*]

We should be civil because we want to live up to the example of public servants like John Roll and Gabby Giffords, who knew first and foremost that we are all Americans, and that we can question each other's ideas without questioning each other's love of country and that our task, working together, is to constantly widen the circle of our concern so that we bequeath the American Dream to future generations. [*Applause*]

They believed—they believed, and I believe that we can be better. Those who died here, those who saved life here—they help me believe. We may not be able to stop all evil in the world, but I know that how we treat one another, that's entirely up to us. [*Applause*]

And I believe that for all our imperfections, we are full of decency and goodness, and that the forces that divide us are not as strong as those that unite us. [*Applause*]

That's what I believe, in part because that's what a child like Christina Taylor Green believed. [*Applause*]

Imagine—imagine for a moment, here was a young girl who was just becoming aware of our democracy; just beginning to understand the obligations of citizenship; just starting to glimpse the fact that some day she, too, might play a part in shaping her nation's future. She had been elected to her student council. She saw public service as something exciting and hopeful. She was off to meet her congresswoman, someone she was sure was good and important and might be a role model. She saw all this through the eyes of a child, undimmed by the cynicism or vitriol that we adults all too often just take for granted.

I want to live up to her expectations. [*Applause*] I want our democracy to be as good as Christina imagined it. I want America to be as good as she imagined it. [*Applause*] All of us—we should do everything we can to make sure this country lives up to our children's expectations. [*Applause*]

As has already been mentioned, Christina was given to us on September 11th, 2001, one of 50 babies born that day to be pictured in a book called *Faces of Hope*. On either side of her photo in that book were simple wishes for a child's life. "I hope you help those in need," read one. "I hope you know all the words to the National Anthem and sing it with your hand over your heart." [*Applause*] "I hope you jump in rain puddles."

If there are rain puddles in Heaven, Christina is jumping in them today. [*Applause*] And here on this Earth—here on this Earth, we place our hands over our hearts, and we commit ourselves as Americans to forging a country that is forever worthy of her gentle, happy spirit.

May God bless and keep those we've lost in restful and eternal peace. May He love and watch over the survivors. And may He bless the United States of America. [*Applause*]

THE INAUGURAL ADDRESS

Inaugural addresses of Presidents John Kennedy, Jimmy Carter, Ronald Reagan, Barack Obama and Donald Trump in the United States and Nelson Mandela in South Africa are included. What purposes are served by inaugurals? Inaugural addresses serve three primary purposes: expressing the essence of the new administration, reunification of the country and energizing the population. A new leader in any organization (and especially a President of the United States) needs to tell his/her constituents what he/she wants to do. Presidents would give inaugural addresses to achieve this aim, even if there were no ritual associated with taking the oath of office.

In order to test whether an inaugural address fulfills the three purposes, it is important to consider whether the address contains the characteristics of form, content, substance, and style that define the inaugural. It also is important to consider whether any aspect of the address violates the norms for the category. Finally, the critic needs to assess whether the speech responds to the specifics of the situation and to consider whether the style of the address is memorable.

Inaugural Address
John F. Kennedy

Mr. Chief Justice, President Eisenhower, Vice President Nixon, President Truman, reverend clergy, fellow citizens, we observe today not a victory of party, but a celebration of freedom—symbolizing an end, as well as a beginning—signifying renewal, as well as change. For I have sworn before you and Almighty God the same solemn oath our forbearers prescribed nearly a century and three-quarters ago.

The world is very different now. For man holds in his mortal hands the power to abolish all forms of human poverty and all forms of human life. And yet the same revolutionary beliefs for which our forebearers fought are still at issue around the globe—the belief that the rights of man come not from the generosity of the State, but from the hand of God.

We dare not forget today that we are the heirs of that first revolution. Let the word go forth from this time and place, to friend and foe alike, that the torch has been passed to a new generation of Americans—born in the century, tempered by war, disciplined by a hard and bitter peace, proud of our ancient heritage—and unwilling to witness or permit the slow undoing of those human rights to which this nation has always been committed, and to which we are committed today at home and around the world.

Let every nation know, whether it wishes us well or ill, that we shall pay any price, bear any burden, meet any hardship, support any friend, oppose any foe, in order to assure the survival and the success of liberty.

January 20, 1961.

This much we pledge—and more.

To those old allies whose cultural and spiritual origins we share, we pledge the loyalty of faithful friends. United, there is little we cannot do in a host of cooperative ventures. Divided, there is little we can do—for we dare not meet a powerful challenge at odds and split asunder.

To those new states whom we welcome to the ranks of the free, we pledge our words that one form of colonial control shall not have passed away merely to be replaced by a far greater iron tyranny. We shall not always expect to find them supporting our view. But we shall always hope to find them strongly supporting their own freedom—and to remember that, in the past, those who foolishly sought power by riding the back of the tiger ended up inside.

To those peoples in the huts and villages across the globe struggling to break the bonds of mass misery, we pledge our best efforts to help them help themselves, for whatever period is required—not because the Communists may be doing it, not because we seek their votes, but because it is right. If a free society cannot help the many who are poor, it cannot save the few who are rich.

To our sister republics south of our border, we offer a special pledge—to convert our good words into good deeds, in a new Alliance for Progress, to assist free men and free governments in casting off the chains of poverty. But this peaceful revolution of hope cannot become the prey of hostile powers. Let all our neighbors know that we shall join with them to oppose aggression or subversion anywhere in the Americas. And let every other power know that this hemisphere intends to remain the master of its own house.

To that world assembly of sovereign states, the United Nations, our last best hope in an age where the instruments of war have far outpaced the instruments of peace, we renew our pledge of support—to prevent it from becoming merely a forum for invective—to strengthen its shield of the new and the weak—and to enlarge the area in which its writ may run.

Finally, to those nations who would make themselves our adversary, we offer not a pledge but a request: that both sides begin anew the quest for peace, before the dark powers of destruction unleashed by science engulf all humanity in planned or accidental self-destruction.

We dare not tempt them with weakness. For only when our arms are sufficient beyond doubt can we be certain beyond doubt that they will never be employed.

But neither can two great and powerful groups of nations take comfort from our present course—both sides overburdened by the cost of modern weapons, both rightly alarmed by the steady spread of the deadly atom, yet both racing to alter that uncertain balance of terror that stays the hand of mankind's final war.

So let us begin anew—remembering on both sides that civility is not a sign of weakness, and sincerity is always subject to proof. Let us never negotiate out of fear. But let us never fear to negotiate.

Let both sides explore what problems unite us instead of laboring those problems which divide us.

Let both sides, for the first time, formulate serious and precise proposals for the inspection and control of arms—and bring the absolute power to destroy other nations under the absolute control of all nations.

Let both sides seek to invoke the wonders of science instead of its terrors. Together let us explore the stars, conquer the deserts, eradicate disease, tap the ocean depths, and encourage the arts and commerce.

Let both sides unite to heed in all corners of the Earth the command of Isaiah—to "undo the heavy burdens and to let the oppressed go free."

And if a beachhead of cooperation may push back the jungle of suspicion, let both sides join in creating a new endeavor, not a new balance of power, but a new world of law, where the strong are just and the weak secure and the peace preserved.

All this will not be finished in the first hundred days. Nor will it be finished in the first thousand days, nor in the life of this Administration nor even perhaps in our lifetime on this planet. But let us begin.

In your hands, my fellow citizen, more than in mine, will rest the final success or failure of our course. Since this country was founded, each generation of America has been summoned to give testimony to its national loyalty. The graves of young Americans who answered the call to service are found around the globe.

Now the trumpet summons us again—not as a call to bear arms, though arms we need; not as a call to battle, though embattled we are; but a call to bear the burden of a long twilight struggle, year in, and year out, "rejoicing in hope, patient in tribulation"—a struggle against the common enemies of man: tyranny, poverty, disease, and war itself.

Can we forge against these enemies a grand and global alliance, north and south, east and west, that can assure a more fruitful life for all mankind? Will you join in that historic effort?

In the long history of the world, only a few generations have been granted the role of defending freedom in its hour of maximum danger. I do not shrink from this responsibility—I welcome it. I do not believe that any of us would exchange places with any other people or any other generation. The energy, the faith, the devotion which we bring to this endeavor will light our country and all who serve it—and the glow from that fire can truly light the world.

And so, my fellow Americans, ask not what your country can do for you. Ask what you can do for your country.

My fellow citizens of the world: Ask not what America will do for you, but what together we can do for the freedom of man.

Finally, whether you are citizens of America or citizens of the world, ask of us the same high standards of strength and sacrifice which we ask of you. With a good conscience our only sure reward, with history the final judge of our deeds, let us go forth to lead the land we love, asking His blessing and His help, but knowing that here on Earth God's work must truly be our own.

Inaugural Address

James Earl Carter

For myself and for our nation, I want to thank my predecessor for all he has done to heal our land. In this outward and physical ceremony we attest once again to the inner and spiritual strength of our nation.

As my high school teacher, Miss Julia Coleman, used to say, "We must adjust to changing times and still hold to unchanging principles."

Here before me is the Bible used in the inauguration of our first President in 1789, and I have just taken the oath of office on the Bible my mother gave me just a few years ago, opened to a timeless admonition from the ancient prophet Micah:

"He hath showed thee, O man, what is good;
and what doth the Lord require of thee, but
to do justly, and to love mercy, and to walk
humbly with thy God." (Micah 6:8)

This inauguration ceremony marks a new beginning, a new dedication within our Government, and a new spirit among us all. A President may sense and proclaim that new spirit, but only a people can provide it.

Two centuries ago our nation's birth was a milestone in the long quest for freedom, but the bold and brilliant dream which excited the founders of this nation still awaits its consummation. I have no new dream to set forth today, but rather urge a fresh faith in the old dream.

Ours was the first society openly to define itself in terms of both spirituality and human liberty. It is that unique self-definition which has given us an exceptional appeal—but it also imposes on us a special obligation, to take on those moral duties which, when assumed, seem invariably to be in our own best interests.

You have given me a great responsibility—to stay close to you, to be worthy of you and to exemplify what you are. Let us create together a new national spirit of unity and trust. Your strength can compensate for my weakness, and your wisdom can help to minimize my mistakes.

Let us learn together and laugh together and work together and pray together, confident that in the end we will triumph together in the right.

The American dream endures. We must once again have faith in our country—and in one another. I believe America can be better. We can be even stronger than before.

Let our recent mistakes bring a resurgent commitment to the basic principles of our nation, for we know that if we despise our own Government we have no future. We recall in special times when we have stood briefly, but magnificently, united; in those times no prize was beyond our grasp.

But we cannot dwell upon remembered glory. We cannot afford to drift. We reject the prospect of failure or mediocrity or an inferior quality of life for any person.

Our Government must at the same time be both competent and compassionate.

We have already found a high degree of personal liberty, and we are now struggling to enhance equality of opportunity. Our commitment to human rights must be absolute, our laws fair, our natural beauty preserved; the powerful must not persecute the weak, and human dignity must be enhanced.

We have learned that "more" is not necessarily "better," that even our great nation has its recognized limits and that we can neither answer all questions nor solve all problems. We cannot afford to do everything, nor can we afford to lack boldness as we meet the future. So together, in a spirit of

January 20, 1977.

individual sacrifice for the common good, we must simply do our best.

Our nation can be strong abroad only if it is strong at home, and we know that the best way to enhance freedom in other lands is to demonstrate here that our democratic system is worthy of emulation.

To be true to ourselves, we must be true to others. We will not behave in foreign places so as to violate our rules and standards here at home, for we know that this trust which our nation earns is essential to our strength.

The world itself is now dominated by a new spirit. Peoples more numerous and more politically aware are craving and now demanding their place in the sun—not just for the benefit of their own physical condition, but for basic human rights.

The passion for freedom is on the rise. Tapping this new spirit, there can be no nobler nor more ambitious task for America to undertake on this day of a new beginning than to help shape a just and peaceful world that is truly humane.

We will be ever vigilant and never vulnerable, and we will fight our wars against poverty, ignorance and injustice, for those are the enemies against which our forces can be honorably marshaled.

We are a proudly idealistic nation, but let no one confuse our idealism with weakness.

Because we are free we can never be indifferent to the fate of freedom elsewhere. Our moral sense dictates a clear cut preference for those societies which share with us an abiding respect for individual human rights. We do not seek to intimidate, but it is clear that a world which others can dominate with impunity would be inhospitable to decency and a threat to the well-being of all people.

The world is still engaged in a massive armaments race designed to insure continuing equivalent strength among potential adversaries. We pledge perseverance and wisdom in our efforts to limit the world's armaments to those necessary for each nation's own domestic safety. We will move this year a step toward our ultimate goal—the elimination of all nuclear weapons from this Earth.

We urge all other people to join us, for success can mean life instead of death.

Within us, the people of the United States, there is evident a serious and purposeful rekindling of confidence, and I join in the hope that when my time as your President has ended, people might say this about our nation:

That we had remembered the words of Micah and renewed our search for humility, mercy and justice;

That we had torn down the barriers that separated those of different race and region and religion, and where there had been mistrust, built unity, with a respect for diversity;

That we had found productive work for those able to perform it;

That we had strengthened the American family, which is the basis our society;

That we had ensured respect for the law, and equal treatment under the law, for the weak and the powerful, for the rich and the poor;

And that we had enabled our people to be proud of their own Government once again.

I would hope that the nations of the world might say that we had built a lasting peace, based not on weapons of war but on international policies which reflect our own most precious values.

These are not just my goals. And they will not be my accomplishments but the affirmation of our nation's continuing moral strength and our belief in an undiminished, ever-expanding American dream.

Inaugural Address

Ronald Reagan

Senator Hatfield, Mr. Chief Justice, Mr. President, Vice President Bush, Vice President Mondale, Senator Baker, Speaker O'Neill, Reverend Moomaw, and my fellow citizens:

To a few of us here today this is a solemn and most momentous occasion, and yet in the history of our nation it is a commonplace occurrence. The orderly transfer of authority as called for in the Constitution routinely takes place, as it has for almost two centuries, and few of us stop to think how unique we really are. In the eyes of many in the world, this every-four-year ceremony we accept as normal is nothing less than a miracle.

Mr. President, I want our fellow citizens to know how much you did to carry on this tradition. By your gracious cooperation in the transition process, you have shown a watching world that we are a united people pledged to maintaining a political system which guarantees individual liberty to a greater degree than any other, and I thank you and your

January 20, 1981.

people for all your help in maintaining the continuity which is the bulwark of our Republic.

The business of our nation goes forward. These United States are confronted with an economic affliction of great proportions. We suffer from the longest and one of the worst sustained inflations in our national history. It distorts our economic decision, penalizes thrift, and crushes the struggling young and the fixed-income elderly alike. It threatens to shatter the lives of millions of our people.

Idle industries have cast workers into unemployment, human misery, and personal indignity. Those who do work are denied a fair return for their labor by a tax system which penalizes successful achievement and keeps us from maintaining full productivity.

But great as our tax burden is, it has not kept pace with public spending. For decades we have piled deficit upon deficit, mortgaging our future and our children's future for the temporary convenience of the present. To continue this long trend is to guarantee tremendous social, cultural, political, and economic upheavals.

You and I, as individuals, can, by borrowing, live beyond our means, but for only a limited period of time. Why, then, should we think that collectively, as a nation, we're not bound by that same limitation? We must act today in order to preserve tomorrow. And let there be no misunderstanding: We are going to begin to act, beginning today.

The economic ills we suffer have come upon us over several decades. They will not go away in days, weeks, or months, but they will go away. They will go away because we as Americans have the capacity now, as we've had in the past, to do whatever needs to be done to preserve this last and greatest bastion of freedom.

In this present crisis, government is not the solution to our problem; government is the problem. From time to time we've been tempted to believe that society has become too complex to be managed by self-rule, that government by an elite group is superior to government for, by, and of the people. Well, if no one among us is capable of governing himself, then who among us has the capacity to govern someone else? All of us together, in and out of government, must bear the burden. The solutions we seek must be equitable, with no one group singled out to pay a higher price.

We hear much of special interest groups. Well, our concern must be for a special interest group that has been too long neglected. It knows no sectional boundaries or ethnic and racial divisions, and

it crosses political party lines. It is made up of men and women who raise our food, patrol our streets, man our mines and factories, teach our children, keep our homes, and heal us when we're sick—professionals, industrialists, shopkeepers, clerks, cabbies, and truck drivers. They are, in short, "We the people," this breed called Americans.

Well, this administration's objective will be a healthy, vigorous, growing economy that provides equal opportunities for all Americans, with no barriers born of bigotry or discrimination. Putting America back to work means putting all Americans back to work. Ending inflation means freeing all Americans from the terror of runaway living costs. All must share in the productive work of this "new beginning," and all must share in the bounty of a revised economy. With the idealism and fair play which are the core of our system and our strength, we can have a strong and prosperous America, at peace with itself and the world.

So, as we begin, let us take inventory. We are a nation that has a government—not the other way around. And this makes us special among the nations of the Earth. Our government has no power except that granted it by the people. It is time to check and reverse the growth of government, which shows signs of having grown beyond the consent of the governed.

It is my intention to curb the size and influence of the Federal establishment and to demand recognition of the distinction between the powers granted to the Federal Government and those reserved to the States or to the people. All of us need to be reminded that the Federal Government did not create the States; the States created the Federal Government.

Now, so there will be no misunderstanding, it's not my intention to do away with government. It is rather to make it work—work with us, not over us; to stand by our side, not ride on our back. Government can and must provide opportunity, not smother it; foster productivity, not stifle it.

If we look to the answer as to why for so many years we achieved so much, prospered as no other people on Earth, it was because here in this land we unleashed the energy and individual genius of man to a greater extent than has ever been done before. Freedom and the dignity of the individual have been more available and assured here than in any other place on Earth. The price for this freedom at times has been high, but we have never been unwilling to pay that price.

It is no coincidence that our present troubles parallel and are proportionate to the intervention and intrusion in our lives that result from unnecessary and excessive growth of government. It is time for us to realize that we're too great a nation to limit ourselves to small dreams. We're not, as some would have us believe, doomed to an inevitable decline. I do not believe in a fate that will fall on us no matter what we do. I do believe in a fate that will fall on us if we do nothing so, with all the creative energy at our command, let us begin an era of national renewal. Let us renew our determination, our courage, and our strength. And let us renew our faith and our hope.

We have every right to dream heroic dreams. Those who say that we're in a time when there are not heroes, they just don't know where to look. You can see heroes every day going in and out of factory gates. Others, a handful in number, produce enough food to feed all of us and then the world beyond. You meet heroes across a counter, and they're on both sides of that counter. There are entrepreneurs with faith in themselves and faith in an idea who create new jobs, new wealth and opportunity. They're individuals and families whose taxes support the government and whose voluntary gifts support church, charity, culture, art, and education. Their patriotism is quiet, but deep. Their values sustain our national life.

Now, I have used the words "they" and "their" in speaking of these heroes. I could say "you" and "your" because I'm addressing the heroes of whom I speak—you, the citizens of this blessed land. Your dreams, your hopes, your goals are going to be the dreams, the hopes, and the goals of this administration, so help me God.

We shall reflect the compassion that is so much a part of your makeup. How can we love our country and not love our countrymen; and loving them, reach out a hand when they fall, heal them when they're sick, and provide opportunity to make them self-sufficient so they will be equal in fact and not just in theory?

Can we solve the problems confronting us? Well, the answer is an unequivocal and emphatic "yes." To paraphrase Winston Churchill, I did not take the oath I've just taken with the intention of presiding over the dissolution of the world's strongest economy.

In the days ahead I will propose removing the roadblocks that have slowed our economy and reduced productivity. Steps will be taken aimed at restoring the balance between the various levels of government. Progress may be slow, measured in inches and feet, not miles, but we will progress. It is time to reawaken this industrial giant, to get government back within its means, and to lighten our punitive tax burden. And these will be our first

priorities, and on these principles there will be no compromise.

On the eve our struggle for independence a man who might have been one of the greatest among the Founding Fathers, Dr. Joseph Warren, president of the Massachusetts Congress, said to his fellow Americans, "Our country is in danger, but not to be despaired of . . . . On you depend the fortunes of America. You are to decide the important questions upon which rests the happiness and the liberty of millions yet unborn. Act worthy of yourselves."

Well, I believe we, the Americans of today, are ready to act worthy of ourselves here in our own land, we will be seen as having greater strength throughout the world. We will again be the exemplar of freedom and a beacon of hope for those who do not now have freedom.

To those neighbors and allies who share our freedom, we will strengthen our historic ties and assure them of our support and firm commitment. We will match loyalty with loyalty. We will strive for mutually beneficial relations. We will not use our friendship to impose on their sovereignty, for our own sovereignty is not for sale.

As for the enemies of freedom, those who are potential adversaries, they will be reminded that peace is the highest aspiration of the American people. We will negotiate for it, sacrifice for it, we will not surrender for it, now or ever.

Our forbearance should never be misunderstood. Our reluctance for conflict should not be misjudged as a failure of will. When action is required to preserve our national security, we will act. We will maintain sufficient strength to prevail if need be, knowing that if we do so we have the best chance of never having to use that strength.

Above all, we must realize that no arsenal or no weapon in the arsenals of the world is so formidable as the will and moral courage of free men and women. It is a weapon our adversaries in today's world do not have. Let that be understood by those who practice terrorism and prey upon their neighbors.

I'm told that tens of thousands of prayer meetings are being held on this day, and for that I'm deeply grateful. We are a nation under God, and I believe God intended for us to be free. It would be fitting and good, I think, if on each Inaugural day in future years it should be declared a day of prayer.

This is the first time in our history that this ceremony has been held, as you've been told, on this West Front of the Capitol. Standing here, one faces a magnificent vista, opening up on this city's special beauty and history. At the end of this open mall are those shrines to the giants on whose shoulders we stand.

Directly in front of me, the monument to a monumental man, George Washington, father of our country. A man of humility who came to greatness reluctantly. He led America out of revolutionary victory into infant nationhood. Off to one side, the stately memorial to Thomas Jefferson. The Declaration of Independence flames with his eloquence. And then, beyond the Reflecting Pool, the dignified columns of the Lincoln Memorial. Whoever would understand in his heart the meaning of America will find it in the life of Abraham Lincoln.

Beyond those monuments to heroism is the Potomac River, and on the far shore the sloping hills of Arlington National Cemetery, with its row upon row of simple white markers bearing crosses or Stars of David. They add up to only a tiny fraction of the price that has been paid for our freedom.

Each one of those markers is a monument to the kind of hero I spoke of earlier. Their lives ended in places call Belleau Wood, The Argonne, Omaha Beach, Salerno, and halfway around the world on Guadalcanal, Tarawa, Pork Chop Hill, the Chosin Reservoir, and in a hundred rice paddies and jungles of a place called Vietnam.

Under one such marker lies a young man, Martin Treptow, who left his job in a small town barbershop in 1917 to go to France with the famed Rainbow Division. There, on the western front, he was killed trying to carry a message between battalions under heavy artillery fire.

We're told that on his body was found a diary. On the flyleaf under the heading, "My Pledge," he had written these words: "America must win this war. Therefore I will work, I will save, I will sacrifice, I will endure, I will fight cheerfully and do my utmost, as if the issue of the whole struggle depended on me alone."

The crisis we are facing today does not require of us the kind of sacrifice that Martin Treptow and so many thousands of others were called upon to make. It does require, however, our best effort and our willingness to believe in ourselves and to believe in our capacity to perform great deeds, to believe that together with God's help we can and will resolve the problems which now confront us.

And after all, why shouldn't we believe that? We are Americans.

God bless you, and thank you.

Inaugural Address
Nelson Mandela

Your majesties, your royal highnesses, distinguished guests, comrades and friends: Today, all of us do, by our presence here, and by our celebration in other parts of our country and the world, confer glory and hope to newborn liberty.

Out of the experience of an extraordinary human disaster that lasted too long must be born a society of which all humanity will be proud.

Our daily deeds as ordinary South Africans must produce an actual South African reality that will reinforce humanity's belief in justice, strengthen its confidence in the nobility of the human soul and sustain all our hopes for a glorious life for all.

All this we owe both to ourselves and to the peoples of the world who are so well represented here today.

To my compatriots, I have no hesitation in saying that each one of us is as intimately attached to the soil of this beautiful country as are the famous jacaranda trees of Pretoria and the mimosa trees of the bushveld.

Each time one of us touches the soil of this land, we feel a sense of personal renewal. The national mood changes as the seasons change.

We are moved by a sense of joy and exhilaration when the grass turns green and the flowers bloom.

That spiritual and physical oneness we all share with this common homeland explains the depth of the pain we all carried in our hearts as we saw our country tear itself apart in terrible conflict, and as we saw it spurned, outlawed, and isolated by the peoples of the world, precisely because it has become the universal base of the pernicious ideology and practice of racism and racial oppression.

We, the people of South Africa, feel fulfilled that humanity has taken us back into its bosom, that we, who were outlaws not so long ago, have today been given the rare privilege to be host to the nations of the world on our own soil.

We thank all our distinguished international guests for having to come to take possession with the people of our country of what is, after all, a common victory for justice, for peace, for human dignity.

Presented May 10, 1994.

We trust that you will continue to stand by us as we tackle the challenges of building peace, prosperity, nonsexism, nonracialism and democracy.

We deeply appreciate the role that the masses of our people and their democratic, religious, women, youth, business, traditional and other leaders have played to bring about this conclusion. Not least among them is my Second Deputy President, the Honorable F.W. de Klerk.

We would also like to pay tribute to our security forces, in all their ranks, for the distinguished role they have played in securing our first democratic elections and the transition to democracy, from bloodthirsty forces which still refuse to see the light.

The time for the healing of the wounds has come.

The moment to bridge the chasms that divide us has come.

The time to build is upon us.

We have, at last, achieved our political emancipation. We pledge ourselves to liberate all our people from the continuing bondage of poverty, deprivation, suffering, gender and other discrimination.

We succeeded to take our last steps to freedom in conditions of relative peace. We commit ourselves to the construction of a complete, just and lasting peace.

We have triumphed in the effort to implant hope in the breasts of the millions of our people. We enter into a covenant that we shall build the society in which all South Africans, both black and white, will be able to walk tall, without any fear in their hearts assured of their inalienable right to human dignity—a rainbow nation at peace with itself and the world.

As a token of its commitment to the renewal of our country, the new Interim Government of National Unity will, as a matter of urgency, address the issue of amnesty for various categories of our people who are currently serving terms of imprisonment.

We dedicate this day to all the heroes and heroines in this country and the rest of the world who sacrificed in many ways and surrendered their lives so that we could be free.

Their dreams have become reality. Freedom is their reward.

We are both humbled and elevated by the honor and privilege that you, the people of South Africa, have bestowed on us, as the first President of a united, democratic, nonracial and nonsexist South Africa, to lead our country out of the valley of darkness.

We understand it still that there is no easy road to freedom.

We know it well that none of us acting alone can achieve success.

We must therefore act together as a united people, for national reconciliation, for nation building, for the birth of a new world.

Let there be justice for all.

Let here be peace for all.

Let there be work, bread, water and salt for all.

Let each know that for each the body, the mind and the soul have been freed to fulfill themselves.

Never, never and never again shall it be that this beautiful land will again experience the oppression of one by another and suffer the indignity of being the skunk of the world.

The sun shall never set on so glorious a human achievement!

Let freedom reign. God bless Africa!

PRESIDENT BARACK OBAMA—INAUGURAL ADDRESS

On January 20, 2009, Barack Obama was sworn in as President of the United States. Obama took office at a time of great economic crisis. At the same time, his many supporters were immensely hopeful that he could bring real change to Washington. Thus, President Obama faced a difficult situation in confronting an economic crisis and high expectations that his presidency would produce rapid change. The situation was less dire on January 20, 2013 when he was sworn in for a second term.

2009 Inaugural Address
Barack Obama

My fellow citizens: I stand here today humbled by the task before us, grateful for the trust you've bestowed, mindful of the sacrifices borne by our ancestors.

I thank President Bush for his service to our nation—[*applause*]—as well as the generosity and cooperation he has shown throughout this transition.

Forty-four Americans have now taken the presidential oath. The words have been spoken during rising tides of prosperity and the still waters of peace. Yet, every so often, the oath is taken amidst gathering clouds and raging storms. At these moments, America has carried on not simply because of the skill or vision of those in high office, but because we, the people, have remained faithful to the ideals of our forebears and true to our founding documents.

So it has been; so it must be with this generation of Americans.

That we are in the midst of crisis is now well understood. Our nation is at war against a far-reaching network of violence and hatred. Our economy is badly weakened, a consequence of greed and irresponsibility on the part of some, but also our collective failure to make hard choices and prepare the nation for a new age. Homes have been lost, jobs shed, businesses shuttered. Our health care is too costly, our schools fail too many—and each day brings further evidence that the ways we use energy strengthen our adversaries and threaten our planet.

These are the indicators of crisis, subject to data and statistics. Less measurable, but no less profound, is a sapping of confidence across our land; a nagging fear that America's decline is inevitable, that the next generation must lower its sights.

Today I say to you that the challenges we face are real. They are serious and they are many. They will not be met easily or in a short span of time. But know this America: They will be met. [*Applause*]

On this day, we gather because we have chosen hope over fear, unity of purpose over conflict and discord. On this day, we come to proclaim an end to the petty grievances and false promises, the recriminations and worn-out dogmas that for far too long have strangled our politics. We remain a young nation. But in the words of Scripture, the time has come to set aside childish things. The time has come to reaffirm our enduring spirit; to choose our better history; to carry forward that precious gift, that noble idea passed on from generation to generation: the God-given promise that all are equal, all are free, and all deserve a chance to pursue their full measure of happiness. [*Applause*]

In reaffirming the greatness of our nation we understand that greatness is never a given. It must be earned. Our journey has never been one of shortcuts or settling for less. It has not been the path for the faint-hearted, for those that prefer leisure over work, or seek only the pleasures of riches and fame. Rather, it has been the risk-takers, the doers, the makers of things—some celebrated, but more often men and women obscure in their labor—who have carried us up the long rugged path towards prosperity and freedom.

For us, they packed up their few worldly possessions and traveled across oceans in search of a new life. For us, they toiled in sweatshops, and settled the West, endured the lash of the whip, and plowed the hard earth. For us, they fought and died in places like Concord and Gettysburg, Normandy and Khe Sahn.

Time and again these men and women struggled and sacrificed and worked till their hands were raw so that we might live a better life. They saw America as bigger than the sum of our individual ambitions, greater than all the differences of birth or wealth or faction.

This is the journey we continue today. We remain the most prosperous, powerful nation on Earth. Our workers are no less productive than when this crisis began. Our minds are no less inventive, our goods and services no less needed than they were last week, or last month, or last year. Our capacity remains undiminished. But our time of standing pat, of protecting narrow interests and putting off unpleasant decisions—that time has surely passed. Starting today, we must pick ourselves up, dust ourselves off, and begin again the work of remaking America. [*Applause*]

For everywhere we look, there is work to be done. The state of our economy calls for action, bold and swift. And we will act, not only to create new jobs, but to lay a new foundation for growth. We will build the roads and bridges, the electric grids and digital lines that feed our commerce and bind us together. We'll restore science to its rightful place, and wield technology's wonders to raise health care's quality and lower its cost. We will harness the sun and the winds and the soil to fuel our cars and run our factories. And we will transform our schools and colleges and universities to meet the demands of a new age. All this we can do. All this we will do.

Now, there are some who question the scale of our ambitions, who suggest that our system cannot tolerate too many big plans. Their memories are short, for they have forgotten what this country has already done, what free men and women can achieve when imagination is joined to common purpose, and necessity to courage. What the cynics fail to understand is that the ground has shifted beneath them, that the stale political arguments that have consumed us for so long no longer apply.

The question we ask today is not whether our government is too big or too small, but whether it works—whether it helps families find jobs at a decent wage, care they can afford, a retirement that is dignified. Where the answer is yes, we intend to move forward. Where the answer is no, programs will end. And those of us who manage the public's dollars will be held to account, to spend wisely, reform bad habits, and do our business in the light of day, because only then can we restore the vital trust between a people and their government.

Nor is the question before us whether the market is a force for good or ill. Its power to generate wealth and expand freedom is unmatched. But this crisis has reminded us that without a watchful eye, the market can spin out of control. The nation cannot prosper long when it favors only the prosperous. The success of our economy has always depended not just on the size of our gross domestic product, but on the reach of our prosperity, on the ability to extend opportunity to every willing heart—not out of charity, but because it is the surest route to our common good. [*Applause*]

As for our common defense, we reject as false the choice between our safety and our ideals. Our Founding Fathers—[*applause*]—our Founding Fathers, faced with perils that we can scarcely imagine, drafted a charter to assure the rule of law and the rights of man—a charter expanded by the blood of generations. Those ideals still light the world, and we will not give them up for expedience sake. [*Applause*]

And so, to all the other peoples and governments who are watching today, from the grandest capitals to the small village where my father was born, know that America is a friend of each nation, and every man, woman, and child who seeks a future of peace and dignity. And we are ready to lead once more. [*Applause*]

Recall that earlier generations faced down fascism and communism not just with missiles and tanks, but with the sturdy alliances and enduring convictions. They understood that our power alone cannot protect us, nor does it entitle us to do as we please. Instead they knew that our power grows through its prudent use; our security emanates from the justness of our cause, the force of our example, the tempering qualities of humility and restraint.

We are the keepers of this legacy. Guided by these principles once more we can meet those new threats that demand even greater effort, even greater cooperation and understanding between nations. We will begin to responsibly leave Iraq to its people and forge a hard-earned peace in Afghanistan. With old friends and former foes, we'll work tirelessly to lessen the nuclear threat, and roll back the specter of a warming planet.

We will not apologize for our way of life, nor will we waver in its defense. And for those who seek to advance their aims by inducing terror and slaughtering innocents, we say to you now that our spirit is stronger and cannot be broken—you cannot outlast us, and we will defeat you. [*Applause*]

For we know that our patchwork heritage is a strength, not a weakness. We are a nation of Christians and Muslims, Jews and Hindus, and nonbelievers. We are shaped by every language and culture, drawn from every end of this Earth; and because we have tasted the bitter swill of civil war and segregation, and emerged from that dark chapter stronger and more united, we cannot help but believe that the old hatreds shall someday pass; that the lines of tribe shall soon dissolve; that as the world grows smaller, our common humanity shall reveal itself; and that America must play its role in ushering in a new era of peace.

To the Muslim world, we seek a new way forward, based on mutual interest and mutual respect. To those leaders around the globe who seek to sow conflict, or blame their society's ills on the West, know that your people will judge you on what you can build, not what you destroy. [*Applause*]

To those who cling to power through corruption and deceit and the silencing of dissent, know that you are on the wrong side of history, but that we will extend a hand if you are willing to unclench your fist. [*Applause*]

To the people of poor nations, we pledge to work alongside you to make your farms flourish and let clean waters flow; to nourish starved bodies and feed hungry minds. And to those nations like ours that enjoy relative plenty, we say we can no longer afford indifference to the suffering outside our borders, nor can we consume the world's resources without regard to effect. For the world has changed, and we must change with it.

As we consider the role that unfolds before us, we remember with humble gratitude those brave Americans who at this very hour patrol far-off deserts and distant mountains. They have something to tell us, just as the fallen heroes who lie in Arlington whisper through the ages.

We honor them not only because they are the guardians of our liberty, but because they embody the spirit of service—a willingness to find meaning in something greater than themselves.

And yet at this moment, a moment that will define a generation, it is precisely this spirit that must inhabit us all. For as much as government can do, and must do, it is ultimately the faith and determination of the American people upon which this nation relies. It is the kindness to take in a stranger when the levees break, the selflessness of workers who would rather cut their hours than see a friend lose their job which sees us through our darkest hours. It is the firefighter's courage to storm a stairway filled with smoke, but also a parent's willingness to nurture a child that finally decides our fate.

Our challenges may be new. The instruments with which we meet them may be new. But those values upon which our success depends—honesty and hard work, courage and fair play, tolerance and curiosity, loyalty and patriotism—these things are old. These things are true. They have been the quiet force of progress throughout our history.

What is demanded, then, is a return to these truths. What is required of us now is a new era of responsibility—a recognition on the part of every American that we have duties to ourselves, our nation and the world; duties that we do not grudgingly accept, but rather seize gladly, firm in the knowledge that there is nothing so satisfying to the spirit, so defining of our character than giving our all to a difficult task.

This is the price and the promise of citizenship. This is the source of our confidence—the knowledge that God calls on us to shape an uncertain destiny. This is the meaning of our liberty and our creed, why men and women and children of every race and every faith can join in celebration across this magnificent mall; and why a man whose father less than 60 years ago might not have been served in a local restaurant can now stand before you to take a most sacred oath. [*Applause*]

So let us mark this day with remembrance of who we are and how far we have traveled. In the year of America's birth, in the coldest of months, a small band of patriots huddled by dying campfires on the shores of an icy river. The capital was abandoned. The enemy was advancing. The snow was stained with blood. At the moment when the outcome of our revolution was most in doubt, the father of our nation ordered these words to be read to the people:

"Let it be told to the future world ... that in the depth of winter, when nothing but hope and virtue could survive ... that the city and the country, alarmed at one common danger, came forth to meet [it]."

America: In the face of our common dangers, in this winter of our hardship, let us remember these timeless words. With hope and virtue, let us brave once more the icy currents, and endure what storms may come. Let it be said by our children's children that when we were tested we refused to let this journey end, that we did not turn back nor did we falter; and with eyes fixed on the horizon and God's grace upon us, we carried forth that great gift of freedom and delivered it safely to future generations.

Thank you. God bless you. And God bless the United States of America. [*Applause*]

2013 Inaugural Address

Barack Obama

Vice President Biden, Mr. Chief Justice, members of the United States Congress, distinguished guests, and fellow citizens:

Each time we gather to inaugurate a President we bear witness to the enduring strength of our Constitution. We affirm the promise of our democracy. We recall that what binds this nation together is not the colors of our skin or the tenets of our faith or the origins of our names. What makes us exceptional— what makes us American—is our allegiance to an idea articulated in a declaration made more than two centuries ago:

"We hold these truths to be self-evident, that all men are created equal; that they are endowed by their Creator with certain unalienable rights; that among these are life, liberty, and the pursuit of happiness."

Today we continue a never-ending journey to bridge the meaning of those words with the realities of our time. For history tells us that while these truths may be self-evident, they've never been self-executing; that while freedom is a gift from God, it must be secured by His people here on Earth. The patriots of 1776 did not fight to replace the tyranny of a king with the privileges of a few or the rule of a mob. They gave to us a republic, a government of, and by, and for the people, entrusting each generation to keep safe our founding creed.

And for more than two hundred years, we have.

Through blood drawn by lash and blood drawn by sword, we learned that no union founded on the principles of liberty and equality could survive half-slave and half-free. We made ourselves anew, and vowed to move forward together.

Together, we determined that a modern economy requires railroads and highways to speed travel and commerce, schools and colleges to train our workers.

Together, we discovered that a free market only thrives when there are rules to ensure competition and fair play.

Together, we resolved that a great nation must care for the vulnerable, and protect its people from life's worst hazards and misfortune.

Through it all, we have never relinquished our skepticism of central authority, nor have we succumbed to the fiction that all society's ills can be cured through government alone. Our celebration of initiative and enterprise, our insistence on hard work and personal responsibility, these are constants in our character.

But we have always understood that when times change, so must we; that fidelity to our founding principles requires new responses to new challenges; that preserving our individual freedoms ultimately requires collective action. For the American people can no more meet the demands of today's world by acting alone than American soldiers could have met the forces of fascism or communism with muskets and militias. No single person can train all the math and science teachers we'll need to equip our children for the future, or build the roads and networks and research labs that will bring new jobs and businesses to our shores. Now, more than ever, we must do these things together, as one nation and one people.

This generation of Americans has been tested by crises that steeled our resolve and proved our resilience. A decade of war is now ending. An economic recovery has begun. America's possibilities are limitless, for we possess all the qualities that this world without boundaries demands: youth and drive; diversity and openness; an endless capacity for risk and a gift for reinvention. My fellow Americans, we are made for this moment, and we will seize it—so long as we seize it together.

For we, the people, understand that our country cannot succeed when a shrinking few do very well and a growing many barely make it. We believe that America's prosperity must rest upon the broad shoulders of a rising middle class. We know that America thrives when every person can find independence and pride in their work; when the wages of honest labor liberate families from the brink of hardship. We are true to our creed when a little girl born into the bleakest poverty knows that she has the same chance to succeed as anybody else, because she is an American; she is free, and she is equal, not just in the eyes of God but also in our own.

We understand that outworn programs are inadequate to the needs of our time. So we must harness new ideas and technology to remake our government, revamp our tax code, reform our schools, and empower our citizens with the skills they need to work harder, learn more, reach higher. But while the means will change, our purpose endures: a nation that rewards the effort and determination of every single American. That is what this moment requires. That is what will give real meaning to our creed.

President Barack Obama, Inaugural Address, January 21, 2013.

We, the people, still believe that every citizen deserves a basic measure of security and dignity. We must make the hard choices to reduce the cost of health care and the size of our deficit. But we reject the belief that America must choose between caring for the generation that built this country and investing in the generation that will build its future. For we remember the lessons of our past, when twilight years were spent in poverty and parents of a child with a disability had nowhere to turn.

We do not believe that in this country freedom is reserved for the lucky, or happiness for the few. We recognize that no matter how responsibly we live our lives, any one of us at any time may face a job loss, or a sudden illness, or a home swept away in a terrible storm. The commitments we make to each other through Medicare and Medicaid and Social Security, these things do not sap our initiative, they strengthen us. They do not make us a nation of takers; they free us to take the risks that make this country great.

We, the people, still believe that our obligations as Americans are not just to ourselves, but to all posterity. We will respond to the threat of climate change, knowing that the failure to do so would betray our children and future generations. Some may still deny the overwhelming judgment of science, but none can avoid the devastating impact of raging fires and crippling drought and more powerful storms.

The path towards sustainable energy sources will be long and sometimes difficult. But America cannot resist this transition, we must lead it. We cannot cede to other nations the technology that will power new jobs and new industries, we must claim its promise. That's how we will maintain our economic vitality and our national treasure—our forests and waterways, our crop lands and snow-capped peaks. That is how we will preserve our planet, commanded to our care by God. That's what will lend meaning to the creed our fathers once declared.

We, the people, still believe that enduring security and lasting peace do not require perpetual war. Our brave men and women in uniform, tempered by the flames of battle, are unmatched in skill and courage. Our citizens, seared by the memory of those we have lost, know too well the price that is paid for liberty. The knowledge of their sacrifice will keep us forever vigilant against those who would do us harm. But we are also heirs to those who won the peace and not just the war; who turned sworn enemies into the surest of friends—and we must carry those lessons into this time as well.

We will defend our people and uphold our values through strength of arms and rule of law. We will show the courage to try and resolve our differences with other nations peacefully—not because we are naïve about the dangers we face, but because engagement can more durably lift suspicion and fear.

America will remain the anchor of strong alliances in every corner of the globe. And we will renew those institutions that extend our capacity to manage crisis abroad, for no one has a greater stake in a peaceful world than its most powerful nation. We will support democracy from Asia to Africa, from the Americas to the Middle East, because our interests and our conscience compel us to act on behalf of those who long for freedom. And we must be a source of hope to the poor, the sick, the marginalized, the victims of prejudice—not out of mere charity, but because peace in our time requires the constant advance of those principles that our common creed describes: tolerance and opportunity, human dignity and justice.

We, the people, declare today that the most evident of truths—that all of us are created equal—is the star that guides us still; just as it guided our forebears through Seneca Falls, and Selma, and Stonewall; just as it guided all those men and women, sung and unsung, who left footprints along this great Mall, to hear a preacher say that we cannot walk alone; to hear a King proclaim that our individual freedom is inextricably bound to the freedom of every soul on Earth.

It is now our generation's task to carry on what those pioneers began. For our journey is not complete until our wives, our mothers and daughters can earn a living equal to their efforts. Our journey is not complete until our gay brothers and sisters are treated like anyone else under the law—for if we are truly created equal, then surely the love we commit to one another must be equal as well. Our journey is not complete until no citizen is forced to wait for hours to exercise the right to vote. Our journey is not complete until we find a better way to welcome the striving, hopeful immigrants who still see America as a land of opportunity—until bright young students and engineers are enlisted in our workforce rather than expelled from our country. Our journey is not complete until all our children, from the streets of Detroit to the hills of Appalachia, to the quiet lanes of Newtown, know that they are cared for and cherished and always safe from harm.

That is our generation's task—to make these words, these rights, these values of life and liberty and the pursuit of happiness real for every American.

Being true to our founding documents does not require us to agree on every contour of life. It does not mean we all define liberty in exactly the same way or follow the same precise path to happiness. Progress does not compel us to settle centuries-long debates about the role of government for all time, but it does require us to act in our time.

For now decisions are upon us and we cannot afford delay. We cannot mistake absolutism for principle, or substitute spectacle for politics, or treat name-calling as reasoned debate. We must act, knowing that our work will be imperfect. We must act, knowing that today's victories will be only partial and that it will be up to those who stand here in four years and 40 years and 400 years hence to advance the timeless spirit once conferred to us in a spare Philadelphia hall.

My fellow Americans, the oath I have sworn before you today, like the one recited by others who serve in this Capitol, was an oath to God and country, not party or faction. And we must faithfully execute that pledge during the duration of our service.

But the words I spoke today are not so different from the oath that is taken each time a soldier signs up for duty or an immigrant realizes her dream. My oath is not so different from the pledge we all make to the flag that waves above and that fills our hearts with pride.

They are the words of citizens and they represent our greatest hope. You and I, as citizens, have the power to set this country's course. You and I, as citizens, have the obligation to shape the debates of our time—not only with the votes we cast, but with the voices we lift in defense of our most ancient values and enduring ideals.

Let us, each of us, now embrace with solemn duty and awesome joy what is our lasting birthright. With common effort and common purpose, with passion and dedication, let us answer the call of history and carry into an uncertain future that precious light of freedom.

Thank you. God bless you, and may He forever bless these United States of America.

Inaugural Address
Donald J. Trump

Chief Justice Roberts, President Carter, President Clinton, President Bush, President Obama, fellow Americans, and people of the world: thank you.

We, the citizens of America, are now joined in a great national effort to rebuild our country and to restore its promise for all of our people.

Together, we will determine the course of America and the world for years to come.

We will face challenges. We will confront hardships. But we will get the job done.

Every four years, we gather on these steps to carry out the orderly and peaceful transfer of power, and we are grateful to President Obama and First Lady Michelle Obama for their gracious aid throughout this transition. They have been magnificent.

Today's ceremony, however, has very special meaning. Because today we are not merely transferring power from one Administration to another, or from one party to another—but we are transferring power from Washington, D.C. and giving it back to you, the American People.

For too long, a small group in our nation's Capital has reaped the rewards of government while the people have borne the cost.

Washington flourished—but the people did not share in its wealth.

Politicians prospered—but the jobs left, and the factories closed.

The establishment protected itself, but not the citizens of our country.

Their victories have not been your victories; their triumphs have not been your triumphs; and while they celebrated in our nation's Capital, there was little to celebrate for struggling families all across our land.

That all changes—starting right here, and right now, because this moment is your moment: it belongs to you.

It belongs to everyone gathered here today and everyone watching all across America.

This is your day. This is your celebration.

And this, the United States of America, is your country.

What truly matters is not which party controls our government, but whether our government is controlled by the people.

January 20th 2017, will be remembered as the day the people became the rulers of this nation again.

The forgotten men and women of our country will be forgotten no longer.

Donald J. Trump, "Inaugural Address," January 20, 2017

Everyone is listening to you now.

You came by the tens of millions to become part of a historic movement the likes of which the world has never seen before.

At the center of this movement is a crucial conviction: that a nation exists to serve its citizens.

Americans want great schools for their children, safe neighborhoods for their families, and good jobs for themselves.

These are the just and reasonable demands of a righteous public.

But for too many of our citizens, a different reality exists: Mothers and children trapped in poverty in our inner cities; rusted-out factories scattered like tombstones across the landscape of our nation; an education system, flush with cash, but which leaves our young and beautiful students deprived of knowledge; and the crime and gangs and drugs that have stolen too many lives and robbed our country of so much unrealized potential.

This American carnage stops right here and stops right now.

We are one nation—and their pain is our pain. Their dreams are our dreams; and their success will be our success. We share one heart, one home, and one glorious destiny.

The oath of office I take today is an oath of allegiance to all Americans.

For many decades, we've enriched foreign industry at the expense of American industry;

Subsidized the armies of other countries while allowing for the very sad depletion of our military;

We've defended other nation's borders while refusing to defend our own;

And spent trillions of dollars overseas while America's infrastructure has fallen into disrepair and decay.

We've made other countries rich while the wealth, strength, and confidence of our country has disappeared over the horizon.

One by one, the factories shuttered and left our shores, with not even a thought about the millions upon millions of American workers left behind.

The wealth of our middle class has been ripped from their homes and then redistributed across the entire world.

But that is the past. And now we are looking only to the future.

We assembled here today are issuing a new decree to be heard in every city, in every foreign capital, and in every hall of power.

From this day forward, a new vision will govern our land.

From this moment on, it's going to be America First.

Every decision on trade, on taxes, on immigration, on foreign affairs, will be made to benefit American workers and American families.

We must protect our borders from the ravages of other countries making our products, stealing our companies, and destroying our jobs. Protection will lead to great prosperity and strength.

I will fight for you with every breath in my body—and I will never, ever let you down.

America will start winning again, winning like never before.

We will bring back our jobs. We will bring back our borders. We will bring back our wealth. And we will bring back our dreams.

We will build new roads, and highways, and bridges, and airports, and tunnels, and railways all across our wonderful nation.

We will get our people off of welfare and back to work—rebuilding our country with American hands and American labor.

We will follow two simple rules: Buy American and Hire American.

We will seek friendship and goodwill with the nations of the world—but we do so with the understanding that it is the right of all nations to put their own interests first.

We do not seek to impose our way of life on anyone, but rather to let it shine as an example for everyone to follow.

We will reinforce old alliances and form new ones—and unite the civilized world against Radical Islamic Terrorism, which we will eradicate completely from the face of the Earth.

At the bedrock of our politics will be a total allegiance to the United States of America, and through our loyalty to our country, we will rediscover our loyalty to each other.

When you open your heart to patriotism, there is no room for prejudice.

The Bible tells us, "how good and pleasant it is when God's people live together in unity."

We must speak our minds openly, debate our disagreements honestly, but always pursue solidarity.

When America is united, America is totally unstoppable.

There should be no fear—we are protected, and we will always be protected.

We will be protected by the great men and women of our military and law enforcement and, most importantly, we are protected by God.

Finally, we must think big and dream even bigger.

In America, we understand that a nation is only living as long as it is striving.

We will no longer accept politicians who are all talk and no action—constantly complaining but never doing anything about it.

The time for empty talk is over.

Now arrives the hour of action.

Do not let anyone tell you it cannot be done. No challenge can match the heart and fight and spirit of America.

We will not fail. Our country will thrive and prosper again.

We stand at the birth of a new millennium, ready to unlock the mysteries of space, to free the Earth from the miseries of disease, and to harness the energies, industries and technologies of tomorrow.

A new national pride will stir our souls, lift our sights, and heal our divisions.

It is time to remember that old wisdom our soldiers will never forget: that whether we are black or brown or white, we all bleed the same red blood of patriots, we all enjoy the same glorious freedoms, and we all salute the same great American Flag.

And whether a child is born in the urban sprawl of Detroit or the windswept plains of Nebraska, they look up at the same night sky, they fill their heart with the same dreams, and they are infused with the breath of life by the same almighty Creator.

So to all Americans, in every city near and far, small and large, from mountain to mountain, and from ocean to ocean, hear these words:

You will never be ignored again.

Your voice, your hopes, and your dreams, will define our American destiny. And your courage and goodness and love will forever guide us along the way.

Together, We Will Make America Strong Again.

We Will Make America Wealthy Again.

We Will Make America Proud Again.

We Will Make America Safe Again.

And, Yes, Together, We Will Make America Great Again. Thank you, God Bless You, And God Bless America.

TEST CASES FOR GENERIC ANALYSIS

The remainder of this chapter contains two test cases for generic analysis. The goal is to discover whether useful genres exist in the two categories of speeches included. The first category is the presidential Farewell Address, a speech presented by successful two-term presidents at the completion of the second term. These examples are included: the famous final speech of Dwight Eisenhower, Ronald Reagan's farewell to the American people, Bill Clinton's final speech to the nation, as well as that of President Obama. Again, the first step in looking at these works should be to lay out the characteristics of the genre as defined by the model. Once those characteristics are identified, the generic analysis can proceed. As in the case of inaugurals, it is important to consider whether people other than presidents give something like a Farewell Address.

The final category is less well-defined. The final category is the speech of self-defense, usually known as an "apologia." Three works are included in this category. The first is the most important of President Reagan's speeches during the Iran-Contra scandal, his Tower Commission address. The second example of apologia is the "Map Room" speech that President Clinton presented to the nation after he admitted in testimony before the Grand Jury investigation of Kenneth Starr that he had had an "inappropriate" relationship with Monica Lewinsky. The final apologia was presented by Senator Al Franken after he was accused of sexual misconduct.

In considering the works in the final category, it is important to lay out the characteristics of the speeches in relation to the generic model in order to test whether the works fit in a useful genre. If a narrow genre does exist, then it can be used to analyze and evaluate the rhetoric.

Notes

1   Seminal research on inaugural addresses has been done by Karlyn Kohrs Campbell and Kathleen Hall Jamieson. Although my analysis of inaugurals is somewhat different from theirs, I have been influenced by their groundbreaking research. See "Inaugurating the Presidency," in *Form, Genre and the Study of Political Discourse*, ed. Herbert W. Simons and Aram A. Aghazarian (Columbia: University of South Carolina Press, 1986), pp. 203–225.

2   Campbell and Jamieson, p. 217.

The remainder of this section will be devoted to further case analyses of rhetorical genres. In carrying out these analyses, one useful tactic is to use the following form as a research aid.

GENRE ANALYSIS

Identify the following situational factors

Recurring Problem

Constraining Purpose

Societal Constraints

Identify the perceived strategic constraints created by the situational factors.

Identify the characteristics of form, content, substance, and style required by the perceived strategic constraints.

FAREWELL ADDRESSES

Successful presidents (and other leaders) often make a speech or other presentation in which they reflect on their accomplishments and point the organization toward a better future. Often, these works contain a warning about problems that must be overcome in the future. In this section, Farewell Addresses by Presidents Dwight Eisenhower, Ronald Reagan, Bill Clinton, and Barack Obama are included. The Clinton address is somewhat different from the others in that his presidency was challenged by the Monica Lewinsky scandal.

Farewell Address
Dwight David Eisenhower

MY FELLOW AMERICANS:

Three days from now, after half a century in the service of our country, I shall lay down the responsibilities of office as, in traditional and solemn ceremony, the authority of the Presidency is vested in my successor.

This evening I come to you with a message of leave-taking and farewell, and to share a few final thoughts with you, my countrymen.

Like every other citizen, I wish the new President, and all who will labor with him, Godspeed. I pray that the coming years will be blessed with peace and prosperity for all.

Our people expect their President and the Congress to find essential agreement on issues of great moment, the wise resolution of which will better shape the future of the Nation.

My own relations with the Congress, which began on a remote and tenuous basis when, long ago, a member of the Senate appointed me to West Point, have since ranged to the intimate during the war and immediate post-war period, and, finally, to the mutually interdependent during these past eight years.

In this final relationship, the Congress and the Administration have, on most vital issues, cooperated well, to serve the national good rather than mere partisanship, and so have assured that the business of the Nation should go forward. So, my official relationship with the Congress ends in a feeling, on my part, of gratitude that we have been able to do so much together.

II.

We now stand ten years past the midpoint of a century that has witnessed four major wars among great nations. Three of these involved our own country. Despite these holocausts America is today the strongest, the most influential and most productive nation in the world. Understandably proud of this pre-eminence, we yet realize that America's leadership and prestige depend, not merely upon our unmatched material progress, riches and military strength, but on how we use our power in the interests of world peace and human betterment.

III.

Throughout America's adventure in free government, our basic purposes have been to keep the peace; to foster progress in human achievement, and to enhance liberty, dignity and integrity among people and among nations. To strive for less would be unworthy of a free and religious people. Any failure traceable to arrogance, or our lack of comprehension or readiness to sacrifice would inflict upon us grievous hurt both at home and abroad.

Progress toward these noble goals is persistently threatened by the conflict now engulfing the world. It commands our whole attention, absorbs our very beings. We face a hostile ideology—global in scope atheistic in character, ruthless in purpose, and insidious in method. Unhappily the danger it poses promises to be of indefinite duration. To meet it successfully, there is called for, not so much the emotional and transitory sacrifices of crisis, but rather those which enable us to carry forward steadily, surely, and without complaint the burdens of prolonged and complex struggle—with liberty the stake. Only thus shall we remain, despite every provocation, on our charted course toward permanent peace and human betterment.

Crises there will continue to be. In meeting them, whether foreign or domestic, great or small, there is a recurring temptation to feel that some spectacular and costly action would become the miraculous solution to all current difficulties. A huge increase in newer elements of our defense; development of unrealistic programs to cure every ill in agriculture; a dramatic expansion in basic and applied research—these and many other possibilities, each possibly promising in itself, may be suggested as the only way to the road we wish to travel.

But each proposal must be weighed in the light of a broader consideration: the need to maintain balance in and among national programs—balance between the private and the public economy, balance between cost and hoped for advantage—balance between the clearly necessary and the comfortably desirable; balance between our essential requirements as a nation and the duties imposed by the nation upon the individual; balance between actions of the member and the national welfare of the future. Good judgment seeks balance and progress; lack of it eventually finds imbalance and frustration.

The record of many decades stands as proof that our people and their government have, in the main, understood these truths and have responded to them well, in the face of stress and threat. But threats, new in kind or degree, constantly arise. I mention two only.

IV.

A vital element in keeping the peace is our military establishment. Our arms must be mighty, ready for instant action, so that no potential aggressor may be tempted to risk his own destruction.

Our military organization today bears little relation to that known by any of my predecessors in peacetime, or indeed by the fighting men of World War II or Korea.

Until the latest of our world conflicts, the United States had no armaments industry. American makers of plowshares could, with time and as required, make swords as well. But now we can no longer risk emergency improvisation of national defense; we have been compelled to create a permanent armaments industry of vast proportions. Added to this, three and a half million men and women are directly engaged in the defense establishment. We annually spend on military security more than the net income of all United States corporations.

This conjunction of an immense military establishment and large arms industry is new in the American experience. The total influence—economic, political, even spiritual—is felt in every city, every State house, every office of the Federal government. We recognize the imperative need for this development. Yet we must not fail to comprehend its grave implications. Our toil, resources and livelihood are all involved; so is the very structure of our society.

In the councils of government, we must guard against the acquisition of unwarranted influence, whether sought or unsought, by the miliary-industrial complex. The potential for the disastrous rise of misplaced power exists and will persist.

We must never let the weight of this combination endanger our liberties or democratic processes. We should take nothing for granted. Only an alert and knowledgeable citizenry can compel the proper

meshing of tho huge industrial and military machinery of defense with our peaceful methods and goals, so that security and liberty may prosper together.

Akin to, and largely responsible for the sweeping changes in our industrial-military posture, has been the technological revolution during recent decades.

In this revolution, research has become central; it also become more formalized, complex, and costly. A steadily increasing share is conducted for, by or at the direction of, the Federal government.

Today, the solitary inventor, tinkering in his shop, has been overshadowed by task forces of scientists in laboratories and testing fields. In the same fashion, the free university, historically the fountainhead of free ideas and scientific discovery, has experienced a revolution in the conduct of research. Partly because of the huge costs involved, a government contract becomes virtually a substitute for intellectual curiosity. For every old blackboard there are now hundreds of new electronic computers.

The prospect of domination of the nation's scholars by Federal employment, project allocations, and the power of money is ever present—and is gravely to be regarded.

Yet, in holding scientific research and discovery in respect, as we should, we must also be alert to the equal and opposite danger that public policy could itself become the captive of a scientific—technological elite.

It is the task of statesmanship to mold, to balance, and to integrate these and other forces, new and old, within the principles of our democratic system—ever aiming toward the supreme goals of our free society.

V.

Another factor in maintaining balance involves the element of time. As we peer into society's future we—you and I, and our government—must avoid the impulse to live only for today, plundering, for our own ease and convenience, the precious resources of tomorrow. We cannot mortgage the material assets of our grandchildren without risking the loss also of their political and spiritual heritage. We want democracy to survive for all generations to come, not to become the insolvent phantom of tomorrow.

VI.

Down the long lane of the history yet to be written America knows that this world of ours, ever growing smaller, must avoid becoming a community of dreadful fear and hate, and be, instead, a proud confederation of mutual trust and respect.

Such a confederation must be one of equals. The weakest must come to the conference table with the same confidence as do we, protected as we are by our moral, economic, and military strength. That table, though scarred by many past frustrations, cannot be abandoned for the certain agony of the battlefield.

Disarmament, with mutual honor and confidence, is a continuing imperative. Together we must learn how to resolve difference, not with arms, but with intellect and decent purpose. Because this need is so sharp and apparent I confess that I lay down my official responsibilities in this field with a definite sense of disappointment. As one who has witnessed the horror and the lingering sadness of war—as one who knows that another war could utterly destroy this civilization which has been so slowly and painfully built over thousands of years—I wish I could say tonight that a lasting peace is in sight.

Happily, I can say that war has been avoided. Steady progress toward our ultimate goal has been made. But, so much remains to be done. As a private citizen, I shall never cease to do what little I can to help the world advance along the road.

VII.

So—in this my last good night to you as your President—I thank you for the many opportunities you have given me for public service in war and peace. I trust that in that service you find some things worthy; as for the rest of it, I know you will find ways to improve performance in the future.

You and I—my fellow citizens—need to be strong in our faith that all nations, under God, will reach the goal of peace with justice. May we be ever unswerving in devotion to principle, confident but humble with power, diligent in pursuit of the Nation's great goals.

To all the peoples of the world, I once more give expression to America's prayerful and continuing aspiration:

We pray that peoples of all faiths, all races, all nations, may have their human needs satisfied; that those now denied opportunity shall come to enjoy it to the full; that all who yearn for freedom may experience its spiritual blessings; that those who have freedom will understand, also, its heavy responsibilities; that all who are insensitive to the needs of others will learn charity; that the scourges of poverty, disease and ignorance will be made to disappear from the earth, and that, in the goodness of time, all peoples will come to live together in a peace guaranteed by the binding force of mutual respect and love.

Farewell Address
Ronald Reagan

MY FELLOW AMERICANS:

This is the 34th time I'll speak to you from the Oval Office and the last. We've been together eight years now, and soon it'll be time for me to go. But before I do, I wanted to share some thoughts, some of which I've been saving for a long time.

It's been the honor of my life to be your President. So many of you have written the past few weeks to say thanks, but I could say as much to you. Nancy and I are grateful for the opportunity you gave us to serve.

One of the things about the Presidency is that you're always somewhat apart. You spend a lot of time going by too fast in a car someone else is driving, and seeing the people through tinted glass—the parents holding up a child, and the wave you saw too late and couldn't return. And so many times I wanted to stop and reach out from behind the glass, and connect. Well, maybe I can do a little of that tonight.

People ask how I feel about leaving. And the fact is, "parting is such sweet sorrow." The sweet part is California, and the ranch, and freedom. The sorrow—the goodbyes, of course, and leaving this beautiful place.

You know, down the hall and up the stairs from this office is the part of the White House where the President and his family live. There are a few favorite windows I have up there that I like to stand and look out of early in the morning. The view is over the grounds here to the Washington Monument, and the Mall and the Jefferson Memorial. But on mornings when the humidity is low, you can see past the Jefferson to the river, the Potomac, and the Virginia shore. Someone said that's the view Lincoln had when he saw the smoke rising from the Battle of Bull Run. I see more prosaic things: the grass on the banks, the morning traffic as people make their way to work, now and then a sailboat on the river.

I've been thinking a bit at that window. I've been reflecting on what the past eight years have meant and mean. And the image that comes to mind like a refrain is a nautical one—a small story about a big ship, and a refugee, and a sailor. It was back in the early eighties, at the height of the boat people. And the sailor was hard at work on the carrier *Midway*, which was patrolling the South China Sea. The sailor, like most American servicemen, was young, smart, and fiercely observant. The crew spied on the horizon a leaky little boat. And crammed inside were refugees from Indochina hoping to get to America. The *Midway* sent a small launch to bring them to the ship and safety. As the refugees made their way through the choppy seas, one spied the sailor on deck, and stood up, and called out to him. He yelled, "Hello, American sailor. Hello, freedom man."

A small moment with a big meaning, a moment the sailor, who wrote it in a letter, couldn't get out of his mind. And, when I saw it, neither could I. Because that's what it was to be an American in the 1980s. We stood, again, for freedom. I know we always have, but in the past few years the world again, and in a way, we ourselves—rediscovered it.

It's been quite a journey this decade, and we held together through some stormy seas. And at the end, together, we are reaching our destination.

The fact is, from Grenada to the Washington and Moscow summits, from the recession of '81 to '82, to the expansion that began in late '82 and continues to this day, we've made a difference. The way I see it, there were two great triumphs, two things that I'm proudest of. One is the economic recovery, in which the people of America created—and filled—19 million new jobs. The other is the recovery of our morale. America is respected again in the world and looked to for leadership.

Something that happened to me a few years ago reflects some of this. It was back in 1981, and I was attending my first big economic summit, which was held that year in Canada. The meeting place rotates among the member countries. The opening meeting was a formal dinner for the heads of government of the seven industrialized nations. Now, I sat there like the new kid in school and listened, and it was all Francois this and Helmut that. They dropped titles and spoke to one another on a first-name basis. Well, at one point I sort of leaned in and said, "My name's Ron." Well, in that same year, we began the actions we felt would ignite an economic comeback—cut taxes and regulation, started to cut spending. And soon the recovery began.

Two years later another economic summit, with pretty much the same cast. At the big opening meeting we all got together, and all of a sudden, just for a moment, I saw that everyone was just sitting there looking at me. And then one of them broke the silence. "Tell us about the American miracle," he said.

Well, back in 1980, when I was running for President, it was all so different. Some pundits said our programs would result in catastrophe. Our views on foreign affairs would cause war. Our plans for the economy would cause inflation to soar and bring about economic collapse. I even remember one highly respected economist saying, back in 1982, that "The engines of economic growth have shut down here, and they're likely to stay that way for years to come." Well, he and other opinion leaders were wrong. The fact is, what they called "radical" was really "right." What they called "dangerous" was just "desperately needed."

And in all of that time I won a nickname, "The Great Communicator." But I never thought it was my style or the words I used that made a difference: It was the content. I wasn't a great communicator, but I communicated great things, and they didn't spring full bloom from my brow, they came from the heart of a great nation—from our experience, our wisdom, and our belief in the principles that have guided us for two centuries. They called it the Reagan revolution. Well, I'll accept that, but for me it always seemed more like the great rediscovery of our values and our common sense.

Common sense told us that when you put a big tax on something, the people will produce less of it. So, we cut the people's tax rates, and the people produced more than ever before. The economy bloomed like a plant that had been cut back and could now grow quicker and stronger. Our economic program brought about the longest peacetime expansion in our history: real family income up, the poverty rate down, entrepreneurship booming, and an explosion in research and new technology. We're exporting more than ever because American industry became more competitive and at the same time, we summoned the national will to knock down protectionist walls abroad instead of erecting them at home. Common sense also told us that to preserve the peace, we'd have to become strong again after years of weakness and confusion. So, we rebuilt our defenses, and this New Year we toasted the new peacefulness around the globe. Not only have the superpowers actually begun to reduce their stockpiles of nuclear weapons—and hope for even more progress is bright—but the regional conflicts that rack the globe are also beginning to cease. The Persian Gulf is no longer a war zone. The Soviets are leaving Afghanistan. The Vietnamese are preparing to pull out of Cambodia, and an American-mediated accord will soon send 50,000 Cuban troops home from Angola.

The lesson of all this was, of course, that because we're a great nation, our challenges seem complex. It will always be this way. But as long as we remember our first principles and believe in ourselves, the future will always be ours. And something else we learned: Once you begin a great movement, there's no telling where it will end. We meant to change a nation, and instead, we changed a world.

Countries across the globe are turning to free markets and free speech and turning away from the ideologies of the past. For them, the great rediscovery of the 1980s has been that, lo and behold, the moral way of government is the practical way of government: Democracy, the profoundly good, is also the profoundly productive.

When you've got to the point when you can celebrate the anniversaries of your 39th birthday you can sit back sometimes, review our life, and see it flowing before you. For me there was a fork in the river, and it was right in the middle of my life. I never meant to go into politics. It wasn't my intention when I was young. But I was raised to believe you had to pay your way for the blessings bestowed on you. I was happy with my career in the entertainment world, but I ultimately went into politics because I wanted to protect something precious.

Ours was the first revolution in the history of mankind that truly reversed the course of government, and with three little words: "We the People." "We the People" tell the government what to do, it doesn't tell us. "We the People" are the driver, the government is the car. And we decide where it should go, and by what route, and how fast. Almost all the worlds' constitutions are documents in which governments tell the people what their privileges are. Our Constitution is a document in which "We the People" tell the government what it is allowed to do. "We the People" are free. This belief has been the underlying basis for everything I've tried to do these past years.

But back in the 1960s, when I began, it seemed to me that we'd been reversing the order of things—that through more and more rules and regulations and confiscatory taxes, the government was taking more of our money, more of our options, and more of our freedom. I went into politics in part to put up my hand and say, "Stop." I was a citizen politician, and it seemed the right thing for a citizen to do.

I think we have stopped a lot of what needed stopping. And I hope we have once again reminded people that man is not free unless government is limited. There's a clear cause and effect here that is as neat and predictable as a law of physics: As government expands, liberty contracts.

Nothing is less free than pure Communism, and yet we have, the past few years, forged a satisfying new closeness with the Soviet Union. I've been asked if this isn't a gamble, and my answer is no because we're basing our actions not on words but deeds. The detente of the 1970s was based not on actions but promises. They'd promise to treat their own people and the people of the world better. But the gulag was still the gulag, and the state was still expansionist, and they still waged proxy wars in Africa, Asia, and Latin America.

Well, this time, so far, it's different. President Gorbachev has brought about some internal democratic reforms and begun the withdrawal from Afghanistan. He has also freed prisoners whose names I've given him every time we've met.

But life has a way of reminding you of big things through small incidents. Once, during the heady days of the Moscow summit, Nancy and I decided to break off from the entourage one afternoon to visit the shops on Arbat Street, that's a little street just off Moscow's main shopping area. Even though our visit was a surprise, every Russian there immediately recognized us, and called out our names, and reached for our hands. We were just about swept away by the warmth. You could almost feel the possibilities in all that joy. But within seconds, a KGB detail pushed their way toward us and began pushing and shoving the people in the crowd. It was an interesting moment. It reminded me that while the man on the street in the Soviet Union yearns for peace, the government is Communist. And those who run it are Communists, and that means we and they view such issues as freedom and human rights very differently.

We must keep up our guard, but we must also continue to work together to lessen and eliminate tension and mistrust. My view is that President Gorbachev is different from previous Soviet leaders. I think he knows some of the things wrong with his society and is trying to fix them. We wish him well. And we'll continue to work to make sure that the Soviet Union that eventually emerges from this process is a less threatening one. What it all boils down to is this. I want the new closeness to continue. And it will, as long as we make it clear that we will continue to act in a certain way as long as they continue to act in a helpful manner. If and when they don't, at first pull your punches. If they persist, pull the plug. It's still trust but verify. It's still play, but cut the cards. It's still watch closely. And don't be afraid to see what you see.

I've been asked if I have any regrets. Well, I do. The deficit is one. I've been talking a great deal about that lately, but tonight isn't for arguments. And I'm going to hold my tongue. But an observation: I've had my share of victories in the Congress, but what few people noticed is that I never won anything you didn't win for me. They never saw my troops, they never saw Reagan's regiments, the American people. You won every battle with every call you made and letter you wrote demanding action. Well, action is still needed. If we're to finish the job, Reagan's regiments will have to become Bush's brigades. Soon he'll be the chief, and he will need you every bit as much as I did.

Finally, there is a great tradition of warnings in Presidential farewells, and I've got one that's been on my mind for some time. But oddly enough it starts with one of the things I'm proudest of in the past eight years: the resurgence of national pride that I called the new patriotism. This national feeling is good, but it won't last unless it's grounded in thoughtfulness and knowledge.

An informed patriotism is what we want. And are we doing a good enough job teaching our children what America is and what she represents in the long history of the world? Those of us who are over 35 or so years of age grew up in a different America. We were taught, very directly, what it means to be an American. And we absorbed, almost in the air, a love of country and an appreciation of its institutions. If you didn't get those things from your family you got them from the neighborhood, from the father down the street who fought in Korea or the family who lost someone at Anzio. Or you could get a sense of patriotism from school. And if all else failed you could get a sense of patriotism from the popular culture. The movies celebrated democratic values and implicitly reinforced the idea that America was special. TV was like that too through the mid-sixties.

But now, we're about to enter the nineties, and some things have changed. Younger parents aren't sure that an unambivalent appreciation of America is the right thing to teach modern children. And as for those who create the popular culture, well-grounded patriotism is no longer the style. Our spirit is back, but we haven't reinstitutionalized it. We've got to do a better job of getting across that America is freedom—freedom of speech, freedom of religion, freedom of enterprise. And freedom is special and rare. It's fragile; it needs protection.

So, we've got to teach history based not on what's in fashion but what's important: Why the Pilgrims came here, who Jimmy Doolittle was, and what those 30 seconds over Tokyo meant. You know, four years ago on the 40th anniversary of D-Day, I read a letter from a young woman writing to her late father, who'd fought on Omaha Beach. Her name was Lisa Zanetta Henn, and she said, "we will always remember, we will never forget what the boys of Normandy did." Well, let's help her keep her word. If we forget what we did, we won't know who we are. I'm warning of an eradication of the American memory that could result, ultimately, in an erosion of the American spirit. Let's start with some basics: more attention to American history and a greater emphasis on civic ritual. And let me offer lesson number one about America: All great change in America begins at the dinner table. So, tomorrow night in the kitchen I hope the talking begins. And children, if your parents haven't been teaching you what it means to be an American, let 'em know and nail 'em on it. That would be a very American thing to do.

And that's about all I have to say tonight. Except for one thing. The past few days when I've been at that window upstairs, I've thought a lot of the "shining city upon a hill." The phrase comes from John Winthrop, who wrote it to describe the America he imagined. What he imagined was important because he was an early Pilgrim, an early freedom man. He journeyed here on what today we'd call a little wooden boat; and like the other Pilgrims, he was looking for a home that would be free.

I've spoken of the shining city all my political life, but I don't know if I ever quite communicated what I saw when I said it. But in the mind it was a tall proud city built on rocks stronger than oceans, wind-swept, God-blessed, and teeming with people of all kinds living in harmony and peace, a city with free ports that hummed with commerce and creativity, and if there had to be city walls, the walls had doors and the doors were open to anyone with the will and the heart to get here. That's how I saw it, and see it still.

And how stands the city on this winter night? More prosperous, more secure and happier than it was eight years ago. But more than that; after 200 years, two centuries, she still stands strong and true on the granite ridge, and her glow has held steady no matter what storm. And she's still a beacon, still a magnet for all who must have freedom, for all the pilgrims from all the lost places who are hurtling through the darkness, toward home.

We've done our part. And as I walk off into the city streets, a final word to the men and women of the Reagan revolution, the men and women across America who for eight years did the work that brought America back. My friends: We did it. We weren't just marking time. We made a difference.

We made the city stronger. We made the city freer, and we left her in good hands. All in all, not bad, not bad at all.

And so, goodbye, God bless you, and God bless the United States of America.

Farewell Address

William J. Clinton

On this, my last opportunity to speak to you from the Oval Office as your president, I am profoundly grateful to you for twice giving me the honor to serve, to work for you and with you to prepare our nation for the 21st century. And I am grateful to Vice President Gore, to my Cabinet secretaries, and to all those who have served with me for the last eight years.

This has been a time of dramatic transformation, and you have risen to every new challenge. You have made our social fabric stronger, our families healthier and safer, our people more prosperous. You, the American people, have made our passage into the global information age an era of great American renewal. In all the work I have done as president—every decision I have made, every executive action I have taken, every bill I proposed and signed—I have tried to give all Americans the tools and conditions to build the future of our dreams, and a good society with a strong economy, a cleaner environment, and a freer, safer, more prosperous world.

I have steered my course by our enduring values—opportunity for all, responsibility from all, a community of all Americans. I have sought to give America a new kind of government—smaller, more modern, more effective, full of ideas and policies appropriate to this new time, always putting people first, always focusing on the future.

Working together, America has done well. Our economy is breaking records, with more than 22 million new jobs, the lowest unemployment in 30 years, the highest home ownership ever, the longest expansion in history.

Our families and communities are stronger. Thirty-five million Americans have used the family leave law; eight million have moved off welfare. Crime is at a 25-year low. Over 10 million Americans receive more college aid, and more people than ever are going to college. Our schools are better—higher standards, greater accountability and larger investments have brought higher test scores and higher graduation rates. More than three million children have health insurance now, and more than seven million Americans have been lifted out of poverty. Incomes are rising across the board. Our air and water are cleaner. Our food and drinking water are safer. And more of our precious land has been preserved in the Continental United States than at any time in 100 years. America has been a force for peace and prosperity in every corner of the globe.

I am very grateful to be able to turn over the reins of leadership to a new president with America in such a strong position to meet the challenges of the future.

Tonight I want to leave you with three thoughts about our future.

First, America must maintain our record of fiscal responsibility. Through our last four budgets, we have turned record deficits to record surpluses, and we have been able to pay down $600 billion of our national debt, on track to be debt-free by the end of the decade for the first time since 1835. Staying on that course will bring lower interest rates, greater prosperity, and the opportunity to meet our big challenges. If we choose wisely, we can pay down the debt, deal with the retirement of the baby boomers, invest more in our future, and provide tax relief.

Second, because the world is more connected every day in every way, America's security and prosperity require us to continue to lead in the world. At this remarkable moment in history, more people live in freedom than ever before. Our alliances are stronger than ever. People all around the world look to America to be a force for peace and prosperity, freedom and security. The global economy is giving more of our own, and billions around the world, the chance to work and live and raise their families with dignity. But the forces of integration that have created these good opportunities also make us more subject to global forces of destruction, to terrorism, organized crime and narco-trafficking, the spread of deadly weapons and disease, the degradation of the global environment.

The expansion of trade hasn't fully closed the gap between those of us who live on the cutting edge of the global economy and the billions around the world who live on the knife's edge of survival. This global gap requires more than compassion; it requires action. Global poverty is a powder keg that can be ignited by our indifference.

In his first inaugural address, Thomas Jefferson warned of entangling alliances. But in our times America cannot and must not disentangle itself from the world. If we want the world to embody our shared values, then we must assume a shared responsibility. If the wars of the 20th century, especially the recent ones in Kosovo and Bosnia, have taught us anything, it is that we achieve our aims by defending our values, and leading the forces of freedom and peace. We embrace boldly and resolutely that duty to lead—to stand with our allies in word and deed, and to put a human face on the global economy so that expanded trade benefits all peoples in all nations, lifting lives and hopes all across the world.

Third, we must remember that America cannot lead in the world unless here at home we weave the threads of our coat of many colors into the fabric of one America. As we become evermore diverse, we must work harder to unite around our common values and our common humanity. We must work harder to overcome our differences, in our hearts and in our laws. We must treat all our people with fairness and dignity, regardless of their race, religion, gender or sexual orientation, and regardless of when they arrived in our country, always moving towards the more perfect union of our founders' dreams.

Hillary, Chelsea and I join all Americans in wishing our very best to the next president, George W. Bush, to his family and his administration in meeting these challenges and in leading freedom's march in this new century. As for me, I leave the presidency more idealistic, more full of hope than the day I arrived, and more confident than ever that America's best days lie ahead.

My days in this office are nearly through, but my days of service I hope are not. In the years ahead I will never hold a position higher or a covenant more sacred than that of president of the United States. But there is no title I will wear more proudly than that of citizen. Thank you, God bless you, and God bless America.

Farewell Address

Barack Obama

Hello, Chicago! It's good to be home! Thank you, everybody. Thank you. Thank you so much. Thank you. All right, everybody sit down. We're on live TV here. I've got to move. You can tell that I'm a lame duck because nobody is following instructions. Everybody have a seat.

My fellow Americans—Michelle and I have been so touched by all the well wishes that we've received over the past few weeks. But tonight, it's my turn to say thanks. Whether we have seen eye-to-eye or rarely agreed at all, my conversations with you, the American people, in living rooms and in schools, at farms, on factory floors, at diners and on distant military outposts—those conversations are what have kept me honest, and kept me inspired, and kept me going. And every day, I have learned from you. You made me a better President, and you made me a better man.

"This is where I learned that change only happens when ordinary people get involved and they get engaged, and they come together to demand it."

So I first came to Chicago when I was in my early 20s. And I was still trying to figure out who I was, still searching for a purpose in my life. And it was a neighborhood not far from here where I began working with church groups in the shadows of closed steel mills. It was on these streets where I witnessed the power of faith, and the quiet dignity of working people in the face of struggle and loss.

AUDIENCE: Four more years! Four more years! Four more years!

THE PRESIDENT: I can't do that.

AUDIENCE: Four more years! Four more years! Four more years!

THE PRESIDENT: This is where I learned that change only happens when ordinary people get involved and they get engaged, and they come together to demand it.

After eight years as your President, I still believe that. And it's not just my belief. It's the beating heart of our American idea—our bold experiment in self-government. It's the conviction that we are all created equal, endowed by our Creator with certain unalienable rights, among them life, liberty, and the pursuit of happiness. It's the insistence that these rights, while self-evident, have never been self-executing; that We, the People, through the instrument of our democracy, can form a more perfect union.

What a radical idea. A great gift that our Founders gave to us: The freedom to chase our individual dreams through our sweat and toil and imagination, and the imperative to strive together, as well, to achieve a common good, a greater good.

For 240 years, our nation's call to citizenship has given work and purpose to each new generation. It's what led patriots to choose republic over tyranny, pioneers to trek west, slaves to brave that makeshift railroad to freedom. It's what pulled immigrants and refugees across oceans and the Rio Grande. It's what pushed women to reach for the ballot. It's what powered workers to organize. It's why GIs gave their lives at Omaha Beach and Iwo Jima, Iraq and

Barack Obama, "Farewell Address," January 10, 2017

Afghanistan. And why men and women from Selma to Stonewall were prepared to give theirs, as well.

So that's what we mean when we say America is exceptional—not that our nation has been flawless from the start, but that we have shown the capacity to change and make life better for those who follow. Yes, our progress has been uneven. The work of democracy has always been hard. It's always been contentious. Sometimes it's been bloody. For every two steps forward, it often feels we take one step back. But the long sweep of America has been defined by forward motion, a constant widening of our founding creed to embrace all and not just some.

If I had told you eight years ago that America would reverse a great recession, reboot our auto industry, and unleash the longest stretch of job creation in our history—if I had told you that we would open up a new chapter with the Cuban people, shut down Iran's nuclear weapons program without firing a shot, take out the mastermind of 9/11—if I had told you that we would win marriage equality, and secure the right to health insurance for another 20 million of our fellow citizens)—if I had told you all that, you might have said our sights were set a little too high. But that's what we did. That's what you did.

You were the change. You answered people's hopes, and because of you, by almost every measure, America is a better, stronger place than it was when we started.

In 10 days, the world will witness a hallmark of our democracy.

AUDIENCE: Nooo —

THE PRESIDENT: No, no, no, no, no—the peaceful transfer of power from one freely elected President to the next. I committed to President-elect Trump that my administration would ensure the smoothest possible transition, just as President Bush did for me. Because it's up to all of us to make sure our government can help us meet the many challenges we still face.

We have what we need to do so. We have everything we need to meet those challenges. After all, we remain the wealthiest, most powerful, and most respected nation on Earth. Our youth, our drive, our diversity and openness, our boundless capacity for risk and reinvention means that the future should be ours. But that potential will only be realized if our democracy works. Only if our politics better reflects the decency of our people. Only if all of us, regardless of party affiliation or particular interests, help restore the sense of common purpose that we so badly need right now.

That's what I want to focus on tonight: The state of our democracy. Understand, democracy does not require uniformity. Our founders argued. They quarreled. Eventually they compromised. They expected us to do the same. But they knew that democracy does require a basic sense of solidarity—the idea that for all our outward differences, we're all in this together; that we rise or fall as one.

There have been moments throughout our history that threatens that solidarity. And the beginning of this century has been one of those times. A shrinking world, growing inequality; demographic change and the specter of terrorism—these forces haven't just tested our security and our prosperity, but are testing our democracy, as well. And how we meet these challenges to our democracy will determine our ability to educate our kids, and create good jobs, and protect our homeland. In other words, it will determine our future.

To begin with, our democracy won't work without a sense that everyone has economic opportunity. And the good news is that today the economy is growing again. Wages, incomes, home values, and retirement accounts are all rising again. Poverty is falling again. The wealthy are paying a fairer share of taxes even as the stock market shatters records. The unemployment rate is near a 10-year low. The uninsured rate has never, ever been lower. Health care costs are rising at the slowest rate in 50 years. And I've said and I mean it—if anyone can put together a plan that is demonstrably better than the improvements we've made to our health care system and that covers as many people at less cost, I will publicly support it.

Because that, after all, is why we serve. Not to score points or take credit, but to make people's lives better.

But for all the real progress that we've made, we know it's not enough. Our economy doesn't work as well or grow as fast when a few prosper at the expense of a growing middle class and ladders for folks who want to get into the middle class. That's the economic argument. But stark inequality is also corrosive to our democratic ideal. While the top one percent has amassed a bigger share of wealth and income, too many families, in inner cities and in rural counties, have been left behind—the laid-off factory worker; the waitress or health care worker who's just barely getting by and struggling to pay the bills—convinced that the game is fixed against them, that their government only serves the interests of the powerful—that's a recipe for more cynicism and polarization in our politics.

But there are no quick fixes to this long-term trend. I agree, our trade should be fair and not just free. But the next wave of economic dislocations won't come from overseas. It will come from the relentless pace of automation that makes a lot of good, middle-class jobs obsolete.

And so we're going to have to forge a new social compact to guarantee all our kids the education they need—to give workers the power to unionize for better wages; to update the social safety net to reflect the way we live now, and make more reforms to the tax code so corporations and individuals who reap the most from this new economy don't avoid their obligations to the country that's made their very success possible.

We can argue about how to best achieve these goals. But we can't be complacent about the goals themselves. For if we don't create opportunity for all people, the disaffection and division that has stalled our progress will only sharpen in years to come.

There's a second threat to our democracy—and this one is as old as our nation itself. After my election, there was talk of a post-racial America. And such a vision, however well-intended, was never realistic. Race remains a potent and often divisive force in our society. Now, I've lived long enough to know that race relations are better than they were 10, or 20, or 30 years ago, no matter what some folks say. You can see it not just in statistics, you see it in the attitudes of young Americans across the political spectrum.

But we're not where we need to be. And all of us have more work to do. If every economic issue is framed as a struggle between a hardworking white middle class and an undeserving minority, then workers of all shades are going to be left fighting for scraps while the wealthy withdraw further into their private enclaves. If we're unwilling to invest in the children of immigrants, just because they don't look like us, we will diminish the prospects of our own children—because those brown kids will represent a larger and larger share of America's workforce. And we have shown that our economy doesn't have to be a zero-sum game. Last year, incomes rose for all races, all age groups, for men and for women.

So if we're going to be serious about race going forward, we need to uphold laws against discrimination—in hiring, and in housing, and in education, and in the criminal justice system. That is what our Constitution and our highest ideals require.

But laws alone won't be enough. Hearts must change. It won't change overnight. Social attitudes oftentimes take generations to change. But if our democracy is to work in this increasingly diverse nation, then each one of us needs to try to heed the advice of a great character in American fiction—Atticus Finch —who said "You never really understand a person until you consider things from his point of view…until you climb into his skin and walk around in it."

For blacks and other minority groups, it means tying our own very real struggles for justice to the challenges that a lot of people in this country face—not only the refugee, or the immigrant, or the rural poor, or the transgender American, but also the middle-aged white guy who, from the outside, may seem like he's got advantages, but has seen his world upended by economic and cultural and technological change. We have to pay attention, and listen.

For white Americans, it means acknowledging that the effects of slavery and Jim Crow didn't suddenly vanish in the '60s—that when minority groups voice discontent, they're not just engaging in reverse racism or practicing political correctness. When they wage peaceful protest, they're not demanding special treatment but the equal treatment that our Founders promised.

For native-born Americans, it means reminding ourselves that the stereotypes about immigrants today were said, almost word for word, about the Irish, and Italians, and Poles—who it was said we're going to destroy the fundamental character of America. And as it turned out, America wasn't weakened by the presence of these newcomers; these newcomers embraced this nation's creed, and this nation was strengthened.

So regardless of the station that we occupy, we all have to try harder. We all have to start with the premise that each of our fellow citizens loves this country just as much as we do; that they value hard work and family just like we do; that their children are just as curious and hopeful and worthy of love as our own.

And that's not easy to do. For too many of us, it's become safer to retreat into our own bubbles, whether in our neighborhoods or on college campuses, or places of worship, or especially our social media feeds, surrounded by people who look like us and share the same political outlook and never challenge our assumptions. The rise of naked partisanship, and increasing economic and regional stratification, the splintering of our media into a channel for every taste—all this makes this great sorting seem natural, even inevitable. And increasingly, we become so secure in our bubbles that we start accepting only information, whether it's true or not, that fits our opinions, instead of basing our opinions on the evidence that is out there.

And this trend represents a third threat to our democracy. But politics is a battle of ideas. That's how our democracy was designed. In the course of a healthy debate, we prioritize different goals, and the different means of reaching them. But without some common baseline of facts, without a willingness to admit new information, and concede that your opponent might be making a fair point, and that science and reason matter—then we're going to keep talking past each other, and we'll make common ground and compromise impossible.

And isn't that part of what so often makes politics dispiriting? How can elected officials rage about deficits when we propose to spend money on preschool for kids, but not when we're cutting taxes for corporations? How do we excuse ethical lapses in our own party, but pounce when the other party does the same thing? It's not just dishonest, this selective sorting of the facts; it's self-defeating. Because, as my mother used to tell me, reality has a way of catching up with you.

Take the challenge of climate change. In just eight years, we've halved our dependence on foreign oil; we've doubled our renewable energy; we've led the world to an agreement that has the promise to save this planet. But without bolder action, our children won't have time to debate the existence of climate change. They'll be busy dealing with its effects: more environmental disasters, more economic disruptions, waves of climate refugees seeking sanctuary.

Now, we can and should argue about the best approach to solve the problem. But to simply deny the problem not only betrays future generations, it betrays the essential spirit of this country—the essential spirit of innovation and practical problem-solving that guided our Founders.

It is that spirit, born of the Enlightenment, that made us an economic powerhouse—the spirit that took flight at Kitty Hawk and Cape Canaveral; the spirit that cures disease and put a computer in every pocket.

It's that spirit—a faith in reason, and enterprise, and the primacy of right over might—that allowed us to resist the lure of fascism and tyranny during the Great Depression; that allowed us to build a post-World War II order with other democracies, an order based not just on military power or national affiliations but built on principles—the rule of law, human rights, freedom of religion, and speech, and assembly, and an independent press.

That order is now being challenged—first by violent fanatics who claim to speak for Islam; more recently by autocrats in foreign capitals who see free markets and open democracies and and civil society itself as a threat to their power. The peril each poses to our democracy is more far-reaching than a car bomb or a missile. It represents the fear of change; the fear of people who look or speak or pray differently; a contempt for the rule of law that holds leaders accountable; an intolerance of dissent and free thought; a belief that the sword or the gun or the bomb or the propaganda machine is the ultimate arbiter of what's true and what's right.

Because of the extraordinary courage of our men and women in uniform, because of our intelligence officers, and law enforcement, and diplomats who support our troops—no foreign terrorist organization has successfully planned and executed an attack on our homeland these past eight years. And although Boston and Orlando and San Bernardino and Fort Hood remind us of how dangerous radicalization can be, our law enforcement agencies are more effective and vigilant than ever. We have taken out tens of thousands of terrorists—including bin Laden. The global coalition we're leading against ISIL has taken out their leaders, and taken away about half their territory. ISIL will be destroyed, and no one who threatens America will ever be safe.

And to all who serve or have served, it has been the honor of my lifetime to be your Commander-in-Chief. And we all owe you a deep debt of gratitude.

But protecting our way of life, that's not just the job of our military. Democracy can buckle when we give in to fear. So, just as we, as citizens, must remain vigilant against external aggression, we must guard against a weakening of the values that make us who we are.

And that's why, for the past eight years, I've worked to put the fight against terrorism on a firmer legal footing. That's why we've ended torture, worked to close Gitmo, reformed our laws governing surveillance to protect privacy and civil liberties. That's why I reject discrimination against Muslim Americans, who are just as patriotic as we are.

That's why we cannot withdraw from big global fights—to expand democracy, and human rights, and women's rights, and LGBT rights. No matter how imperfect our efforts, no matter how expedient ignoring such values may seem, that's part of defending America. For the fight against extremism and intolerance and sectarianism and chauvinism are of a piece with the fight against authoritarianism and nationalist aggression. If the scope of freedom and respect for the rule of law shrinks around the world, the likelihood of war within and between nations increases, and our own freedoms will eventually be threatened.

So let's be vigilant, but not afraid. ISIL will try to kill innocent people. But they cannot defeat America unless we betray our Constitution and our principles in the fight. Rivals like Russia or China cannot match our influence around the world—unless we give up what we stand for—and turn ourselves into just another big country that bullies smaller neighbors.

Which brings me to my final point: Our democracy is threatened whenever we take it for granted. All of us, regardless of party, should be throwing ourselves into the task of rebuilding our democratic institutions. When voting rates in America are some of the lowest among advanced democracies, we should be making it easier, not harder, to vote. When trust in our institutions is low, we should reduce the corrosive influence of money in our politics, and insist on the principles of transparency and ethics in public service. When Congress is dysfunctional, we should draw our congressional districts to encourage politicians to cater to common sense and not rigid extremes.

But remember, none of this happens on its own. All of this depends on our participation; on each of us accepting the responsibility of citizenship, regardless of which way the pendulum of power happens to be swinging.

Our Constitution is a remarkable, beautiful gift. But it's really just a piece of parchment. It has no power on its own. We, the people, give it power. We, the people, give it meaning. With our participation, and with the choices that we make, and the alliances that we forge. Whether or not we stand up for our freedoms. Whether or not we respect and enforce the rule of law. That's up to us. America is no fragile thing. But the gains of our long journey to freedom are not assured.

In his own farewell address, George Washington wrote that self-government is the underpinning of our safety, prosperity, and liberty, but "from different causes and from different quarters much pains will be taken…to weaken in your minds the conviction of this truth." And so we have to preserve this truth with "jealous anxiety;" that we should reject "the first dawning of every attempt to alienate any portion of our country from the rest or to enfeeble the sacred ties" that make us one.

America, we weaken those ties when we allow our political dialogue to become so corrosive that people of good character aren't even willing to enter into public service; so coarse with rancor that Americans with whom we disagree are seen not just as misguided but as malevolent. We weaken those ties when we define some of us as more American than others; when we write off the whole system as inevitably corrupt, and when we sit back and blame the leaders we elect without examining our own role in electing them.

It falls to each of us to be those those anxious, jealous guardians of our democracy; to embrace the joyous task we've been given to continually try to improve this great nation of ours. Because for all our outward differences, we, in fact, all share the same proud title, the most important office in a democracy: Citizen. Citizen.

So, you see, that's what our democracy demands. It needs you. Not just when there's an election, not just when your own narrow interest is at stake, but over the full span of a lifetime. If you're tired of arguing with strangers on the Internet, try talking with one of them in real life. If something needs fixing, then lace up your shoes and do some organizing. If you're disappointed by your elected officials, grab a clipboard, get some signatures, and run for office yourself. Show up. Dive in. Stay at it.

Sometimes you'll win. Sometimes you'll lose. Presuming a reservoir of goodness in other people, that can be a risk, and there will be times when the process will disappoint you. But for those of us fortunate enough to have been a part of this work, and to see it up close, let me tell you, it can energize and inspire. And more often than not, your faith in America—and in Americans—will be confirmed.

Mine sure has been. Over the course of these eight years, I've seen the hopeful faces of young graduates and our newest military officers. I have mourned with grieving families searching for answers, and found grace in a Charleston church. I've seen our scientists help a paralyzed man regain his sense of touch. I've seen wounded warriors who at points were given up for dead walk again. I've seen our doctors and volunteers rebuild after earthquakes and stop pandemics in their tracks. I've seen the youngest of children remind us through their actions and through their generosity of our obligations to care for refugees, or work for peace, and, above all, to look out for each other.

So that faith that I placed all those years ago, not far from here, in the power of ordinary Americans to bring about change—that faith has been rewarded in ways I could not have possibly imagined. And I hope your faith has, too. Some of you here tonight or watching at home, you were there with us in 2004, in 2008, 2012—maybe you still can't believe we pulled this whole thing off. Let me tell you, you're not the only ones.

Michelle—Michelle LaVaughn Robinson, girl of the South Side—for the past 25 years, you have not only been my wife and mother of my children, you have been my best friend. You took on a role you didn't ask for and you made it your own, with grace and with grit and with style and good humor. You made the White House a place that belongs to everybody. And the new generation sets its sights higher because it has you as a role model. So you have made me proud. And you have made the country proud.

Malia and Sasha, under the strangest of circumstances, you have become two amazing young women. You are smart and you are beautiful, but more importantly, you are kind and you are thoughtful and you are full of passion. You wore the burden of years in the spotlight so easily. Of all that I've done in my life, I am most proud to be your dad.

To Joe Biden—the scrappy kid from Scranton who became Delaware's favorite son—you were the first decision I made as a nominee, and it was the best. Not just because you have been a great Vice President, but because in the bargain, I gained a brother. And we love you and Jill like family, and your friendship has been one of the great joys of our lives.

To my remarkable staff: For eight years—and for some of you, a whole lot more—I have drawn from your energy, and every day I tried to reflect back what you displayed—heart, and character, and idealism. I've watched you grow up, get married, have kids, start incredible new journeys of your own. Even when times got tough and frustrating, you never let Washington get the better of you. You guarded against cynicism. And the only thing that makes me prouder than all the good that we've done is the thought of all the amazing things that you're going to achieve from here.

And to all of you out there—every organizer who moved to an unfamiliar town, every kind family who welcomed them in, every volunteer who knocked on doors, every young person who cast a ballot for the first time, every American who lived and breathed the hard work of change—you are the best supporters and organizers anybody could ever hope for, and I will be forever grateful. Because you did change the world. You did.

And that's why I leave this stage tonight even more optimistic about this country than when we started. Because I know our work has not only helped so many Americans, it has inspired so many Americans—especially so many young people out there—to believe that you can make a difference to hitch your wagon to something bigger than yourselves.

Let me tell you, this generation coming up—unselfish, altruistic, creative, patriotic—I've seen you in every corner of the country. You believe in a fair, and just, and inclusive America. You know that constant change has been America's hallmark; that it's not something to fear but something to embrace. You are willing to carry this hard work of democracy forward. You'll soon outnumber all of us, and I believe as a result the future is in good hands.

My fellow Americans, it has been the honor of my life to serve you. I won't stop. In fact, I will be right there with you, as a citizen, for all my remaining days. But for now, whether you are young or whether you're young at heart, I do have one final ask of you as your President—the same thing I asked when you took a chance on me eight years ago. I'm asking you to believe. Not in my ability to bring about change—but in yours.

I am asking you to hold fast to that faith written into our founding documents; that idea whispered by slaves and abolitionists; that spirit sung by immigrants and homesteaders and those who marched for justice; that creed reaffirmed by those who planted flags from foreign battlefields to the surface of the moon; a creed at the core of every American whose story is not yet written: Yes, we can.

Yes, we did. Yes, we can.

Thank you. God bless you. May God continue to bless the United States of America.

Presidents and other leaders often use rhetoric to advocate for policy change for the nation or for their organization. On occasion, however, the issue is not about public policy, but about the personal actions of the president or other leader. Speeches in which the leader defends him/herself against allegations of misconduct are known as apologia. Two examples of presidential apologia by Ronald Reagan and Bill Clinton are included, as is an example of a Senatorial apologia from Senator Al Franken.

Address to the Nation on the Iran Arms and *Contra* Aid Controversy

Ronald Reagan

MY FELLOW AMERICANS:

I've spoken to you from this historic office on many occasions and about many things. The power of the Presidency is often thought to reside within this Oval Office. Yet it doesn't rest here; it rests in you, the American people, and in your trust. Your trust is what gives a President his powers of leadership and his personal strength, and it's what I want to talk to you about this evening.

For the past three months, I've been silent on the revelations about Iran. And you must have been thinking: "Well, why doesn't he tell us what's happening? Why doesn't he just speak to us as he has in the past when we've faced troubles or tragedies?" Others of you, I guess, were thinking: "What's he doing hiding out in the White House?" Well, the reason I haven't spoken to you before now is this: You deserve the truth. And as frustrating as the waiting has been, I felt it was improper to come to you with sketchy reports, or possibly even erroneous statements, which would then have to be corrected, creating even more doubt and confusion. There's been enough of that. I've paid a price for my silence in terms of your trust and confidence. But I've had to wait, as you have, for the complete story. That's why I appointed Ambassador David Abshire as my Special Counselor to help get out the thousands of documents to the various investigations. And I appointed a Special Review Board, the Tower Board, which took on the chore of pulling the truth together for me and getting to the bottom of things. It has now issued its findings.

I'm often accused of being an optimist, and it's true I had to hunt pretty hard to find any good news in the Board's report. As you know, it's well-stocked with criticisms, which I'll discuss in a moment; but

I was very relieved to read this sentence: ". . . The Board is convinced that the President does indeed want the full story to be told." And that will continue to be my pledge to you as the other investigations go forward. I want to thank the members of the panel: former Senator John Tower, Former Secretary of State Edmund Muskie, and former national security adviser Brent Scowcroft. They have done the Nation, as well as me personally, a great service by submitting a report of such integrity and depth. They have my genuine and enduring gratitude.

I've studied the Board's report. Its findings are honest, convincing, and highly critical; and I accept them. And tonight I want to share with you my thoughts on these findings and report to you on the actions I'm taking to implement the Board's recommendations. First, let me say I take full responsibility for my own actions and for those of my administration. As angry as I may be about activities undertaken without my knowledge, I am still accountable for those activities. As disappointed as I may be in some who served me, I'm still the one who must answer to the American people for this behavior. And as personally distasteful as I find secret bank accounts and diverted funds—well, as the Navy would say, this happened on my watch.

Let's start with the part that is the most controversial. A few months ago I told the American people I did not trade arms for hostages. My heart and my best intentions still tell me that's true, but the facts and the evidence tell me it is not. As the Tower Board reported, what began as a strategic opening to Iran deteriorated, in its implementation, into trading arms for hostages. This runs counter to my own beliefs, to administration policy, and to the original strategy we had in mind. There are reasons why it happened, but no excuses. It was a mistake. I undertook the original Iran initiative in order to develop relations with those who might assume leadership in a post-Khomeni government.

It's clear from the Board's report, however, that I let my personal concern for the hostages spill over into the geopolitical strategy of reaching out to Iran. I asked so many questions about the hostages

March 4, 1987.

welfare that I didn't ask enough about the specifics of the total Iran plan. Let me say to the hostage families: We have not given up. We never will. And I promise you we'll use every legitimate means to free your loved ones from captivity. But I must also caution that those Americans who freely remain in such dangerous areas must know that they're responsible for their own safety.

Now, another major aspect of the Board's findings regards the transfer of funds to the Nicaraguan contras. The Tower Board wasn't able to find out what happened to this money, so the facts here will be left to the continuing investigations of the court-appointed Independent Counsel and the two congressional investigating committees. I'm confident the truth will come out about this matter, as well. As I told the Tower Board, I didn't know about any diversion of funds to the contras. But as President, I cannot escape responsibility.

Much has been said about my management style, a style that's worked successfully for me during eight years as Governor of California and for most of my Presidency. The way I work is to identify the problem, find the right individuals to do the job, and then let them go to it. I've found this invariably brings out the best in people. They seem to rise to their full capability, and in the long run you get more done. When it came to managing the NSC staff, let's face it, my style didn't match its previous track record. I've already begun correcting this. As a start, yesterday I met with the entire professional staff of the National Security Council. I defined for them the values I want to guide the national security policies of this country. I told them that I wanted a policy that was as justifiable and understandable in public as it was in secret. I wanted a policy that reflected the will of the Congress as well as the White House. And I told them that there'll be no more freelancing by individuals when it comes to our national security.

You've heard a lot about the staff of the National Security Council in recent months. Well, I can tell you, they are good and dedicated government employees, who put in long hours for the Nation's benefit. They are eager and anxious to serve their country. One thing still upsetting me, however, is that no one kept proper records of meetings or decisions. This led to my failure to recollect whether I approved an arms shipment before or after the fact. I did approve it; I just can't say specifically when. Well, rest assured, there's plenty of recordkeeping now going on at 1600 Pennsylvania Avenue.

For nearly a week now, I've been studying the Board's report. I want the American people to know that this wrenching ordeal of recent months has not been in vain. I endorse every one of the Tower Board's recommendations. In fact, I'm going beyond their recommendations so as to put the house in even better order. I'm taking action in three basic areas: personnel, national security policy, and the process for making sure that the system works.

First, personnel—I've brought in an accomplished and highly respected new team here at the White House. They bring new blood, new energy, and new credibility and experience. Former Senator Howard Baker, my new Chief of Staff, possesses a breadth of legislative and foreign affairs skills that's impossible to match. I'm hopeful that his experience as minority and majority leader of the Senate can help us forge a new partnership with the Congress, especially on foreign and national security policies. I'm genuinely honored that he's given up his own Presidential aspirations to serve the country as my Chief of Staff. Frank Carlucci, my new national security adviser, is respected for his experience in government and trusted for his judgment and counsel. Under him, the NSC staff is being rebuilt with proper management discipline. Already, almost half the NSC professional staff is comprised of new people.

Yesterday I nominated William Webster, a man of sterling reputation, to be Director of the Central Intelligence Agency. Mr. Webster has served as Director of the FBI and as a U.S. District Court judge. He understands the meaning of "rule of law." So that his knowledge of national security matters can be available to me on a continuing basis, I will also appoint John Tower to serve as a member of my Foreign Intelligence Advisory Board. I am considering other changes in personnel, and I'll move more furniture, as I see fit, in the weeks and months ahead.

Second, in the area of national security policy. I have ordered the NSC to begin a comprehensive review of all covert operations. I have also directed that any covert activity be in support of clear policy objectives and in compliance with American values. I expect a covert policy that, if Americans saw it on the front page of their newspaper, they'd say, "That makes sense." I have had issued a directive prohibiting the NSC staff itself from undertaking covert operations—no ifs, ands, or buts. I have asked Vice President Bush to reconvene his task force on terrorism to review our terrorist policy in light of the events that have occurred.

Third, in terms of the process of reaching national security decisions, I am adopting in total the Tower report's model of how the NSC process and staff should work. I am directing Mr. Carlucci to take the necessary steps to make it happen. He will report back to me on further reforms that might be needed.

I've created the post of NSC legal adviser to assure a greater sensitivity to matters of law. I am also determined to make the congressional oversight process work. Proper procedures for consultation with the Congress will be followed, not only in letter but in spirit. Before the end of March, I will report to the Congress on all steps I've taken in line with the Tower Board's conclusions.

Now, what should happen when you make a mistake is this: You take your knocks, you learn your lessons, and then you move on. That's the healthiest way to deal with a problem. This in no way diminishes the importance of the other continuing investigations, but the business of our country and our people must proceed. I've gotten this message from Republicans and Democrats in Congress, from allies around the world, and—if we're reading the signals right—even from the Soviets. And of course, I've heard the message from you, the American people. You know, by the time you reach my age, you've made plenty of mistakes. And if you've lived your life properly—so, you learn. You put things in perspective. You pull your energies together. You change. You go forward.

My fellow Americans, I have a great deal that I want to accomplish with you and for you over the next two years. And the Lord willing, that's exactly what I intend to do.

Good night, and God bless you.

Map Room Speech
William Clinton

Good evening. This afternoon in this room, from this chair, I testified before the Office of Independent Counsel and the grand jury.

I answered their questions truthfully, including questions about my private life, questions no American citizen would ever want to answer.

Still, I must take complete responsibility for all my actions, both public and private. And that is why I am speaking to you tonight.

As you know, in a deposition in January, I was asked questions about my relationship with Monica Lewinsky. While my answers were legally accurate, I did not volunteer information.

Indeed, I did have a relationship with Ms. Lewinsky that was not appropriate. In fact, it was wrong. It constituted a critical lapse in judgment and a personal failure on my part for which I am solely and completely responsible.

But I told the grand jury today and I say to you now that at no time did I ask anyone to lie, to hide or destroy evidence or to take any other unlawful action.

I know that my public comments and my silence about this matter gave a false impression. I misled people, including even my wife. I deeply regret that.

I can only tell you I was motivated by many factors. First, by a desire to protect myself from the embarrassment of my own conduct.

I was also very concerned about protecting my family. The fact that these questions were being asked in a politically inspired lawsuit, which has since been dismissed, was a consideration, too.

In addition, I had real and serious concerns about an independent counsel investigation that began with private business dealings 20 years ago, dealings, I might add, about which an independent federal agency found no evidence of any wrongdoing by me or my wife over two years ago.

The independent counsel investigation moved on to my staff and friends, then into my private life. And now the investigation itself is under investigation.

This has gone on too long, cost too much and hurt too many innocent people.

Now, this matter is between me, the two people I love most—my wife and our daughter—and our God. I must put it right, and I am prepared to do whatever it takes to do so.

Nothing is more important to me personally. But it is private, and I intend to reclaim my family life for my family. It's nobody's business but ours.

Even presidents have private lives. It is time to stop the pursuit of personal destruction and the prying into private lives and get on with our national life.

Our country has been distracted by this matter for too long, and I take my responsibility for my part in all of this. That is all I can do.

Now it is time—in fact, it is past time—to move on.

We have important work to do—real opportunities to seize, real problems to solve, real security matters to face.

And so tonight, I ask you to turn away from the spectacle of the past seven months, to repair the fabric of our national discourse, and to return our attention to all the challenges and all the promise of the next American century.

Thank you for watching. And good night.

Statement of Apology

Al Franken

The first thing I want to do is apologize: to Leeann, to everyone else who was part of that tour, to everyone who has worked for me, to everyone I represent, and to everyone who counts on me to be an ally and supporter and champion of women. There's more I want to say, but the first and most important thing—and if it's the only thing you care to hear, that's fine—is: I'm sorry.

I respect women. I don't respect men who don't. And the fact that my own actions have given people a good reason to doubt that makes me feel ashamed.

But I want to say something else, too. Over the last few months, all of us—including and especially men who respect women—have been forced to take a good, hard look at our own actions and think (perhaps, shamefully, for the first time) about how those actions have affected women.

For instance, that picture. I don't know what was in my head when I took that picture, and it doesn't matter. There's no excuse. I look at it now and I feel disgusted with myself. It isn't funny. It's completely inappropriate. It's obvious how Leeann would feel violated by that picture. And, what's more, I can see how millions of other women would feel violated by it—women who have had similar experiences in their own lives, women who fear having those experiences, women who look up to me, women who have counted on me.

Coming from the world of comedy, I've told and written a lot of jokes that I once thought were funny but later came to realize were just plain offensive. But the intentions behind my actions aren't the point at all. It's the impact these jokes had on others that matters. And I'm sorry it's taken me so long to come to terms with that.

While I don't remember the rehearsal for the skit as Leeann does, I understand why we need to listen to and believe women's experiences.

I am asking that an ethics investigation be undertaken, and I will gladly cooperate.

And the truth is, what people think of me in light of this is far less important than what people think of women who continue to come forward to tell their stories. They deserve to be heard, and believed. And they deserve to know that I am their ally and supporter. I have let them down and am committed to making it up to them.

Senator Al Franken, Statement of Apology Issued, November 16, 2017

CHAPTER 9
The Informed Citizen

The Informed Citizen system is designed to help the individual protect himself/herself from deceptive andmanipulative rhetoric. The system moves through four stages that are summarized below in order to achieve these aims.

Stages in the Informed Citizen

I. Determine the need for critical self protection by asking:

    1. Is a major claim on beliefs/attitudes/values or actions being made?

    2. Is the person merely relaying information or is he/she strategically presenting the material?

II. Identify the claims that are being made

III. Test the Quality of the Case for the Claims

    1. Does the rhetor provide evidence and reasoning for every claim?

    2. Does the support material meet the tests of evidence?

    3. Is the reasoning consistent?

    4. Does the reasoning lead to the conclusion directly or could there be alternative factors that invalidate the conclusion?

    5. Are there counterarguments or facts that invalidate the conclusion?

IV. Test the Rhetoric for Manipulation

    1. Does the rhetoric attempt to prevent other voices from being heard?

    2. Does the rhetoric attempt to overwhelm our reason?

    3. Does the rhetoric attack groups or individual people, rather than their ideas or actions?

Four works of rhetoric are included to illustrate application of the system. In each case, the critic carefully should move through the four stages in order to make a judgment about whether a strong and ethical case is made in the rhetoric. No assumption should be made that simply because a work is included that it must violate the standards. Critics need to be vigilant to protect themselves from deceptive and manipulative rhetoric, but at the same time they should not be over critical.

It is important to note that the Informed Citizen System, could be applied to any of the works contained in earlier sections of this workbook.

In "The Election is About Who We Are," Republican Presidential Candidate Pat Buchanan presented his vision of the Republican party and the nation. Buchanan's speech is one of the most discussed speeches of the last thirty years. Buchanan, who is generally thought of as extremely conservative, supports major cuts in social programs. He also favors a nationalist agenda that would dramatically limit immigration to the United States and would reject free trade in favor of a protectionist policy.

Buchanan is one of those political figures who is both beloved and hated. His supporters find him to be perhaps the most appealing Republican politician since Ronald Reagan. His opponents (and that includes many Republicans and moderates) find him extremist. Application of the Informed Citizen can reveal whether Buchanan made a strong and ethical case for his position or violated standards for ethical rhetoric.

The Election Is About Who We Are

Taking Back Our Country

Pat Buchanan, Presidential Candidate and Columnist

What a terrific crowd this is. What a terrific crowd. This may even be larger than the crowd I had in Eligay, Georgia. Don't laugh. We carried Eligay.

Listen my friends, we may have taken the long way home, but we finally got here.

The first thing I want to do is to congratulate President Bush, and remove any doubt about where we stand: The primaries are over, the heart is strong again, and the Buchanan brigades are enlisted—all the way to a great comeback victory in November.

My friends, like many of you last month, I watched that giant masquerade ball up at Madison Square Garden—where 20,000 radicals and liberals came dressed up as moderates and centrists—in the greatest single exhibition of cross-dressing in American political history.

One by one, the prophets of doom appeared at the podium. The Reagan decade, they moaned, was a terrible time in America; and they said the only way to prevent even worse times is to entrust our nation's fate and future to the party that gave us McGovern, Mondale, Carter and Michael Dukakis.

Where do they find these leaders? No way, my friends. The American people are not going to go back to the discredited liberalism of the 1960s and the failed liberalism of the 1970s—no matter how slick the package in 1992.

No, the malcontents of Madison Square Garden notwithstanding, the 1980s were not terrible years in America. They were great years. You know it. And I know it. And everyone knows it except for the carping critics who sat on the sidelines of history, jeering at one of the great statesmen of modern time, Ronald Reagan.

Remember the time of Jimmy Carter's days of malaise? Ronald Reagan crafted the greatest peacetime recovery in U.S. history—three million new businesses created, and 20 million new jobs.

Under the Reagan Doctrine, one by one, it was the communist dominos that began to fall. First, Grenada was liberated by U.S. airborne troops and the U.S. Marine Corps.

Then, the mighty Red Army was driven out of Afghanistan with American weapons. In Nicaragua, that squalid Marxist regime was forced to hold free elections—by Ronald Reagan's contra army—and the communists were thrown out of power.

Fellow Americans, we ought to remember, it was under our party that the Berlin Wall came down, and Europe was reunited. It was under our party that the Soviet Empire collapsed, and the captive nations broke free.

You know, it is said that every president will be remembered in history with but a single sentence. George Washington was the father of our country. Abraham Lincoln preserved the Union. And Ronald Reagan won the Cold War. And it is just about time that my old colleagues, the columnists and commentators, looking down on us tonight from their sky boxes and anchor booths and sky boxes, gave Ronald Reagan the full credit he deserves—for leading America to victory in the Cold War.

Most of all, my friends, Ronald Reagan made us proud to be Americans again. We never felt better about our country; and we never stood taller in the eyes of the world than when the Gipper was at the helm.

But we are here tonight, my friends, not only to celebrate, but to nominate. And an American president has many, many roles.

Delivered at the Republican National Convention, Houston, Texas, August 17, 1992.

He is our first diplomat, the architect of American foreign policy. And which of these two men is more qualified for that role? George Bush has been U.N. ambassador, director of the CIA, envoy to China. As vice president, George Bush co-authored and co-signed the policies that won the Cold War. As president, George Bush presided over the liberation of Eastern Europe and the termination of the Warsaw Pact.

And what about Mr. Clinton? Well, Bill Clinton couldn't find 150 words to discuss foreign policy in an acceptance speech that lasted almost an hour. You know, as was said of another Democratic candidate, Bill Clinton's foreign policy experience is pretty much confined to having had breakfast once at the International House of Pancakes.

You know, let's recall what happened. Let us look at the record and recall what happened. Under President George Bush, more human beings escaped from the prison house of tyranny to freedom than in any other four-year period in history.

And for any man, let me tell you for any man to call this the record of failure is the cheap political rhetoric of politicians who only know how to build themselves up by tearing America down, and we don't want that kind of leadership in the United States.

The presidency, my friends, the presidency is also an office that Theodore Roosevelt called America's bully pulpit. Harry Truman said it was preeminently a place of moral leadership. George Bush is a defender of right-to-life, and a champion of the Judeo-Christian values and beliefs upon which this America was founded.

Mr. Clinton, however, has a different agenda.

At its top is unrestricted, unrestricted abortion on demand. When the Irish-Catholic governor of Pennsylvania, Robert Casey, asked to say a few words on behalf of the 25 million unborn children destroyed since Roe v. Wade, Bob Casey was told there was no room for him at the podium at Bill Clinton's convention and no room at the inn.

Yet a militant leader of the homosexual rights movement could rise at that convention and say:

"Bill Clinton and Al Gore represent the most pro-lesbian and pro-gay ticket in history." And so they do.

Bill Clinton says he supports school choice—but only for state-run schools. Parents who send their children to Christian schools, or private schools or Jewish schools or Catholic schools need not apply.

Elect me, and you get two for the price of one, Mr. Clinton says of his lawyer-spouse.

And what does Hillary believe? Well, Hillary believes that 12-year-olds should have the right to sue their parents.

And Hillary has compared marriage and the family as institutions to slavery and life on an Indian reservation.

Well, speak for yourself, Hillary.

Friends, my friends, this is radical feminism. The agenda that Clinton and Clinton would impose on America—abortion on demand, a litmus test for the Supreme Court, homosexual rights, discrimination against religious schools, women in combat units—that's change, all right. That's not the kind of change America needs. It's not the kind of change America wants. And it is not the kind of change we can abide in a nation that we still call God's country.

A president of the United States is also America's commander-in-chief. He's the man we authorize to send fathers and sons and brothers and friends into battle.

George Bush was 17 years old when they bombed Pearl Harbor. He left his high school graduation, he walked down to the recruiting office, and signed up to become the youngest fighter pilot in the Pacific war.

And Mr. Clinton? And Bill Clinton?

I'll tell you where he was. I'll tell you where he was.

I'll tell you where he was. When Bill Clinton's time came in Vietnam, he sat up in a dormitory in Oxford, England, and figured out how to dodge the draft.

Let me ask the question of this convention. Which of these two men has won the moral authority to send young Americans into battle? I suggest, respectfully, it is the American patriot and war hero, Navy Lieutenant J. G. George Herbert Walker Bush.

My fellow Americans, my fellow Americans, this campaign is about philosophy, and it is about character; and George Bush wins on both counts.

And it is time all of us came home and stood beside him.

As his running mate, Mr. Clinton chose Albert Gore. But just how moderate is Prince Albert? Well, according to the Taxpayers Union, Al Gore beat out Teddy Kennedy, two straight years, for the title of biggest spender in the U.S. Senate, and Teddy Kennedy isn't moderate about anything.

I'm not kidding. I'm not kidding about Teddy. How many other 60-year-olds do you know who still go to Florida for spring break?

You know, at that great big costume party they held up in New York, Mr. Gore made a startling declaration. Henceforth, Albert Gore said, the central organizing principle of governments everywhere must be the environment.

Wrong, Albert!

The central organizing principle of this republic is freedom.

And from the ancient forests of Oregon and Washington, to the Inland Empire of California, America's great middle class has got to start standing up to these environmental extremists who put birds and rats and insects ahead of families, workers and jobs.

One year ago, my friends, I could not have dreamt that I would be here tonight. I was just one of many panelists on what President Bush calls "those crazy Sunday talk shows."

But I disagreed with the president; and so we challenged the president in the Republican primaries and we fought as best we could. From February to June, President Bush won 33 primaries. I can't recall exactly how many we won.

I'll get you the figure tomorrow.

But tonight I want to speak from the heart, to the three million Americans who voted for Pat Buchanan for president. I will never forget you, nor the great honor you have done me. But I do believe, I do believe deep in my heart, that the right place for us to be now—in this presidential campaign—is right beside George Bush.

This party is my home. This party is our home, and we've got to come home to it. And don't let anyone tell you any different.

Yes, we disagreed with President Bush, but we stand with him for the freedom of choice religious schools. And we stand with him against the amoral idea that gay and lesbian couples should have the same standing in law as married men and women.

We stand with President Bush for right-to-life, and for voluntary prayer in the public schools.

And we stand against putting our wives and daughters and sisters into combat units of the United States Army. And we stand, my friends, we also stand with President Bush in favor of the right of small towns and communities to control the raw sewage of pornography that so terribly pollutes our popular culture.

We stand with President Bush in favor of federal judges who interpret the law as written, and against would-be Supreme Court justices like Mario Cuomo who think they have a mandate to re-write the Constitution.

My friends, this election is about more than who gets what. It is about who we are. It is about what we believe and what we stand for as Americans. There is a religious war going on in this country for the soul of America. It is a cultural war as critical to the kind of nation we shall be as the Cold War itself, for this war is for the soul of America. And in that struggle for the soul of America, Clinton and Clinton are on the other side, and George Bush is on our side.

And so, to the Buchanan brigades out there, we have to come home, and stand beside George Bush.

In those six months campaigning from Concord, New Hampshire to California, I came to know our country better than I had known it ever before in my life, and I gathered up memories that are going to be with me the rest of my days.

There was that day-long ride through the great state of Georgia in a bus Vice President Bush himself had used in 1988 called Asphalt One. The ride ended in a 9:00 p.m. speech in a tiny town in southern Georgia called Fitzgerald.

There were those workers at the James River Paper Mill, in northern New Hampshire in a town called Groveton—tough, hardy men. None of them would say a word to me as I came down the line, shaking their hands one by one. They were under threat of losing their jobs at Christmas. As I moved down the line, one tough fellow about my age just looked up and said to me, "Save our jobs."

Then there was the legal secretary that I met at the Manchester airport Christmas Day who came running up to me and said, "Mr. Buchanan, I'm going to vote for you." And then she broke down weeping and she said, "I've lost my job, I don't have any money, and they're going to take away my little girl. What am I going to do?"

My friends, these people are our people. They don't read Adam Smith or Edmund Burke, but they came from the same schoolyards and the same playgrounds and town as we came from. They share our beliefs and convictions, our hopes and our dreams. These are the conservatives of the heart. They are our people. And we need to reconnect with them. We need to let them know we know how bad they're hurting. They don't expect miracles of us, but they need to know we care.

There were the people, of Hayfork, a tiny town up in California's Trinity Alps, a town that is now under a sentence of death because a federal judge has set aside nine million acres for the habitat of the spotted owl—forgetting about the habitat of the men and women who live and work in Hayfork.

And there were the brave people of Koreatown who took the worst of those L.A. riots, but still live the family values we treasure, and who still believe deeply in the American dream.

Friends, in those wonderful 25 weeks of our campaign, the saddest days were the days of that riot in L.A., the worst riot in American history. But out of that awful tragedy can come a message of hope.

Hours after that awful tragedy can come a message of hope.

Hours after that riot ended I went down to the Army compound in south Los Angeles where I met the troopers of the 18th Cavalry who had come to save the city of Los Angeles. An officer of the 18th Cav said, "Mr. Buchanan, I want you to talk to a couple of our troopers." And I went over and I met these young fellas. They couldn't have been 20 years old, and they recounted their story.

They had come into Los Angeles late in the evening of the second day, when the rioting was still going on, and two of them walked up a dark street, where the mob had burned and looted every building on the block but one, a convalescent home for the aged. And the mob was headed in to ransack and loot the apartments of the terrified old men and women inside. The troopers came up the street, M-16s at the ready, and the mob threatened and cursed, but the mob retreated because it had met the one thing that could stop it: force, rooted in justice, and backed by moral courage.

Greater love than this hath no man than that he lay down his life for his friend. Here were 19-year-old boys ready to lay down their lives to stop a mob from molesting old people they did not even know. And as those boys took back the streets of Los Angeles, block by block, my friends, we must take back our cities, and take back our culture, and take back our country.

God bless you, and God bless America.

GEORGE W. BUSH, PRESIDENT BUSH OUTLINES IRAQI THREAT

One of the most important actions of President George W. Bush was to expand the Global War on Terror by attacking Iraq in March 2003. The decision to go to war with Iraq has been widely praised by conservatives and widely attacked by many others. President Bush laid out his case for war in a major speech in Cincinnati in October 2002. It is important to consider whether the President made a strong case for going to war.

President Bush Outlines Iraqi Threat

George W. Bush

Thank you all. Thank you for that very gracious and warm Cincinnati welcome. I'm honored to be here tonight; I appreciate you all coming.

Tonight I want to take a few minutes to discuss a grave threat to peace, and America's determination to lead the world in confronting that threat.

The threat comes from Iraq. It arises directly from the Iraqi regime's own actions—its history of aggression, and its drive toward an arsenal of terror. Eleven years ago, as a condition for ending the Persian Gulf War, the Iraqi regime was required to destroy its weapons of mass destruction, to cease all development of such weapons, and to stop all support for terrorist groups. The Iraqi regime has violated all of those obligations. It possesses and produces chemical and biological weapons. It is seeking nuclear weapons. It has given shelter and support to terrorism, and practices terror against its own people. The entire world has witnessed Iraq's eleven-year history of defiance, deception and bad faith.

We also must never forget the most vivid events of recent history. On September the 11th, 2001, America felt its vulnerability—even to threats that gather on the other side of the earth. We resolved then, and we are resolved today, to confront every threat, from any source, that could bring sudden terror and suffering to America.

Members of the Congress of both political parties, and members of the United Nations Security Council, agree that Saddam Hussein is a threat to peace and must disarm. We agree that the Iraqi dictator must not be permitted to threaten America and the world with horrible poisons and diseases and gases and atomic weapons. Since we all agree on this goal, the issues is: how can we best achieve it?

Many Americans have raised legitimate questions: about the nature of the threat; about the urgency of action—why be concerned now; about the link between Iraq developing weapons of terror, and the wider war on terror. These are all issues we've discussed broadly and fully within my administration. And tonight, I want to share those discussions with you.

First, some ask why Iraq is different from other countries or regimes that also have terrible weapons. While there are many dangers in the world, the threat from Iraq stands alone—because it gathers the most serious dangers of our age in one place. Iraq's weapons of mass destruction are controlled by a murderous tyrant who has already used chemical

October 7, 2002.

weapons to kill thousands of people. This same tyrant has tried to dominate the Middle East, has invaded and brutally occupied a small neighbor, has struck other nations without warning, and holds an unrelenting hostility toward the United States.

By its past and present actions, by its technological capabilities, by the merciless nature of its regime, Iraq is unique. As a former chief weapons inspector of the U.N. has said, "The fundamental problem with Iraq remains the nature of the regime, itself. Saddam Hussein is a homicidal dictator who is addicted to weapons of mass destruction."

Some ask how urgent this danger is to America and the world. The danger is already significant, and it only grows worse with time. If we know Saddam Hussein has dangerous weapons today—and we do—does it make any sense for the world to wait to confront him as he grows even stronger and develops even more dangerous weapons?

In 1995, after several years of deceit by the Iraqi regime, the head of Iraq's military industries defected. It was then that the regime was forced to admit that it had produced more than 30,000 liters of anthrax and other deadly biological agents. The inspectors, however, concluded that Iraq had likely produced two to four times that amount. This is a massive stockpile of biological weapons that has never been accounted for, and capable of killing millions.

We know that the regime has produced thousands of tons of chemical agents, including mustard gas, sarin nerve gas, VX nerve gas. Saddam Hussein also has experience in using chemical weapons. He has ordered chemical attacks on Iran, and on more than forty villages in his own country. These actions killed or injured at least 20,000 people, more than six times the number of people who died in the attacks of September the 11th.

And surveillance photos reveal that the regime is rebuilding facilities that it had used to produce chemical and biological weapons. Every chemical and biological weapon that Iraq has or makes is a direct violation of the truce that ended the Persian Gulf War in 1991. Yet, Saddam Hussein has chosen to build and keep these weapons despite international sanctions, U.N. demands, and isolation from the civilized world.

Iraq possesses ballistic missiles with a likely range of hundreds of miles—far enough to strike Saudi Arabia, Israel, Turkey, and other nations—in a region where more than 135,000 American civilians and service members live and work. We've also discovered through intelligence that Iraq has a growing fleet of manned and unmanned aerial vehicles that could be used to disperse chemical or biological weapons across broad areas. We're concerned that Iraq is exploring ways of using these UAVS for missions targeting the United States. And, of course, sophisticated delivery systems aren't required for a chemical or biological attack; all that might be required are a small container and one terrorist or Iraqi intelligence operative to deliver it.

And that is the source of our urgent concern about Saddam Hussein's links to international terrorist groups. Over the years, Iraq has provided safe haven to terrorists such as Abu Nidal, whose terror organization carried out more than 90 terrorist attacks in 20 countries that killed or injured nearly 900 people, including 12 Americans. Iraq has also provided safe haven to Abu Abbas, who was responsible for seizing the Achille Lauro and killing an American passenger. And we know that Iraq is continuing to finance terror and gives assistance to groups that use terrorism to undermine Middle East peace.

We know that Iraq and the al Qaeda terrorist network share a common enemy—the United States of America. We know that Iraq and al Qaeda have had high-level contacts that go back a decade. Some al Qaeda leaders who fled Afghanistan went to Iraq. These include one very senior al Qaeda leader who received medical treatment in Baghdad this year, and who has been associated with planning for chemical and biological attacks. We've learned that Iraq has trained al Qaeda members in bomb-making and poisons and deadly gases. And we know that after September the 11th, Saddam Hussein's regime gleefully celebrated the terrorist attacks on America.

Iraq could decide on any given day to provide a biological or chemical weapon to a terrorist group or individual terrorists. Alliance with terrorists could allow the Iraqi regime to attack America without leaving any fingerprints.

Some have argued that confronting the threat from Iraq could detract from the war against terror. To the contrary; confronting the threat posed by Iraq is crucial to winning the war on terror. When I spoke to Congress more than a year ago, I said that those who harbor terrorists are as guilty as the terrorists themselves. Saddam Hussein is harboring terrorists and the instruments of terror, the instruments of mass death and destruction. And he cannot be trusted. The risk is simply too great that he will use them, or provide them to a terror network.

Terror cells and outlaw regimes building weapons of mass destruction are different faces of the same evil. Our security requires that we confront both. And the United States military is capable of confronting both.

Many people have asked how close Saddam Hussein is to developing a nuclear weapon. Well, we don't know exactly, and that's the problem. Before the Gulf War, the best intelligence indicated that Iraq was eight to ten years away from developing a nuclear weapon. After the war, international inspectors learned that the regime had been much closer—the regime in Iraq would likely have possessed a nuclear weapon no later than 1993. The inspectors discovered that Iraq had an advanced nuclear weapons development program, had a design for a workable nuclear weapon, and was pursuing several different methods of enriching uranium for a bomb.

Before being barred from Iraq in 1998, the International Atomic Energy Agency dismantled extensive nuclear weapons-related facilities, including three uranium enrichment sites. That same year, information from a high-ranking Iraqi nuclear engineer who had defected revealed that despite his public promises, Saddam Hussein had ordered his nuclear program to continue.

The evidence indicates that Iraq is reconstituting its nuclear weapons program. Saddam Hussein has held numerous meetings with Iraqi nuclear scientists, a group he calls his "nuclear mujahideen"—his nuclear holy warriors. Satellite photographs reveal that Iraq is rebuilding facilities at sites that have been part of its nuclear program in the past. Iraq has attempted to purchase high-strength aluminum tubes and other equipment needed for gas centrifuges, which are used to enrich uranium for nuclear weapons.

If the Iraqi regime is able to produce, buy, or steal an amount of highly enriched uranium a little larger than a single softball, it could have a nuclear weapon in less than a year. And if we allow that to happen, a terrible line would be crossed. Saddam Hussein would be in a position to blackmail anyone who opposes his aggression. He would be in a position to dominate the Middle East. He would be in a position to threaten America. And Saddam Hussein would be in a position to pass nuclear technology to terrorists.

Some citizens wonder, after 11 years of living with this problem, why do we need to confront it now? And there's a reason. We've experienced the horror of September the 11th. We have seen that those who hate America are willing to crash airplanes into buildings full of innocent people. Our enemies would be no less willing, in fact, they would be eager, to use biological or chemical, or a nuclear weapon.

Knowing these realities, America must not ignore the threat gathering against us. Facing clear evidence of peril, we cannot wait for the final proof—the smoking gun—that could come in the form of a mushroom cloud. As President Kennedy said in October of 1962, "Neither the United States of America, nor the world community of nations can tolerate deliberate deception and offensive threats on the part of any nation, large or small. We no longer live in a world," he said, "where only the actual firing of weapons represents a sufficient challenge to a nations security to constitute maximum peril."

Understanding the threats of our time, knowing the designs and deceptions of the Iraqi regime, we have every reason to assume the worst, and we have an urgent duty to prevent the worst from occurring.

Some believe we can address this danger by simply resuming the old approach to inspections, and applying diplomatic and economic pressure. Yet this is precisely what the world has tried to do since 1991. The U.N. inspections program was met with systematic deception. The Iraqi regime bugged hotel rooms and offices of inspectors to find where they were going next; they forged documents, destroyed evidence, and developed mobile weapons facilities to keep a step ahead of inspectors. Eight so-called presidential palaces were declared off-limits to unfettered inspections. These sites actually encompass twelve square miles, with hundreds of structures, both above and below the ground, where sensitive materials could be hidden.

The world has also tried economic sanctions—and watched Iraq use billions of dollars in illegal oil revenues to fund more weapons purchases, rather than providing for the needs of the Iraqi people.

The world has tried limited military strikes to destroy Iraq's weapons of mass destruction capabilities—only to see them openly rebuilt, while the regime again denies they even exist.

The world has tried no-fly zones to keep Saddam from terrorizing his own people—and in the last year alone, the Iraqi military has fired upon American and British pilots more than 750 times.

After eleven years during which we have tried containment, sanctions, inspections, even selected military action, the end result is that Saddam Hussein still has chemical and biological weapons and is increasing his capabilities to make more. And he is moving ever closer to developing a nuclear weapon.

Clearly, to actually work, any new inspections, sanctions or enforcement mechanisms will have to be very different. America wants the U.N. to be an effective organization that helps keep the peace. And that is why we are urging the Security Council to adopt a new resolution setting out tough, immediate requirements. Among those requirements: the Iraqi regime must reveal and destroy, under U.N. supervision, all existing weapons of mass destruction.

To ensure that we learn the truth, the regime must allow witnesses to its illegal activities to be interviewed outside the country—and these witnesses must be free to bring their families with them so they are beyond the reach of Saddam Hussein's terror and murder. And inspectors must have access to any site, at any time, without pre-clearance, without delay, without exceptions.

The time for denying, deceiving, and delaying has come to an end. Saddam Hussein must disarm himself—or, for the sake of peace, we will lead a coalition to disarm him.

Many nations are joining us in insisting that Saddam Hussein's regime be held accountable. They are committed to defending the international security that protects the lives of both our citizens and theirs. And that's why America is challenging all nations to take the resolutions of the U.N. Security Council seriously.

And these resolutions are clear. In addition to declaring and destroying all of its weapons of mass destruction, Iraq must end its support for terrorism. It must cease the persecution of its civilian population. It must stop all illicit trade outside the Oil For Food program. It must release or account for all Gulf War personnel, including an American pilot, whose fate is still unknown.

By taking these steps, and by only taking these steps, the Iraqi regime has an opportunity to avoid conflict. Taking these steps would also change the nature of the Iraqi regime itself. America hopes the regime will make that choice. Unfortunately, at least so far, we have little reason to expect it. And that's why two administrations—mine and President Clinton's—have stated that regime change in Iraq is the only certain means of removing a great danger to our nation.

I hope this will not require military action, but it may. And military conflict could be difficult. An Iraqi regime faced with its own demise may attempt cruel and desperate measures. If Saddam Hussein orders such measures, his generals would be well advised to refuse those orders. If they do not refuse, they must understand that all war criminals will be pursued and punished. If we have to act, we will take every precaution that is possible. We will plan carefully; we will act with the full power of the United States military; we will act with allies at our side, and we will prevail. (*Applause.*)

There is no easy or risk-free course of action. Some have argued we should wait—and that's an option. In my view, it's the riskiest of all options, because the longer we wait, the stronger and bolder Saddam Hussein will become. We could wait and

hope that Saddam does not give weapons to terrorists, or develop a nuclear weapon to blackmail the world. But I'm convinced that is a hope against all evidence. As Americans, we want peace—we work and sacrifice for peace. But there can be no peace if our security depends on the will and whims of a ruthless and aggressive dictator. I'm not willing to stake one American life on trusting Saddam Hussein.

Failure to act would embolden other tyrants, allow terrorists access to new weapons and new resources, and make blackmail a permanent feature of world events. The United Nations would betray the purpose of its founding, and prove irrelevant to the problems of our time. And through its inaction, the United States would resign itself to a future of fear.

That is not the America I know. That is not the America I serve. We refuse to live in fear. (*Applause.*) This nation, in world war and in Cold War, has never permitted the brutal and lawless to set history's course. Now, as before, we will secure our nation, protect our freedom, and help others to find freedom of their own.

Some worry that a change of leadership in Iraq could create instability and make the situation worse. The situation could hardly get worse, for world security and for the people of Iraq. The lives of Iraqi citizens would improve dramatically if Saddam Hussein were no longer in power, just as the lives of Afghanistan's citizens improved after the Taliban. The dictator of Iraq is a student of Stalin, using murder as a tool of terror and control, within his own cabinet, within his own army, and even within his own family.

On Saddam Hussein's orders, opponents have been decapitated, wives and mothers of political opponents have been systematically raped as a method of intimidation, and political prisoners have been forced to watch their own children being tortured.

America believes that all people are entitled to hope and human rights, to the non-negotiable demands of human dignity. People everywhere prefer freedom to slavery; prosperity to squalor; self-government to the rule of terror and torture. America is a friend to the people of Iraq. Our demands are directed only at the regime that enslaves them and threatens us. When these demands are met, the first and greatest benefit will come to Iraqi men, women and children. The oppression of Kurds, Assyrians, Turkomans, Shi'a, Sunnis and others will be lifted. The long captivity of Iraq will end, and an era of new hope will begin.

Iraq is a land rich in culture, resources, and talent. Freed from the weight of oppression, Iraq's people will be able to share in the progress and prosperity of our time. If military action is necessary, the United

States and our allies will help the Iraqi people rebuild their economy, and create the institutions of liberty in a unified Iraq at peace with its neighbors.

Later this week, the United States Congress will vote on this matter. I have asked Congress to authorize the use of America's military, if it proves necessary, to enforce U.N. Security Council demands. Approving this resolution does not mean that military action is imminent or unavoidable. The resolution will tell the United Nations, and all nations, that America speaks with one voice and is determined to make the demands of the civilized world mean something. Congress will also be sending a message to the dictator in Iraq: that his only chance—his only choice is full compliance, and the time remaining for that choice is limited.

Members of Congress are nearing an historic vote. I'm confident they will fully consider the facts, and their duties.

The attacks of September the 11th showed our country that vast oceans no longer protect us from danger. Before that tragic date, we had only hints of al Qaeda's plans and designs. Today in Iraq, we see a threat whose outlines are far more clearly defined, and whose consequences could be far more deadly. Saddam Hussein's actions have put us on notice, and there is no refuge from our responsibilities.

We did not ask for this present challenge, but we accept it. Like other generations of Americans, we will meet the responsibility of defending human liberty against violence and aggression. By our resolve, we will give strength to others. By our courage, we will give hope to others. And by our actions, we will secure the peace, and lead the world to a better day.

May God bless America.

SARAH PALIN—STATEMENT ON CURRENT HEALTH CARE DEBATE

Former Alaska governor and 2008 Republican vice presidential candidate Sarah Palin is an immensely popular (and unpopular) figure in American politics. In early August 2009, during a period in which the nation was sharply debating a health care proposal from the Obama administration, Palin made a controversial comment through Facebook. The posting was widely cited and played a role in the debate. For these reasons, it merits analysis.

Statement on the Current Health Care Debate

Sarah Palin
Friday, August 7, 2009 at 3:53pm

As more Americans delve into the disturbing details of the nationalized health care plan that the current administration is rushing through Congress, our collective jaw is dropping, and we're saying not just no, but hell no!

The Democrats promise that a government health care system will reduce the cost of health care, but as the economist Thomas Sowell has pointed out, government health care will not reduce the cost; it will simply refuse to pay the cost. And who will suffer the most when they ration care? The sick, the elderly, and the disabled, of course. The America I know and love is not one in which my parents or my baby with Down Syndrome will have to stand in front of Obama's "death panel" so his bureaucrats can decide, based on a subjective judgment of their "level of productivity in society," whether they are worthy of health care. Such a system is downright evil.

Health care by definition involves life and death decisions. Human rights and human dignity must be at the center of any health care discussion.

Rep. Michele Bachmann highlighted the Orwellian thinking of the president's health care advisor, Dr. Ezekiel Emanuel, the brother of the White House chief of staff, in a floor speech to the House of Representatives. I commend her for being a voice for the most precious members of our society, our children and our seniors.

We must step up and engage in this most crucial debate. Nationalizing our health care system is a point of no return for government interference in the lives of its citizens. If we go down this path, there will be no turning back. Ronald Reagan once wrote, "Government programs, once launched, never disappear. Actually, a government bureau is the nearest thing to eternal life we'll ever see on this earth." Let's stop and think and make our voices heard before it's too late.

—Sarah Palin

President Barack Obama made health care reform the focus of his advocacy for much of 2009 and 2010. Ultimately, he was successful and Congress passed major health care reform legislation in spring 2010. The most important place where President Obama laid out his health care reform proposal was in a major speech to a Joint Session of Congress. Given the importance of health care reform as a political, medical, and economic issue, it is important to test the case made by the president.

Remarks by the President to a Joint Session of Congress on Health Care

U.S. Capitol, Washington, D.C.

THE PRESIDENT: Madam Speaker, Vice President Biden, members of Congress, and the American people:

When I spoke here last winter, this nation was facing the worst economic crisis since the Great Depression. We were losing an average of 700,000 jobs per month. Credit was frozen. And our financial system was on the verge of collapse.

As any American who is still looking for work or a way to pay their bills will tell you, we are by no means out of the woods. A full and vibrant recovery is still many months away. And I will not let up until those Americans who seek jobs can find them—[applause]—until those businesses that seek capital and credit can thrive; until all responsible homeowners can stay in their homes. That is our ultimate goal. But thanks to the bold and decisive action we've taken since January, I can stand here with confidence and say that we have pulled this economy back from the brink. [Applause]

I want to thank the members of this body for your efforts and your support in these last several months, and especially those who've taken the difficult votes that have put us on a path to recovery. I also want to thank the American people for their patience and resolve during this trying time for our nation.

But we did not come here just to clean up crises. We came here to build a future. [Applause] So tonight, I return to speak to all of you about an issue that is central to that future—and that is the issue of health care.

I am not the first President to take up this cause, but I am determined to be the last. [Applause] It has now been nearly a century since Theodore Roosevelt first called for health care reform. And ever since, nearly every President and Congress, whether Democrat or Republican, has attempted to meet this challenge in some way. A bill for comprehensive health reform was first introduced by John Dingell Sr. in 1943. Sixty-five years later, his son continues to introduce that same bill at the beginning of each session. [Applause]

Our collective failure to meet this challenge—year after year, decade after decade—has led us to the breaking point. Everyone understands the extraordinary hardships that are placed on the uninsured, who live every day just one accident or illness away from bankruptcy. These are not primarily people on welfare. These are middle-class Americans. Some can't get insurance on the job. Others are self-employed, and can't afford it, since buying insurance on your own costs you three times as much as the coverage you get from your employer. Many other Americans who are willing and able to pay are still denied insurance due to previous illnesses or conditions that insurance companies decide are too risky or too expensive to cover.

We are the only democracy—the only advanced democracy on Earth—the only wealthy nation—that allows such hardship for millions of its people. There are now more than 30 million American citizens who cannot get coverage. In just a two-year period, one in every three Americans goes without health care coverage at some point. And every day, 14,000 Americans lose their coverage. In other words, it can happen to anyone.

But the problem that plagues the health care system is not just a problem for the uninsured. Those who do have insurance have never had less security and stability than they do today. More and more Americans worry that if you move, lose your job, or change your job, you'll lose your health insurance too. More and more Americans pay their premiums, only to discover that their insurance company has dropped their coverage when they get sick, or won't pay the full cost of care. It happens every day.

One man from Illinois lost his coverage in the middle of chemotherapy because his insurer found that he hadn't reported gallstones that he didn't even know about. They delayed his treatment, and he died because of it. Another woman from Texas was about to get a double mastectomy when her insurance company canceled her policy because she forgot to declare a case of acne. By the time she had her insurance reinstated, her breast cancer had more than doubled in size. That is heart-breaking, it is wrong, and no one should be treated that way in the United States of America. [*Applause*]

Then there's the problem of rising cost. We spend one and a half times more per person on health care than any other country, but we aren't any healthier for it. This is one of the reasons that insurance premiums have gone up three times faster than wages. It's why so many employers—especially small businesses—are forcing their employees to pay more for insurance, or are dropping their coverage entirely. It's why so many aspiring entrepreneurs cannot afford to open a business in the first place, and why American businesses that compete internationally—like our automakers—are at a huge disadvantage. And it's why those of us with health insurance are also paying a hidden and growing tax for those without it—about $1,000 per year that pays for somebody else's emergency room and charitable care.

Finally, our health care system is placing an unsustainable burden on taxpayers. When health care costs grow at the rate they have, it puts greater pressure on programs like Medicare and Medicaid. If we do nothing to slow these skyrocketing costs, we will eventually be spending more on Medicare and Medicaid than every other government program combined. Put simply, our health care problem is our deficit problem. Nothing else even comes close. Nothing else. [*Applause*]

Now, these are the facts. Nobody disputes them. We know we must reform this system. The question is how.

There are those on the left who believe that the only way to fix the system is through a single-payer system like Canada's—[*applause*]—where we would severely restrict the private insurance market and have the government provide coverage for everybody. On the right, there are those who argue that we should end employer-based systems and leave individuals to buy health insurance on their own.

I've said—I have to say that there are arguments to be made for both these approaches. But either one would represent a radical shift that would disrupt the health care most people currently have. Since health care represents one-sixth of our economy, I believe it makes more sense to build on what works and fix what doesn't, rather than try to build an entirely new system from scratch. [*Applause*] And that is precisely what those of you in Congress have tried to do over the past several months.

During that time, we've seen Washington at its best and at its worst.

We've seen many in this chamber work tirelessly for the better part of this year to offer thoughtful ideas about how to achieve reform. Of the five committees asked to develop bills, four have completed their work, and the Senate Finance Committee announced today that it will move forward next week. That has never happened before. Our overall efforts have been supported by an unprecedented coalition of doctors and nurses; hospitals, seniors' groups, and even drug companies—many of whom opposed reform in the past. And there is agreement in this chamber on about 80 percent of what needs to be done, putting us closer to the goal of reform than we have ever been.

But what we've also seen in these last months is the same partisan spectacle that only hardens the disdain many Americans have towards their own government. Instead of honest debate, we've seen scare tactics. Some have dug into unyielding ideological camps that offer no hope of compromise. Too many have used this as an opportunity to score short-term political points, even if it robs the country of our opportunity to solve a long-term challenge. And out of this blizzard of charges and counter-charges, confusion has reigned.

Well, the time for bickering is over. The time for games has passed. [*Applause*] Now is the season for action. Now is when we must bring the best ideas of both parties together, and show the American people that we can still do what we were sent here to do. Now is the time to deliver on health care. Now is the time to deliver on health care.

The plan I'm announcing tonight would meet three basic goals. It will provide more security and stability to those who have health insurance. It will provide insurance for those who don't. And it will slow the growth of health care costs for our families, our businesses, and our government. [*Applause*] It's a plan that asks everyone to take responsibility for meeting this challenge—not just government, not just insurance companies, but everybody including employers and individuals. And it's a plan that incorporates ideas from senators and congressmen, from Democrats and Republicans—and yes, from some of my opponents in both the primary and general election.

Here are the details that every American needs to know about this plan. First, if you are among the hundreds of millions of Americans who already have health insurance through your job, or Medicare, or Medicaid, or the VA, nothing in this plan will require you or your employer to change the coverage or the doctor you have. [*Applause*] Let me repeat this:

Nothing in our plan requires you to change what you have.

What this plan will do is make the insurance you have work better for you. Under this plan, it will be against the law for insurance companies to deny you coverage because of a preexisting condition. [Applause] As soon as I sign this bill, it will be against the law for insurance companies to drop your coverage when you get sick or water it down when you need it the most. [Applause] They will no longer be able to place some arbitrary cap on the amount of coverage you can receive in a given year or in a lifetime. [Applause] We will place a limit on how much you can be charged for out-of-pocket expenses, because in the United States of America, no one should go broke because they get sick. [Applause] And insurance companies will be required to cover, with no extra charge, routine checkups and preventive care, like mammograms and colonoscopies—[applause]—because there's no reason we shouldn't be catching diseases like breast cancer and colon cancer before they get worse. That makes sense, it saves money, and it saves lives. [Applause]

Now, that's what Americans who have health insurance can expect from this plan—more security and more stability.

Now, if you're one of the tens of millions of Americans who don't currently have health insurance, the second part of this plan will finally offer you quality, affordable choices. [Applause] If you lose your job or you change your job, you'll be able to get coverage. If you strike out on your own and start a small business, you'll be able to get coverage. We'll do this by creating a new insurance exchange—a marketplace where individuals and small businesses will be able to shop for health insurance at competitive prices. Insurance companies will have an incentive to participate in this exchange because it lets them compete for millions of new customers. As one big group, these customers will have greater leverage to bargain with the insurance companies for better prices and quality coverage. This is how large companies and government employees get affordable insurance. It's how everyone in this Congress gets affordable insurance. And it's time to give every American the same opportunity that we give ourselves. [Applause]

Now, for those individuals and small businesses who still can't afford the lower-priced insurance available in the exchange, we'll provide tax credits, the size of which will be based on your need. And all insurance companies that want access to this new marketplace will have to abide by the consumer protections I already mentioned. This exchange will take effect in four years, which will give us time to do it right. In the meantime, for those Americans who can't get insurance today because they have preexisting medical conditions, we will immediately offer low-cost coverage that will protect you against financial ruin if you become seriously ill. [Applause] This was a good idea when Senator John McCain proposed it in the campaign, it's a good idea now, and we should all embrace it. [Applause]

Now, even if we provide these affordable options, there may be those—especially the young and the healthy—who still want to take the risk and go without coverage. There may still be companies that refuse to do right by their workers by giving them coverage. The problem is, such irresponsible behavior costs all the rest of us money. If there are affordable options and people still don't sign up for health insurance, it means we pay for these people's expensive emergency room visits. If some businesses don't provide workers health care, it forces the rest of us to pick up the tab when their workers get sick, and gives those businesses an unfair advantage over their competitors. And unless everybody does their part, many of the insurance reforms we seek—especially requiring insurance companies to cover preexisting conditions—just can't be achieved.

And that's why under my plan, individuals will be required to carry basic health insurance—just as most states require you to carry auto insurance. [Applause] Likewise—likewise, businesses will be required to either offer their workers health care, or chip in to help cover the cost of their workers. There will be a hardship waiver for those individuals who still can't afford coverage, and 95 percent of all small businesses, because of their size and narrow profit margin, would be exempt from these requirements. [Applause] But we can't have large businesses and individuals who can afford coverage game the system by avoiding responsibility to themselves or their employees. Improving our health care system only works if everybody does their part.

And while there remain some significant details to be ironed out, I believe—[laughter]—I believe a broad consensus exists for the aspects of the plan I just outlined: consumer protections for those with insurance, an exchange that allows individuals and small businesses to purchase affordable coverage, and a requirement that people who can afford insurance get insurance.

And I have no doubt that these reforms would greatly benefit Americans from all walks of life, as well as the economy as a whole. Still, given all the misinformation that's been spread over the past few months, I realize—[applause]—I realize that many Americans have grown nervous about reform. So tonight I want to address some of the key controversies that are still out there.

Some of people's concerns have grown out of bogus claims spread by those whose only agenda is to kill reform at any cost. The best example is the claim made not just by radio and cable talk show hosts, but by prominent politicians, that we plan to set up panels of bureaucrats with the power to kill off senior citizens. Now, such a charge would be laughable if it weren't so cynical and irresponsible. It is a lie, plain and simple. [*Applause*]

There are also those who claim that our reform efforts would insure illegal immigrants. This, too, is false. The reforms—the reforms I'm proposing would not apply to those who are here illegally.

AUDIENCE MEMBER: You lie! [*Boos*]

THE PRESIDENT: It's not true. And one more misunderstanding I want to clear up—under our plan, no federal dollars will be used to fund abortions, and federal conscience laws will remain in place. [*Applause*]

Now, my health care proposal has also been attacked by some who oppose reform as a "government takeover" of the entire health care system. As proof, critics point to a provision in our plan that allows the uninsured and small businesses to choose a publicly sponsored insurance option, administered by the government just like Medicaid or Medicare. [*Applause*]

So let me set the record straight here. My guiding principle is, and always has been, that consumers do better when there is choice and competition. That's how the market works. [*Applause*] Unfortunately, in 34 states, 75 percent of the insurance market is controlled by five or fewer companies. In Alabama, almost 90 percent is controlled by just one company. And without competition, the price of insurance goes up and quality goes down. And it makes it easier for insurance companies to treat their customers badly—by cherry-picking the healthiest individuals and trying to drop the sickest, by overcharging small businesses who have no leverage, and by jacking up rates.

Insurance executives don't do this because they're bad people; they do it because it's profitable. As one former insurance executive testified before Congress, insurance companies are not only encouraged to find reasons to drop the seriously ill, they are rewarded for it. All of this is in service of meeting what this former executive called "Wall Street's relentless profit expectations."

Now, I have no interest in putting insurance companies out of business. They provide a legitimate service, and employ a lot of our friends and neighbors. I just want to hold them accountable. [*Applause*] And the insurance reforms that I've already mentioned would do just that. But an additional step we can take to keep insurance companies honest is by making a not-for-profit public option available in the insurance exchange. [*Applause*] Now, let me be clear. Let me be clear. It would only be an option for those who don't have insurance. No one would be forced to choose it, and it would not impact those of you who already have insurance. In fact, based on Congressional Budget Office estimates, we believe that less than five percent of Americans would sign up.

Despite all this, the insurance companies and their allies don't like this idea. They argue that these private companies can't fairly compete with the government. And they'd be right if taxpayers were subsidizing this public insurance option. But they won't be. I've insisted that like any private insurance company, the public insurance option would have to be self-sufficient and rely on the premiums it collects. But by avoiding some of the overhead that gets eaten up at private companies by profits and excessive administrative costs and executive salaries, it could provide a good deal for consumers, and would also keep pressure on private insurers to keep their policies affordable and treat their customers better, the same way public colleges and universities provide additional choice and competition to students without in any way inhibiting a vibrant system of private colleges and universities. [*Applause*]

Now, it is—it's worth noting that a strong majority of Americans still favor a public insurance option of the sort I've proposed tonight. But its impact shouldn't be exaggerated—by the left or the right or the media. It is only one part of my plan, and shouldn't be used as a handy excuse for the usual Washington ideological battles. To my progressive friends, I would remind you that for decades, the driving idea behind reform has been to end insurance company abuses and make coverage available for those without it. [*Applause*] The public option—the public option is only a means to that end—and we should remain open to other ideas that accomplish our ultimate goal. And to my Republican friends, I say that rather than making wild claims about a government takeover of health care, we should work together to address any legitimate concerns you may have. [*Applause*]

For example—for example, some have suggested that the public option go into effect only in those markets where insurance companies are not providing affordable policies. Others have proposed a co-op or another nonprofit entity to administer the plan. These are all constructive ideas worth exploring. But

I will not back down on the basic principle that if Americans can't find affordable coverage, we will provide you with a choice. [*Applause*] And I will make sure that no government bureaucrat or insurance company bureaucrat gets between you and the care that you need. [*Applause*]

Finally, let me discuss an issue that is a great concern to me, to members of this chamber, and to the public—and that's how we pay for this plan.

And here's what you need to know. First, I will not sign a plan that adds one dime to our deficits—either now or in the future. [*Applause*] I will not sign it if it adds one dime to the deficit, now or in the future, period. And to prove that I'm serious, there will be a provision in this plan that requires us to come forward with more spending cuts if the savings we promised don't materialize. [*Applause*] Now, part of the reason I faced a trillion-dollar deficit when I walked in the door of the White House is because too many initiatives over the last decade were not paid for—from the Iraq war to tax breaks for the wealthy. [*Applause*] I will not make that same mistake with health care.

Second, we've estimated that most of this plan can be paid for by finding savings within the existing health care system, a system that is currently full of waste and abuse. Right now, too much of the hard-earned savings and tax dollars we spend on health care don't make us any healthier. That's not my judgment—it's the judgment of medical professionals across this country. And this is also true when it comes to Medicare and Medicaid.

In fact, I want to speak directly to seniors for a moment, because Medicare is another issue that's been subjected to demagoguery and distortion during the course of this debate.

More than four decades ago, this nation stood up for the principle that after a lifetime of hard work, our seniors should not be left to struggle with a pile of medical bills in their later years. That's how Medicare was born. And it remains a sacred trust that must be passed down from one generation to the next. [*Applause*] And that is why not a dollar of the Medicare trust fund will be used to pay for this plan. [*Applause*]

The only thing this plan would eliminate is the hundreds of billions of dollars in waste and fraud, as well as unwarranted subsidies in Medicare that go to insurance companies—subsidies that do everything to pad their profits but don't improve the care of seniors. And we will also create an independent commission of doctors and medical experts charged with identifying more waste in the years ahead. [*Applause*]

Now, these steps will ensure that you—America's seniors—get the benefits you've been promised. They will ensure that Medicare is there for future generations. And we can use some of the savings to fill the gap in coverage that forces too many seniors to pay thousands of dollars a year out of their own pockets for prescription drugs. [*Applause*] That's what this plan will do for you. So don't pay attention to those scary stories about how your benefits will be cut, especially since some of the same folks who are spreading these tall tales have fought against Medicare in the past and just this year supported a budget that would essentially have turned Medicare into a privatized voucher program. That will not happen on my watch. I will protect Medicare. [*Applause*]

Now, because Medicare is such a big part of the health care system, making the program more efficient can help usher in changes in the way we deliver health care that can reduce costs for everybody. We have long known that some places—like the Intermountain Healthcare in Utah or the Geisinger Health System in rural Pennsylvania—offer high-quality care at costs below average. So the commission can help encourage the adoption of these commonsense best practices by doctors and medical professionals throughout the system—everything from reducing hospital infection rates to encouraging better coordination between teams of doctors.

Reducing the waste and inefficiency in Medicare and Medicaid will pay for most of this plan. [*Applause*] Now, much of the rest would be paid for with revenues from the very same drug and insurance companies that stand to benefit from tens of millions of new customers. And this reform will charge insurance companies a fee for their most expensive policies, which will encourage them to provide greater value for the money—an idea which has the support of Democratic and Republican experts. And according to these same experts, this modest change could help hold down the cost of health care for all of us in the long run.

Now, finally, many in this chamber—particularly on the Republican side of the aisle—have long insisted that reforming our medical malpractice laws can help bring down the cost of health care. [*Applause*] Now—there you go. There you go. Now, I don't believe malpractice reform is a silver bullet, but I've talked to enough doctors to know that defensive medicine may be contributing to unnecessary costs. [*Applause*] So I'm proposing that we move forward on a range of ideas about how to put patient safety first and let doctors focus on practicing medicine. [*Applause*] I know that the Bush administration considered authorizing demonstration projects in individual states to test these ideas. I think it's a good idea, and I'm directing my Secretary of Health and Human Services to move forward on this initiative today. [*Applause*]

Now, add it all up, and the plan I'm proposing will cost around $900 billion over 10 years—less than we have spent on the Iraq and Afghanistan wars, and less than the tax cuts for the wealthiest few Americans that Congress passed at the beginning of the previous administration. [*Applause*] Now, most of these costs will be paid for with money already being spent—but spent badly—in the existing health care system. The plan will not add to our deficit. The middle class will realize greater security, not higher taxes. And if we are able to slow the growth of health care costs by just one-tenth of one percent each year—one-tenth of one percent—it will actually reduce the deficit by four trillion over the long term.

Now, this is the plan I'm proposing. It's a plan that incorporates ideas from many of the people in this room tonight—Democrats and Republicans. And I will continue to seek common ground in the weeks ahead. If you come to me with a serious set of proposals, I will be there to listen. My door is always open.

But know this: I will not waste time with those who have made the calculation that it's better politics to kill this plan than to improve it. [*Applause*] I won't stand by while the special interests use the same old tactics to keep things exactly the way they are. If you misrepresent what's in this plan, we will call you out. [*Applause*] And I will not—and I will not accept the status quo as a solution. Not this time. Not now.

Everyone in this room knows what will happen if we do nothing. Our deficit will grow. More families will go bankrupt. More businesses will close. More Americans will lose their coverage when they are sick and need it the most. And more will die as a result. We know these things to be true.

That is why we cannot fail. Because there are too many Americans counting on us to succeed—the ones who suffer silently, and the ones who shared their stories with us at town halls, in e-mails, and in letters.

I received one of those letters a few days ago. It was from our beloved friend and colleague, Ted Kennedy. He had written it back in May, shortly after he was told that his illness was terminal. He asked that it be delivered upon his death.

In it, he spoke about what a happy time his last months were, thanks to the love and support of family and friends, his wife, Vicki, his amazing children, who are all here tonight. And he expressed confidence that this would be the year that health care reform—"that great unfinished business of our society," he called it—would finally pass. He repeated the truth that health care is decisive for our future prosperity, but he also reminded me that "it concerns more than material things." "What we face," he wrote, "is above all a moral issue; at stake are not just the details of policy, but fundamental principles of social justice and the character of our country."

I've thought about that phrase quite a bit in recent days—the character of our country. One of the unique and wonderful things about America has always been our self-reliance, our rugged individualism, our fierce defense of freedom and our healthy skepticism of government. And figuring out the appropriate size and role of government has always been a source of rigorous and, yes, sometimes angry debate. That's our history.

For some of Ted Kennedy's critics, his brand of liberalism represented an affront to American liberty. In their minds, his passion for universal health care was nothing more than a passion for big government.

But those of us who knew Teddy and worked with him here—people of both parties—know that what drove him was something more. His friend Orrin Hatch—he knows that. They worked together to provide children with health insurance. His friend John McCain knows that. They worked together on a Patient's Bill of Rights. His friend Chuck Grassley knows that. They worked together to provide health care to children with disabilities.

On issues like these, Ted Kennedy's passion was born not of some rigid ideology, but of his own experience. It was the experience of having two children stricken with cancer. He never forgot the sheer terror and helplessness that any parent feels when a child is badly sick. And he was able to imagine what it must be like for those without insurance, what it would be like to have to say to a wife or a child or an aging parent, there is something that could make you better, but I just can't afford it.

That large-heartedness—that concern and regard for the plight of others—is not a partisan feeling. It's not a Republican or a Democratic feeling. It, too, is part of the American character—our ability to stand in other people's shoes; a recognition that we are all in this together, and when fortune turns against one of us, others are there to lend a helping hand; a belief that in this country, hard work and responsibility should be rewarded by some measure of security and fair play; and an acknowledgment that sometimes government has to step in to help deliver on that promise.

This has always been the history of our progress. In 1935, when over half of our seniors could not support themselves and millions had seen their savings wiped away, there were those who argued that Social Security would lead to socialism, but the men and women of Congress stood fast, and we are all the better for it. In 1965, when some argued that Medicare represented a government takeover of health care, members of Congress—Democrats and Republicans—did not back down. They joined together so that all of us could enter our golden years with some basic peace of mind.

You see, our predecessors understood that government could not, and should not, solve every problem. They understood that there are instances when the gains in security from government action are not worth the added constraints on our freedom. But they also understood that the danger of too much government is matched by the perils of too little; that without the leavening hand of wise policy, markets can crash, monopolies can stifle competition, the vulnerable can be exploited. And they knew that when any government measure, no matter how carefully crafted or beneficial, is subject to scorn; when any efforts to help people in need are attacked as un-American; when facts and reason are thrown overboard and only timidity passes for wisdom, and we can no longer even engage in a civil conversation with each other over the things that truly matter—that at that point we don't merely lose our capacity to solve big challenges. We lose something essential about ourselves.

That was true then. It remains true today. I understand how difficult this health care debate has been. I know that many in this country are deeply skeptical that government is looking out for them. I understand that the politically safe move would be to kick the can further down the road—to defer reform one more year, or one more election, or one more term.

But that is not what the moment calls for. That's not what we came here to do. We did not come to fear the future. We came here to shape it. I still believe we can act even when it's hard. [*Applause*] I still believe—I still believe that we can act when it's hard. I still believe we can replace acrimony with civility, and gridlock with progress. I still believe we can do great things, and that here and now we will meet history's test.

Because that's who we are. That is our calling. That is our character. Thank you, God bless you, and may God bless the United States of America. [*Applause*]

END 9:03 P.M. EDT

APPENDIX ONE

OUTLINE OF
RHETORICAL AND CONTEXTUAL
ANALYSIS CATEGORIES

Outline of Rhetorical and Contextual Analysis Categories

I. Goals

    A. Themes

    B. Requested Actions

II. Organization

    A. Introduction

    B. Conclusion

    C. Main Body—identify the organizational pattern

III. Role of Rhetor

IV. Linguistic Tone

V. Implied Audience

VI. Strategy Categories—use all that are relevant and identify sub-strategies as specifically as possible.

    A. Rational Argument

    B. Narrative

    C. Aesthetic

    D. Values, Needs and Symbols

    E. Credibility

    F. Confrontation

VII. Rhetorical Barriers and Advantages

    Audience—beliefs, attitudes, values, attention

    Situational—culture, complexity, specific events

    Occasion—appropriateness, prior rhetoric

    Reputation of the speaker

VIII. On-Balance evaluation—are the strategies well designed to overcome the barriers in order to achieve the purpose?

Outline of Rhetorical and Contextual Analysis Categories

I. Goals

    A. Themes

    B. Requested Actions

II. Organization

    A. Introduction

    B. Conclusion

    C. Main Body—identify the organizational pattern

III. Role of Rhetor

IV. Linguistic Tone

V. Implied Audience

VI. Strategy Categories—use all that are relevant and identify sub-strategies as specifically as possible.

    A. Rational Argument

    B. Narrative

    C. Aesthetic

    D. Values, Needs and Symbols

    E. Credibility

    F. Confrontation

VII. Rhetorical Barriers and Advantages

    Audience—beliefs, attitudes, values, attention

    Situational—culture, complexity, specific events

    Occasion—appropriateness, prior rhetoric

    Reputation of the speaker

VIII. On-Balance evaluation—are the strategies well designed to overcome the barriers in order to achieve the purpose?

Outline of Rhetorical and Contextual Analysis Categories

I. Goals

    A. Themes

    B. Requested Actions

II. Organization

    A. Introduction

    B. Conclusion

    C. Main Body—identify the organizational pattern

III. Role of Rhetor

IV. Linguistic Tone

V. Implied Audience

VI. Strategy Categories—use all that are relevant and identify sub-strategies as specifically as possible.

    A. Rational Argument

    B. Narrative

    C. Aesthetic

    D. Values, Needs and Symbols

    E. Credibility

    F. Confrontation

VII. Rhetorical Barriers and Advantages

    Audience—beliefs, attitudes, values, attention

    Situational—culture, complexity, specific events

    Occasion—appropriateness, prior rhetoric

    Reputation of the speaker

VIII. On-Balance evaluation—are the strategies well designed to overcome the barriers in order to achieve the purpose?

Outline of Rhetorical and Contextual Analysis Categories

I. Goals

    A. Themes

    B. Requested Actions

II. Organization

    A. Introduction

    B. Conclusion

    C. Main Body—identify the organizational pattern

III. Role of Rhetor

IV. Linguistic Tone

V. Implied Audience

VI. Strategy Categories—use all that are relevant and identify sub-strategies as specifically as possible.

    A. Rational Argument

    B. Narrative

    C. Aesthetic

    D. Values, Needs and Symbols

    E. Credibility

    F. Confrontation

VII. Rhetorical Barriers and Advantages

    Audience—beliefs, attitudes, values, attention

    Situational—culture, complexity, specific events

    Occasion—appropriateness, prior rhetoric

    Reputation of the speaker

VIII. On-Balance evaluation—are the strategies well designed to overcome the barriers in order to achieve the purpose?

Outline of Rhetorical and Contextual Analysis Categories

I. Goals

    A. Themes

    B. Requested Actions

II. Organization

    A. Introduction

    B. Conclusion

    C. Main Body—identify the organizational pattern

III. Role of Rhetor

IV. Linguistic Tone

V. Implied Audience

VI. Strategy Categories—use all that are relevant and identify sub-strategies as specifically as possible.

    A. Rational Argument

    B. Narrative

    C. Aesthetic

    D. Values, Needs and Symbols

    E. Credibility

    F. Confrontation

VII. Rhetorical Barriers and Advantages

    Audience—beliefs, attitudes, values, attention

    Situational—culture, complexity, specific events

    Occasion—appropriateness, prior rhetoric

    Reputation of the speaker

VIII. On-Balance evaluation—are the strategies well designed to overcome the barriers in order to achieve the purpose?

Outline of Rhetorical and Contextual Analysis Categories

I. Goals

    A. Themes

    B. Requested Actions

II. Organization

    A. Introduction

    B. Conclusion

    C. Main Body—identify the organizational pattern

III. Role of Rhetor

IV. Linguistic Tone

V. Implied Audience

VI. Strategy Categories—use all that are relevant and identify sub-strategies as specifically as possible.

    A. Rational Argument

    B. Narrative

    C. Aesthetic

    D. Values, Needs and Symbols

    E. Credibility

    F. Confrontation

VII. Rhetorical Barriers and Advantages

    Audience—beliefs, attitudes, values, attention

    Situational—culture, complexity, specific events

    Occasion—appropriateness, prior rhetoric

    Reputation of the speaker

VIII. On-Balance evaluation—are the strategies well designed to overcome the barriers in order to achieve the purpose?

Outline of Rhetorical and Contextual Analysis Categories

I. Goals

    A. Themes

    B. Requested Actions

II. Organization

    A. Introduction

    B. Conclusion

    C. Main Body—identify the organizational pattern

III. Role of Rhetor

IV. Linguistic Tone

V. Implied Audience

VI. Strategy Categories—use all that are relevant and identify sub-strategies as specifically as possible.

    A. Rational Argument

    B. Narrative

    C. Aesthetic

    D. Values, Needs and Symbols

    E. Credibility

    F. Confrontation

VII. Rhetorical Barriers and Advantages

    Audience—beliefs, attitudes, values, attention

    Situational—culture, complexity, specific events

    Occasion—appropriateness, prior rhetoric

    Reputation of the speaker

VIII. On-Balance evaluation—are the strategies well designed to overcome the barriers in order to achieve the purpose?

Outline of Rhetorical and Contextual Analysis Categories

I. Goals

    A. Themes

    B. Requested Actions

II. Organization

    A. Introduction

    B. Conclusion

    C. Main Body—identify the organizational pattern

III. Role of Rhetor

IV. Linguistic Tone

V. Implied Audience

VI. Strategy Categories—use all that are relevant and identify sub-strategies as specifically as possible.

    A. Rational Argument

    B. Narrative

    C. Aesthetic

    D. Values, Needs and Symbols

    E. Credibility

    F. Confrontation

VII. Rhetorical Barriers and Advantages

    Audience—beliefs, attitudes, values, attention

    Situational—culture, complexity, specific events

    Occasion—appropriateness, prior rhetoric

    Reputation of the speaker

VIII. On-Balance evaluation—are the strategies well designed to overcome the barriers in order to achieve the purpose?

Outline of Rhetorical and Contextual Analysis Categories

I. Goals

    A. Themes

    B. Requested Actions

II. Organization

    A. Introduction

    B. Conclusion

    C. Main Body—identify the organizational pattern

III. Role of Rhetor

IV. Linguistic Tone

V. Implied Audience

VI. Strategy Categories—use all that are relevant and identify sub-strategies as specifically as possible.

    A. Rational Argument

    B. Narrative

    C. Aesthetic

    D. Values, Needs and Symbols

    E. Credibility

    F. Confrontation

VII. Rhetorical Barriers and Advantages

    Audience—beliefs, attitudes, values, attention

    Situational—culture, complexity, specific events

    Occasion—appropriateness, prior rhetoric

    Reputation of the speaker

VIII. On-Balance evaluation—are the strategies well designed to overcome the barriers in order to achieve the purpose?

Outline of Rhetorical and Contextual Analysis Categories

I. Goals

    A. Themes

    B. Requested Actions

II. Organization

    A. Introduction

    B. Conclusion

    C. Main Body—identify the organizational pattern

III. Role of Rhetor

IV. Linguistic Tone

V. Implied Audience

VI. Strategy Categories—use all that are relevant and identify sub-strategies as specifically as possible.

    A. Rational Argument

    B. Narrative

    C. Aesthetic

    D. Values, Needs and Symbols

    E. Credibility

    F. Confrontation

VII. Rhetorical Barriers and Advantages

    Audience—beliefs, attitudes, values, attention

    Situational—culture, complexity, specific events

    Occasion—appropriateness, prior rhetoric

    Reputation of the speaker

VIII. On-Balance evaluation—are the strategies well designed to overcome the barriers in order to achieve the purpose?

Outline of Rhetorical and Contextual Analysis Categories

I. Goals

    A. Themes

    B. Requested Actions

II. Organization

    A. Introduction

    B. Conclusion

    C. Main Body—identify the organizational pattern

III. Role of Rhetor

IV. Linguistic Tone

V. Implied Audience

VI. Strategy Categories—use all that are relevant and identify sub-strategies as specifically as possible.

    A. Rational Argument

    B. Narrative

    C. Aesthetic

    D. Values, Needs and Symbols

    E. Credibility

    F. Confrontation

VII. Rhetorical Barriers and Advantages

    Audience—beliefs, attitudes, values, attention

    Situational—culture, complexity, specific events

    Occasion—appropriateness, prior rhetoric

    Reputation of the speaker

VIII. On-Balance evaluation—are the strategies well designed to overcome the barriers in order to achieve the purpose?

Outline of Rhetorical and Contextual Analysis Categories

I. Goals

    A. Themes

    B. Requested Actions

II. Organization

    A. Introduction

    B. Conclusion

    C. Main Body—identify the organizational pattern

III. Role of Rhetor

IV. Linguistic Tone

V. Implied Audience

VI. Strategy Categories—use all that are relevant and identify sub-strategies as specifically as possible.

    A. Rational Argument

    B. Narrative

    C. Aesthetic

    D. Values, Needs and Symbols

    E. Credibility

    F. Confrontation

VII. Rhetorical Barriers and Advantages

    Audience—beliefs, attitudes, values, attention

    Situational—culture, complexity, specific events

    Occasion—appropriateness, prior rhetoric

    Reputation of the speaker

VIII. On-Balance evaluation—are the strategies well designed to overcome the barriers in order to achieve the purpose?

Outline of Rhetorical and Contextual Analysis Categories

I. Goals

    A. Themes

    B. Requested Actions

II. Organization

    A. Introduction

    B. Conclusion

    C. Main Body—identify the organizational pattern

III. Role of Rhetor

IV. Linguistic Tone

V. Implied Audience

VI. Strategy Categories—use all that are relevant and identify sub-strategies as specifically as possible.

   A. Rational Argument

   B. Narrative

   C. Aesthetic

   D. Values, Needs and Symbols

   E. Credibility

   F. Confrontation

VII. Rhetorical Barriers and Advantages

   Audience—beliefs, attitudes, values, attention

   Situational—culture, complexity, specific events

   Occasion—appropriateness, prior rhetoric

   Reputation of the speaker

VIII. On-Balance evaluation—are the strategies well designed to overcome the barriers in order to achieve the purpose?

Outline of Rhetorical and Contextual Analysis Categories

I. Goals

    A. Themes

    B. Requested Actions

II. Organization

    A. Introduction

    B. Conclusion

    C. Main Body—identify the organizational pattern

III. Role of Rhetor

IV. Linguistic Tone

V. Implied Audience

VI. Strategy Categories—use all that are relevant and identify sub-strategies as specifically as possible.

    A. Rational Argument

    B. Narrative

    C. Aesthetic

    D. Values, Needs and Symbols

    E. Credibility

    F. Confrontation

VII. Rhetorical Barriers and Advantages

    Audience—beliefs, attitudes, values, attention

    Situational—culture, complexity, specific events

    Occasion—appropriateness, prior rhetoric

    Reputation of the speaker

VIII. On-Balance evaluation—are the strategies well designed to overcome the barriers in order to achieve the purpose?

Outline of Rhetorical and Contextual Analysis Categories

I. Goals

    A. Themes

    B. Requested Actions

II. Organization

    A. Introduction

    B. Conclusion

    C. Main Body—identify the organizational pattern

III. Role of Rhetor

IV. Linguistic Tone

V. Implied Audience

VI. Strategy Categories—use all that are relevant and identify sub-strategies as specifically as possible.

    A. Rational Argument

    B. Narrative

    C. Aesthetic

    D. Values, Needs and Symbols

    E. Credibility

    F. Confrontation

VII. Rhetorical Barriers and Advantages

    Audience—beliefs, attitudes, values, attention

    Situational—culture, complexity, specific events

    Occasion—appropriateness, prior rhetoric

    Reputation of the speaker

VIII. On-Balance evaluation—are the strategies well designed to overcome the barriers in order to achieve the purpose?

Outline of Rhetorical and Contextual Analysis Categories

I. Goals

    A. Themes

    B. Requested Actions

II. Organization

    A. Introduction

    B. Conclusion

    C. Main Body—identify the organizational pattern

III. Role of Rhetor

IV. Linguistic Tone

V. Implied Audience

VI. Strategy Categories—use all that are relevant and identify sub-strategies as specifically as possible.

    A. Rational Argument

    B. Narrative

    C. Aesthetic

    D. Values, Needs and Symbols

    E. Credibility

    F. Confrontation

VII. Rhetorical Barriers and Advantages

    Audience—beliefs, attitudes, values, attention

    Situational—culture, complexity, specific events

    Occasion—appropriateness, prior rhetoric

    Reputation of the speaker

VIII. On-Balance evaluation—are the strategies well designed to overcome the barriers in order to achieve the purpose?

Outline of Rhetorical and Contextual Analysis Categories

I. Goals

    A. Themes

    B. Requested Actions

II. Organization

    A. Introduction

    B. Conclusion

    C. Main Body—identify the organizational pattern

III. Role of Rhetor

IV. Linguistic Tone

V. Implied Audience

VI. Strategy Categories—use all that are relevant and identify sub-strategies as specifically as possible.

    A. Rational Argument

    B. Narrative

    C. Aesthetic

    D. Values, Needs and Symbols

    E. Credibility

    F. Confrontation

VII. Rhetorical Barriers and Advantages

    Audience—beliefs, attitudes, values, attention

    Situational—culture, complexity, specific events

    Occasion—appropriateness, prior rhetoric

    Reputation of the speaker

VIII. On-Balance evaluation—are the strategies well designed to overcome the barriers in order to achieve the purpose?

Outline of Rhetorical and Contextual Analysis Categories

I. Goals

    A. Themes

    B. Requested Actions

II. Organization

    A. Introduction

    B. Conclusion

    C. Main Body—identify the organizational pattern

III. Role of Rhetor

IV. Linguistic Tone

V. Implied Audience

VI. Strategy Categories—use all that are relevant and identify sub-strategies as specifically as possible.

    A. Rational Argument

    B. Narrative

    C. Aesthetic

    D. Values, Needs and Symbols

    E. Credibility

    F. Confrontation

VII. Rhetorical Barriers and Advantages

    Audience—beliefs, attitudes, values, attention

    Situational—culture, complexity, specific events

    Occasion—appropriateness, prior rhetoric

    Reputation of the speaker

VIII. On-Balance evaluation—are the strategies well designed to overcome the barriers in order to achieve the purpose?

Outline of Rhetorical and Contextual Analysis Categories

I. Goals

    A. Themes

    B. Requested Actions

II. Organization

    A. Introduction

    B. Conclusion

    C. Main Body—identify the organizational pattern

III. Role of Rhetor

IV. Linguistic Tone

V. Implied Audience

VI. Strategy Categories—use all that are relevant and identify sub-strategies as specifically as possible.

    A. Rational Argument

    B. Narrative

    C. Aesthetic

    D. Values, Needs and Symbols

    E. Credibility

    F. Confrontation

VII. Rhetorical Barriers and Advantages

    Audience—beliefs, attitudes, values, attention

    Situational—culture, complexity, specific events

    Occasion—appropriateness, prior rhetoric

    Reputation of the speaker

VIII. On-Balance evaluation—are the strategies well designed to overcome the barriers in order to achieve the purpose?

Outline of Rhetorical and Contextual Analysis Categories

I. Goals

   A. Themes

   B. Requested Actions

II. Organization

   A. Introduction

   B. Conclusion

   C. Main Body—identify the organizational pattern

III. Role of Rhetor

IV. Linguistic Tone

V. Implied Audience

VI. Strategy Categories—use all that are relevant and identify sub-strategies as specifically as possible.

    A. Rational Argument

    B. Narrative

    C. Aesthetic

    D. Values, Needs and Symbols

    E. Credibility

    F. Confrontation

VII. Rhetorical Barriers and Advantages

    Audience—beliefs, attitudes, values, attention

    Situational—culture, complexity, specific events

    Occasion—appropriateness, prior rhetoric

    Reputation of the speaker

VIII. On-Balance evaluation—are the strategies well designed to overcome the barriers in order to achieve the purpose?

Outline of Rhetorical and Contextual Analysis Categories

I. Goals

    A. Themes

    B. Requested Actions

II. Organization

    A. Introduction

    B. Conclusion

    C. Main Body—identify the organizational pattern

III. Role of Rhetor

IV. Linguistic Tone

V. Implied Audience

VI. Strategy Categories—use all that are relevant and identify sub-strategies as specifically as possible.

    A. Rational Argument

    B. Narrative

    C. Aesthetic

    D. Values, Needs and Symbols

    E. Credibility

    F. Confrontation

VII. Rhetorical Barriers and Advantages

    Audience—beliefs, attitudes, values, attention

    Situational—culture, complexity, specific events

    Occasion—appropriateness, prior rhetoric

    Reputation of the speaker

VIII. On-Balance evaluation—are the strategies well designed to overcome the barriers in order to achieve the purpose?

Outline of Rhetorical and Contextual Analysis Categories

I. Goals

    A. Themes

    B. Requested Actions

II. Organization

    A. Introduction

    B. Conclusion

    C. Main Body—identify the organizational pattern

III. Role of Rhetor

IV. Linguistic Tone

V. Implied Audience

VI. Strategy Categories—use all that are relevant and identify sub-strategies as specifically as possible.

    A. Rational Argument

    B. Narrative

    C. Aesthetic

    D. Values, Needs and Symbols

    E. Credibility

    F. Confrontation

VII. Rhetorical Barriers and Advantages

    Audience—beliefs, attitudes, values, attention

    Situational—culture, complexity, specific events

    Occasion—appropriateness, prior rhetoric

    Reputation of the speaker

VIII. On-Balance evaluation—are the strategies well designed to overcome the barriers in order to achieve the purpose?

Outline of Rhetorical and Contextual Analysis Categories

I. Goals

    A. Themes

    B. Requested Actions

II. Organization

    A. Introduction

    B. Conclusion

    C. Main Body—identify the organizational pattern

III. Role of Rhetor

IV. Linguistic Tone

V. Implied Audience

VI. Strategy Categories—use all that are relevant and identify sub-strategies as specifically as possible.

   A. Rational Argument

   B. Narrative

   C. Aesthetic

   D. Values, Needs and Symbols

   E. Credibility

   F. Confrontation

VII. Rhetorical Barriers and Advantages

   Audience—beliefs, attitudes, values, attention

   Situational—culture, complexity, specific events

   Occasion—appropriateness, prior rhetoric

   Reputation of the speaker

VIII. On-Balance evaluation—are the strategies well designed to overcome the barriers in order to achieve the purpose?

Outline of Rhetorical and Contextual Analysis Categories

I. Goals

    A. Themes

    B. Requested Actions

II. Organization

    A. Introduction

    B. Conclusion

    C. Main Body—identify the organizational pattern

III. Role of Rhetor

IV. Linguistic Tone

V. Implied Audience

VI. Strategy Categories—use all that are relevant and identify sub-strategies as specifically as possible.

    A. Rational Argument

    B. Narrative

    C. Aesthetic

    D. Values, Needs and Symbols

    E. Credibility

    F. Confrontation

VII. Rhetorical Barriers and Advantages

    Audience—beliefs, attitudes, values, attention

    Situational—culture, complexity, specific events

    Occasion—appropriateness, prior rhetoric

    Reputation of the speaker

VIII. On-Balance evaluation—are the strategies well designed to overcome the barriers in order to achieve the purpose?

Outline of Rhetorical and Contextual Analysis Categories

I. Goals

    A. Themes

    B. Requested Actions

II. Organization

    A. Introduction

    B. Conclusion

    C. Main Body—identify the organizational pattern

III. Role of Rhetor

IV. Linguistic Tone

V. Implied Audience

VI. Strategy Categories—use all that are relevant and identify sub-strategies as specifically as possible.

    A. Rational Argument

    B. Narrative

    C. Aesthetic

    D. Values, Needs and Symbols

    E. Credibility

    F. Confrontation

VII. Rhetorical Barriers and Advantages

    Audience—beliefs, attitudes, values, attention

    Situational—culture, complexity, specific events

    Occasion—appropriateness, prior rhetoric

    Reputation of the speaker

VIII. On-Balance evaluation—are the strategies well designed to overcome the barriers in order to achieve the purpose?

Outline of Rhetorical and Contextual Analysis Categories

I. Goals

    A. Themes

    B. Requested Actions

II. Organization

    A. Introduction

    B. Conclusion

    C. Main Body—identify the organizational pattern

III. Role of Rhetor

IV. Linguistic Tone

V. Implied Audience

VI. Strategy Categories—use all that are relevant and identify sub-strategies as specifically as possible.

    A. Rational Argument

    B. Narrative

    C. Aesthetic

    D. Values, Needs and Symbols

    E. Credibility

    F. Confrontation

VII. Rhetorical Barriers and Advantages

    Audience—beliefs, attitudes, values, attention

    Situational—culture, complexity, specific events

    Occasion—appropriateness, prior rhetoric

    Reputation of the speaker

VIII. On-Balance evaluation—are the strategies well designed to overcome the barriers in order to achieve the purpose?

Outline of Rhetorical and Contextual Analysis Categories

I. Goals

    A. Themes

    B. Requested Actions

II. Organization

    A. Introduction

    B. Conclusion

    C. Main Body—identify the organizational pattern

III. Role of Rhetor

IV. Linguistic Tone

V. Implied Audience

VI. Strategy Categories—use all that are relevant and identify sub-strategies as specifically as possible.

    A. Rational Argument

    B. Narrative

    C. Aesthetic

    D. Values, Needs and Symbols

    E. Credibility

    F. Confrontation

VII. Rhetorical Barriers and Advantages

    Audience—beliefs, attitudes, values, attention

    Situational—culture, complexity, specific events

    Occasion—appropriateness, prior rhetoric

    Reputation of the speaker

VIII. On-Balance evaluation—are the strategies well designed to overcome the barriers in order to achieve the purpose?

Outline of Rhetorical and Contextual Analysis Categories

I. Goals

    A. Themes

    B. Requested Actions

II. Organization

    A. Introduction

    B. Conclusion

    C. Main Body—identify the organizational pattern

III. Role of Rhetor

IV. Linguistic Tone

V. Implied Audience

VI. Strategy Categories—use all that are relevant and identify sub-strategies as specifically as possible.

    A. Rational Argument

    B. Narrative

    C. Aesthetic

    D. Values, Needs and Symbols

    E. Credibility

    F. Confrontation

VII. Rhetorical Barriers and Advantages

    Audience—beliefs, attitudes, values, attention

    Situational—culture, complexity, specific events

    Occasion—appropriateness, prior rhetoric

    Reputation of the speaker

VIII. On-Balance evaluation—are the strategies well designed to overcome the barriers in order to achieve the purpose?

Outline of Rhetorical and Contextual Analysis Categories

I. Goals

    A. Themes

    B. Requested Actions

II. Organization

    A. Introduction

    B. Conclusion

    C. Main Body—identify the organizational pattern

III. Role of Rhetor

IV. Linguistic Tone

V. Implied Audience

VI. Strategy Categories—use all that are relevant and identify sub-strategies as specifically as possible.

    A. Rational Argument

    B. Narrative

    C. Aesthetic

    D. Values, Needs and Symbols

    E. Credibility

    F. Confrontation

VII. Rhetorical Barriers and Advantages

    Audience—beliefs, attitudes, values, attention

    Situational—culture, complexity, specific events

    Occasion—appropriateness, prior rhetoric

    Reputation of the speaker

VIII. On-Balance evaluation—are the strategies well designed to overcome the barriers in order to achieve the purpose?

Outline of Rhetorical and Contextual Analysis Categories

I. Goals

    A. Themes

    B. Requested Actions

II. Organization

    A. Introduction

    B. Conclusion

    C. Main Body—identify the organizational pattern

III. Role of Rhetor

IV. Linguistic Tone

V. Implied Audience

VI. Strategy Categories—use all that are relevant and identify sub-strategies as specifically as possible.

  A. Rational Argument

  B. Narrative

  C. Aesthetic

  D. Values, Needs and Symbols

  E. Credibility

  F. Confrontation

VII. Rhetorical Barriers and Advantages

  Audience—beliefs, attitudes, values, attention

  Situational—culture, complexity, specific events

  Occasion—appropriateness, prior rhetoric

  Reputation of the speaker

VIII. On-Balance evaluation—are the strategies well designed to overcome the barriers in order to achieve the purpose?

Outline of Rhetorical and Contextual Analysis Categories

I. Goals

    A. Themes

    B. Requested Actions

II. Organization

    A. Introduction

    B. Conclusion

    C. Main Body—identify the organizational pattern

III. Role of Rhetor

IV. Linguistic Tone

V. Implied Audience

VI. Strategy Categories—use all that are relevant and identify sub-strategies as specifically as possible.

    A. Rational Argument

    B. Narrative

    C. Aesthetic

    D. Values, Needs and Symbols

    E. Credibility

    F. Confrontation

VII. Rhetorical Barriers and Advantages

    Audience—beliefs, attitudes, values, attention

    Situational—culture, complexity, specific events

    Occasion—appropriateness, prior rhetoric

    Reputation of the speaker

VIII. On-Balance evaluation—are the strategies well designed to overcome the barriers in order to achieve the purpose?

Outline of Rhetorical and Contextual Analysis Categories

I. Goals

    A. Themes

    B. Requested Actions

II. Organization

    A. Introduction

    B. Conclusion

    C. Main Body—identify the organizational pattern

III. Role of Rhetor

IV. Linguistic Tone

V. Implied Audience

VI. Strategy Categories—use all that are relevant and identify sub-strategies as specifically as possible.

    A. Rational Argument

    B. Narrative

    C. Aesthetic

    D. Values, Needs and Symbols

    E. Credibility

    F. Confrontation

VII. Rhetorical Barriers and Advantages

    Audience—beliefs, attitudes, values, attention

    Situational—culture, complexity, specific events

    Occasion—appropriateness, prior rhetoric

    Reputation of the speaker

VIII. On-Balance evaluation—are the strategies well designed to overcome the barriers in order to achieve the purpose?

Outline of Rhetorical and Contextual Analysis Categories

I. Goals

    A. Themes

    B. Requested Actions

II. Organization

    A. Introduction

    B. Conclusion

    C. Main Body—identify the organizational pattern

III. Role of Rhetor

IV. Linguistic Tone

V. Implied Audience

VI. Strategy Categories—use all that are relevant and identify sub-strategies as specifically as possible.

    A. Rational Argument

    B. Narrative

    C. Aesthetic

    D. Values, Needs and Symbols

    E. Credibility

    F. Confrontation

VII. Rhetorical Barriers and Advantages

    Audience—beliefs, attitudes, values, attention

    Situational—culture, complexity, specific events

    Occasion—appropriateness, prior rhetoric

    Reputation of the speaker

VIII. On-Balance evaluation—are the strategies well designed to overcome the barriers in order to achieve the purpose?

Outline of Rhetorical and Contextual Analysis Categories

I. Goals

    A. Themes

    B. Requested Actions

II. Organization

    A. Introduction

    B. Conclusion

    C. Main Body—identify the organizational pattern

III. Role of Rhetor

IV. Linguistic Tone

V. Implied Audience

VI. Strategy Categories—use all that are relevant and identify sub-strategies as specifically as possible.

    A. Rational Argument

    B. Narrative

    C. Aesthetic

    D. Values, Needs and Symbols

    E. Credibility

    F. Confrontation

VII. Rhetorical Barriers and Advantages

    Audience—beliefs, attitudes, values, attention

    Situational—culture, complexity, specific events

    Occasion—appropriateness, prior rhetoric

    Reputation of the speaker

VIII. On-Balance evaluation—are the strategies well designed to overcome the barriers in order to achieve the purpose?

Outline of Rhetorical and Contextual Analysis Categories

I. Goals

    A. Themes

    B. Requested Actions

II. Organization

    A. Introduction

    B. Conclusion

    C. Main Body—identify the organizational pattern

III. Role of Rhetor

IV. Linguistic Tone

V. Implied Audience

VI. Strategy Categories—use all that are relevant and identify sub-strategies as specifically as possible.

    A. Rational Argument

    B. Narrative

    C. Aesthetic

    D. Values, Needs and Symbols

    E. Credibility

    F. Confrontation

VII. Rhetorical Barriers and Advantages

    Audience—beliefs, attitudes, values, attention

    Situational—culture, complexity, specific events

    Occasion—appropriateness, prior rhetoric

    Reputation of the speaker

VIII. On-Balance evaluation—are the strategies well designed to overcome the barriers in order to achieve the purpose?

APPENDIX TWO

GENRE ANALYSIS

Genre Analysis

Identify the following situational factors

    Recurring Problem

    Constraining Purpose

    Societal Constraints

Identify the perceived strategic constraints created by the situational factors

Identify the characteristics of form, content, substance, and style required by the perceived strategic constraints.

Generic evaluation:

1. Does the rhetoric contain all of the defining characteristics of the genre?
2. Does the rhetoric violate any of the defining characteristics of the genre?
3. Are there specific circumstances or purposes that demand adaptation of the genre?

Genre Analysis

Identify the following situational factors

> Recurring Problem

> Constraining Purpose

> Societal Constraints

Identify the perceived strategic constraints created by the situational factors

Identify the characteristics of form, content, substance, and style required by the perceived strategic constraints.

Generic evaluation:

1. Does the rhetoric contain all of the defining characteristics of the genre?
2. Does the rhetoric violate any of the defining characteristics of the genre?
3. Are there specific circumstances or purposes that demand adaptation of the genre?

Genre Analysis

Identify the following situational factors

Recurring Problem

Constraining Purpose

Societal Constraints

Identify the perceived strategic constraints created by the situational factors

Identify the characteristics of form, content, substance, and style required by the perceived strategic constraints.

Generic evaluation:
1. Does the rhetoric contain all of the defining characteristics of the genre?
2. Does the rhetoric violate any of the defining characteristics of the genre?
3. Are there specific circumstances or purposes that demand adaptation of the genre?

Genre Analysis

Identify the following situational factors

Recurring Problem

Constraining Purpose

Societal Constraints

Identify the perceived strategic constraints created by the situational factors

Identify the characteristics of form, content, substance, and style required by the perceived strategic constraints.

Generic evaluation:
1. Does the rhetoric contain all of the defining characteristics of the genre?
2. Does the rhetoric violate any of the defining characteristics of the genre?
3. Are there specific circumstances or purposes that demand adaptation of the genre?

Genre Analysis

Identify the following situational factors

    Recurring Problem

    Constraining Purpose

    Societal Constraints

Identify the perceived strategic constraints created by the situational factors

Identify the characteristics of form, content, substance, and style required by the perceived strategic constraints.

Generic evaluation:
1. Does the rhetoric contain all of the defining characteristics of the genre?
2. Does the rhetoric violate any of the defining characteristics of the genre?
3. Are there specific circumstances or purposes that demand adaptation of the genre?

Genre Analysis

Identify the following situational factors

Recurring Problem

Constraining Purpose

Societal Constraints

Identify the perceived strategic constraints created by the situational factors

Identify the characteristics of form, content, substance, and style required by the perceived strategic constraints.

Generic evaluation:
1. Does the rhetoric contain all of the defining characteristics of the genre?
2. Does the rhetoric violate any of the defining characteristics of the genre?
3. Are there specific circumstances or purposes that demand adaptation of the genre?

Genre Analysis

Identify the following situational factors

    Recurring Problem

    Constraining Purpose

    Societal Constraints

Identify the perceived strategic constraints created by the situational factors

Identify the characteristics of form, content, substance, and style required by the perceived strategic constraints.

Generic evaluation:

1. Does the rhetoric contain all of the defining characteristics of the genre?
2. Does the rhetoric violate any of the defining characteristics of the genre?
3. Are there specific circumstances or purposes that demand adaptation of the genre?

Genre Analysis

Identify the following situational factors

Recurring Problem

Constraining Purpose

Societal Constraints

Identify the perceived strategic constraints created by the situational factors

Identify the characteristics of form, content, substance, and style required by the perceived strategic constraints.

Generic evaluation:
1. Does the rhetoric contain all of the defining characteristics of the genre?
2. Does the rhetoric violate any of the defining characteristics of the genre?
3. Are there specific circumstances or purposes that demand adaptation of the genre?

Genre Analysis

Identify the following situational factors

Recurring Problem

Constraining Purpose

Societal Constraints

Identify the perceived strategic constraints created by the situational factors

Identify the characteristics of form, content, substance, and style required by the perceived strategic constraints.

Generic evaluation:

1. Does the rhetoric contain all of the defining characteristics of the genre?
2. Does the rhetoric violate any of the defining characteristics of the genre?
3. Are there specific circumstances or purposes that demand adaptation of the genre?

Genre Analysis

Identify the following situational factors

    Recurring Problem

    Constraining Purpose

    Societal Constraints

Identify the perceived strategic constraints created by the situational factors

Identify the characteristics of form, content, substance, and style required by the perceived strategic constraints.

Generic evaluation:
1. Does the rhetoric contain all of the defining characteristics of the genre?
2. Does the rhetoric violate any of the defining characteristics of the genre?
3. Are there specific circumstances or purposes that demand adaptation of the genre?

Genre Analysis

Identify the following situational factors

Recurring Problem

Constraining Purpose

Societal Constraints

Identify the perceived strategic constraints created by the situational factors

Identify the characteristics of form, content, substance, and style required by the perceived strategic constraints.

Generic evaluation:
1. Does the rhetoric contain all of the defining characteristics of the genre?
2. Does the rhetoric violate any of the defining characteristics of the genre?
3. Are there specific circumstances or purposes that demand adaptation of the genre?

Genre Analysis

Identify the following situational factors

    Recurring Problem

    Constraining Purpose

    Societal Constraints

Identify the perceived strategic constraints created by the situational factors

Identify the characteristics of form, content, substance, and style required by the perceived strategic constraints.

Generic evaluation:

1. Does the rhetoric contain all of the defining characteristics of the genre?
2. Does the rhetoric violate any of the defining characteristics of the genre?
3. Are there specific circumstances or purposes that demand adaptation of the genre?

Genre Analysis

Identify the following situational factors

    Recurring Problem

    Constraining Purpose

    Societal Constraints

Identify the perceived strategic constraints created by the situational factors

Identify the characteristics of form, content, substance, and style required by the perceived strategic constraints.

Generic evaluation:
1. Does the rhetoric contain all of the defining characteristics of the genre?
2. Does the rhetoric violate any of the defining characteristics of the genre?
3. Are there specific circumstances or purposes that demand adaptation of the genre?

Genre Analysis

Identify the following situational factors

  Recurring Problem

  Constraining Purpose

  Societal Constraints

Identify the perceived strategic constraints created by the situational factors

Identify the characteristics of form, content, substance, and style required by the perceived strategic constraints.

Generic evaluation:

1. Does the rhetoric contain all of the defining characteristics of the genre?
2. Does the rhetoric violate any of the defining characteristics of the genre?
3. Are there specific circumstances or purposes that demand adaptation of the genre?

Genre Analysis

Identify the following situational factors

    Recurring Problem

    Constraining Purpose

    Societal Constraints

Identify the perceived strategic constraints created by the situational factors

Identify the characteristics of form, content, substance, and style required by the perceived strategic constraints.

Generic evaluation:

1. Does the rhetoric contain all of the defining characteristics of the genre?
2. Does the rhetoric violate any of the defining characteristics of the genre?
3. Are there specific circumstances or purposes that demand adaptation of the genre?

APPENDIX THREE

THE INFORMED CITIZEN

Summary of Stages in the Informed Citizen

I. Determine the need for critical self protection by asking:

    1. Is a major claim on beliefs/attitudes/values or actions being made?

    2. Is the person merely relaying information or is he/she strategically presenting the material?

II. Identify the claims that are being made

III. Test the Quality of the Case for the Claims

    1. Does the rhetor provide evidence and reasoning for every claim?

    2. Does the support material meet the tests of evidence?

    3. Is the reasoning consistent?

    4. Does the reasoning lead to the conclusion directly or could there be alternative factors that invalidate the conclusion?

    5. Are there counter arguments or facts that invalidate the conclusion?

Consider whether on-balance a strong argument is made.

IV. Test the Rhetoric for Manipulation

1. Does the rhetoric attempt to prevent other voices from being heard?

2. Does the rhetoric attempt to overwhelm our reason?

3. Does the rhetoric attack groups or individual people, rather than their ideas or actions?

Summary of Stages in the Informed Citizen

I. Determine the need for critical self protection by asking:

    1. Is a major claim on beliefs/attitudes/values or actions being made?

    2. Is the person merely relaying information or is he/she strategically presenting the material?

II. Identify the claims that are being made

III. Test the Quality of the Case for the Claims

    1. Does the rhetor provide evidence and reasoning for every claim?

    2. Does the support material meet the tests of evidence?

    3. Is the reasoning consistent?

    4. Does the reasoning lead to the conclusion directly or could there be alternative factors that invalidate the conclusion?

    5. Are there counter arguments or facts that invalidate the conclusion?

Consider whether on-balance a strong argument is made.

IV. Test the Rhetoric for Manipulation

    1. Does the rhetoric attempt to prevent other voices from being heard?

    2. Does the rhetoric attempt to overwhelm our reason?

    3. Does the rhetoric attack groups or individual people, rather than their ideas or actions?

Summary of Stages in the Informed Citizen

I. Determine the need for critical self protection by asking:

    1. Is a major claim on beliefs/attitudes/values or actions being made?

    2. Is the person merely relaying information or is he/she strategically presenting the material?

II. Identify the claims that are being made

III. Test the Quality of the Case for the Claims

    1. Does the rhetor provide evidence and reasoning for every claim?

    2. Does the support material meet the tests of evidence?

    3. Is the reasoning consistent?

    4. Does the reasoning lead to the conclusion directly or could there be alternative factors that invalidate the conclusion?

    5. Are there counter arguments or facts that invalidate the conclusion?

Consider whether on-balance a strong argument is made.

IV. Test the Rhetoric for Manipulation

    1. Does the rhetoric attempt to prevent other voices from being heard?

    2. Does the rhetoric attempt to overwhelm our reason?

    3. Does the rhetoric attack groups or individual people, rather than their ideas or actions?

Summary of Stages in the Informed Citizen

I. Determine the need for critical self protection by asking:

    1. Is a major claim on beliefs/attitudes/values or actions being made?

    2. Is the person merely relaying information or is he/she strategically presenting the material?

II. Identify the claims that are being made

III. Test the Quality of the Case for the Claims

    1. Does the rhetor provide evidence and reasoning for every claim?

    2. Does the support material meet the tests of evidence?

    3. Is the reasoning consistent?

    4. Does the reasoning lead to the conclusion directly or could there be alternative factors that invalidate the conclusion?

    5. Are there counter arguments or facts that invalidate the conclusion?

Consider whether on-balance a strong argument is made.

IV. Test the Rhetoric for Manipulation

    1. Does the rhetoric attempt to prevent other voices from being heard?

    2. Does the rhetoric attempt to overwhelm our reason?

    3. Does the rhetoric attack groups or individual people, rather than their ideas or actions?

Summary of Stages in the Informed Citizen

I. Determine the need for critical self protection by asking:

    1. Is a major claim on beliefs/attitudes/values or actions being made?

    2. Is the person merely relaying information or is he/she strategically presenting the material?

II. Identify the claims that are being made

III. Test the Quality of the Case for the Claims

    1. Does the rhetor provide evidence and reasoning for every claim?

    2. Does the support material meet the tests of evidence?

    3. Is the reasoning consistent?

    4. Does the reasoning lead to the conclusion directly or could there be alternative factors that invalidate the conclusion?

    5. Are there counter arguments or facts that invalidate the conclusion?

Consider whether on-balance a strong argument is made.

IV. Test the Rhetoric for Manipulation

    1. Does the rhetoric attempt to prevent other voices from being heard?

    2. Does the rhetoric attempt to overwhelm our reason?

    3. Does the rhetoric attack groups or individual people, rather than their ideas or actions?

Summary of Stages in the Informed Citizen

I. Determine the need for critical self protection by asking:

    1. Is a major claim on beliefs/attitudes/values or actions being made?

    2. Is the person merely relaying information or is he/she strategically presenting the material?

II. Identify the claims that are being made

III. Test the Quality of the Case for the Claims

    1. Does the rhetor provide evidence and reasoning for every claim?

    2. Does the support material meet the tests of evidence?

    3. Is the reasoning consistent?

    4. Does the reasoning lead to the conclusion directly or could there be alternative factors that invalidate the conclusion?

    5. Are there counter arguments or facts that invalidate the conclusion?

Consider whether on-balance a strong argument is made.

IV. Test the Rhetoric for Manipulation

    1. Does the rhetoric attempt to prevent other voices from being heard?

    2. Does the rhetoric attempt to overwhelm our reason?

    3. Does the rhetoric attack groups or individual people, rather than their ideas or actions?

Summary of Stages in the Informed Citizen

I. Determine the need for critical self protection by asking:

    1. Is a major claim on beliefs/attitudes/values or actions being made?

    2. Is the person merely relaying information or is he/she strategically presenting the material?

II. Identify the claims that are being made

III. Test the Quality of the Case for the Claims

    1. Does the rhetor provide evidence and reasoning for every claim?

    2. Does the support material meet the tests of evidence?

    3. Is the reasoning consistent?

    4. Does the reasoning lead to the conclusion directly or could there be alternative factors that invalidate the conclusion?

    5. Are there counter arguments or facts that invalidate the conclusion?

Consider whether on-balance a strong argument is made.

IV. Test the Rhetoric for Manipulation

   1. Does the rhetoric attempt to prevent other voices from being heard?

   2. Does the rhetoric attempt to overwhelm our reason?

   3. Does the rhetoric attack groups or individual people, rather than their ideas or actions?

Summary of Stages in the Informed Citizen

I. Determine the need for critical self protection by asking:

    1. Is a major claim on beliefs/attitudes/values or actions being made?

    2. Is the person merely relaying information or is he/she strategically presenting the material?

II. Identify the claims that are being made

III. Test the Quality of the Case for the Claims

    1. Does the rhetor provide evidence and reasoning for every claim?

    2. Does the support material meet the tests of evidence?

    3. Is the reasoning consistent?

    4. Does the reasoning lead to the conclusion directly or could there be alternative factors that invalidate the conclusion?

    5. Are there counter arguments or facts that invalidate the conclusion?

Consider whether on-balance a strong argument is made.

IV. Test the Rhetoric for Manipulation

    1. Does the rhetoric attempt to prevent other voices from being heard?

    2. Does the rhetoric attempt to overwhelm our reason?

    3. Does the rhetoric attack groups or individual people, rather than their ideas or actions?

Summary of Stages in the Informed Citizen

I. Determine the need for critical self protection by asking:

    1. Is a major claim on beliefs/attitudes/values or actions being made?

    2. Is the person merely relaying information or is he/she strategically presenting the material?

II. Identify the claims that are being made

III. Test the Quality of the Case for the Claims

    1. Does the rhetor provide evidence and reasoning for every claim?

    2. Does the support material meet the tests of evidence?

    3. Is the reasoning consistent?

    4. Does the reasoning lead to the conclusion directly or could there be alternative factors that invalidate the conclusion?

    5. Are there counter arguments or facts that invalidate the conclusion?

Consider whether on-balance a strong argument is made.

IV. Test the Rhetoric for Manipulation

    1. Does the rhetoric attempt to prevent other voices from being heard?

    2. Does the rhetoric attempt to overwhelm our reason?

    3. Does the rhetoric attack groups or individual people, rather than their ideas or actions?

Summary of Stages in the Informed Citizen

I. Determine the need for critical self protection by asking:

    1. Is a major claim on beliefs/attitudes/values or actions being made?

    2. Is the person merely relaying information or is he/she strategically presenting the material?

II. Identify the claims that are being made

III. Test the Quality of the Case for the Claims

    1. Does the rhetor provide evidence and reasoning for every claim?

    2. Does the support material meet the tests of evidence?

    3. Is the reasoning consistent?

    4. Does the reasoning lead to the conclusion directly or could there be alternative factors that invalidate the conclusion?

    5. Are there counter arguments or facts that invalidate the conclusion?

Consider whether on-balance a strong argument is made.

IV. Test the Rhetoric for Manipulation

    1. Does the rhetoric attempt to prevent other voices from being heard?

    2. Does the rhetoric attempt to overwhelm our reason?

    3. Does the rhetoric attack groups or individual people, rather than their ideas or actions?